COMPANION
TO THE ALPS

Hugh Merrick

COMPANION
TO THE ALPS

Hastings House Publishers
New York, New York 10016

Library of Congress Cataloging in Publication Data:
DQ823.5.M45   914.94'7'0470222   73–22228

ISBN 0–8038–0365–6

Printed in Great Britain
Published in the USA by
Hastings House Publishers, New York

Contents

Illustrations

Acknowledgements

The photographs in this book are reproduced by kind permission of:

The Swiss National Tourist Office (nos 2, 4, 6, 7, 8, 21, 22, 25)
The French Government Tourist Office (no. 13)
and by arrangement with:
A. F. Kersting (no. 5)
J. Allan Cash (no. 24)
Beringer & Pampaluchi, Zürich (nos 10, 11, 26)
Albert Steiner, St Moritz (no. 28)
The remainder of the photographs are by the author.
Map by Patrick Leeson

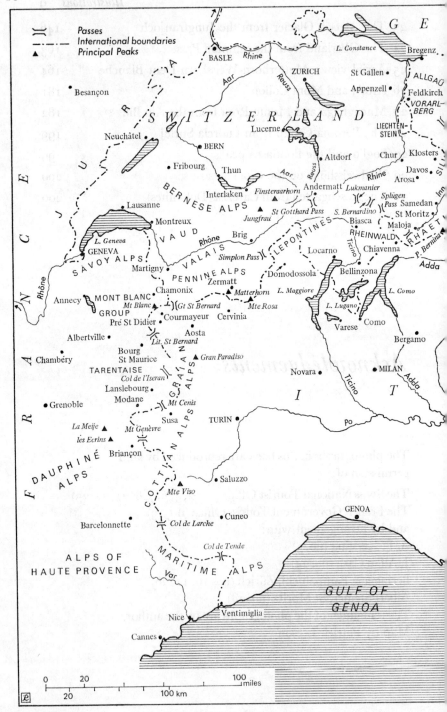

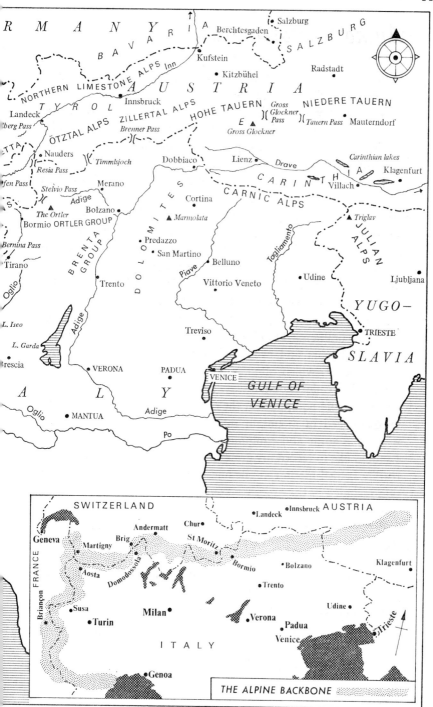

THE ALPINE BACKBONE

Author's Foreword

I am very conscious of the many gaps and omissions in this attempt to cover in a slim volume the multifarious aspects and activities of the Alpine world. This book is aimed primarily at the reader who is neither an experienced mountaineer nor a habitué but who, visiting the Alps in summer, perhaps for the first time, would like to know where he can stroll or 'hike', gently or more strenuously, and where the scenery is at its grandest and most beautiful; in winter, where he can find the facilities he requires. With the universal advent of the cable-car and a variety of lifts, the distinction between summer and winter resorts has largely disappeared; almost every centre has become ambi-seasonal, so any serious attempt at segregation has become unnecessary. Assuming that, in summer at least, visitors will in increasing numbers be travelling by road, I have devoted considerable attention to the great motoring passes and their approaches. I would like to stress that where I have recommended modest mountaineering expeditions, including glacier-tours and even high tracks to club huts and over 'walking-cols' (which often provide the finest views of the great peaks), the reader should always assure himself that he is in every way fitted and equipped for the chosen enterprise; and, if himself inexperienced in mountain matters, he should establish locally whether a guide and equipment are necessary or advisable.

I should like to record my grateful thanks to all those who have so readily helped me to compile and check so much of the information included in the text: Mr Bourda of the Austrian, Mr Greenwood of the Italian, Pauline Hallam of the French, Messrs Schmid and Kunz of the Swiss, Mr. Sternbeck of the German National Tourist Agencies (the order being alphabetical); and to Mrs Parkinson at the Alpine Club. Special thanks are due to the Editor for his encouragement throughout the preparation of the book, and to Katharine Cowherd for a final reading of the proofs, in the light of her extensive knowledge of the subject.

Hugh Merrick

To K

because she loved and shared them with me.

Introduction

Round the world in eighty days was the problem Jules Verne set his Phineas Fogg a century ago. Round the Alps in 80,000 words is that which the editor has cheerfully imposed on me. Phineas, we know, won his bet because by travelling eastwards he gained a bonus day. Though my pen, too, will travel eastwards, that will not gain it a single bonus word. As I set out on our journey through one of the world's great mountain-tracts I am glad not to be on the wrong end of a wager; for it looks an impossible assignment.

How many people, for instance, realise that to all intents and purposes the Alps start with the swell of the first bikini-clad breasts sunning themselves on the beach at Nice or Cannes? For not ten miles behind the Promenade des Anglais the first gentle foothills, orange- and olive-clad, studded with modern villas and rich in ancient walled townships, surge up abruptly in a sheer limestone rampart, 3,000 feet high. Indeed, the steep slopes falling from the Corniche and the cliffs between Nice and Ventimiglia to their east dip their very feet in the Mediterranean blue, and the Alps have begun. To the west, near Marseilles, the great seaboard walls of the Calanques lift to form the southern rim of the Alpine upheaval.

Northwards it surges from the shores of the Inland Sea for 150 miles, through the Alpes Maritimes and the Provençal Alps to Grenoble, to swing eastwards there in a great arc, and then ever on eastwards for another 300, by way of Dauphiné and Savoy, where Mont Blanc lords it over all, to the Oberland and the Pennines, the Gotthard and the Grisons; on into northern Italy's Dolomites and Ortler; Austria's Tyrol, Ötztal, Zillertal and Tauern ranges, with southeastern outlines reaching long fingers down through Carinthia into Jugoslavia, to lose height gradually and fade away at last in the green wooded hills of the Wienerwald, where on Sundays and holidays the amiable citizens of Vienna relax in the enjoyment of their family rambles and munch their *brödchen* and their *pretzel*. This is not a country or a place; it is a whole world of half a dozen countries, of hundreds of peaks, rivers, valleys, lakes, forests and places. Eighty thousand words?

Nowadays, as you fly across the wide French plain, bound for an Alpine holiday, it is possible to get some idea of the immensity of this mighty mountain-world, 600 miles long and less than 100 across at its widest points.

On the northern approach to Zürich, at a point where Mont Blanc's huge mass is seen rising only some 40 miles southeast with the Valaisian giants small and remote beyond, the aircraft swings north, to fly parallel with the long rampart of the Bernese Oberland, the Alps of Uri and finally Zürich's own Glärnisch and Säntis groups – 50 miles of snowy peak and glacier, yet only a small sector of the Alpine chain.

If Geneva is your destination, that sector stretches away to the north as you lose height; Mont Blanc and its satellites form the tremendous centre-piece, flanked by 50 miles of Savoy and the Tarentaise reaching out to the great Dauphiné peaks to the west; while ahead and beyond, to the east of the Monarch, the tumbled ranges of the Pennines, spiked with their familiar giants, sweep endlessly away into the haze of Austria and Italy above the deep blue gulf of the Rhône Valley. The greatest peaks these, it is true, but yet not one half of the Alpine complex.

Perhaps the most overwhelming impression of the immensity of this mountain territory is obtained, in conditions of good visibility, from a jetliner flying diagonally across its heart at 30,000 feet, bound for Rome. Nothing will ever efface the memory of a flight in 1960, even at the lower cruising-altitude of a Viscount, on an October day, described by our captain as the clearest he had ever experienced in years of trans-Alpine flying.

2   *The Via Mala Gorge, near Thusis*

3 *Summit view from the Mönch, looking southwards to the Valais Alps*

4 *Fétan, in the Lower Engadine*

'As we veered steadily towards Geneva,' I wrote at the time, 'first of all the distant Oberland peaks filed past above the red port-wing; then, in mid-distance ahead, with a surf of thin cloud breaking at their feet, the Valaisian giants wheeled into sight, while the Lake unrolled its dark velvet beneath the trailing-edge. Suddenly Mont Blanc was sliding swiftly under the starboard wing, the Midi's rocks, where we had stood last year on just such a day of blue and gold, whirled astern past our feet, as we burst out across the dazzling glacier world – seemingly close enough to touch – into the wide Italian air above the Aosta Valley, dreaming nearly 20,000 feet below.

'Glacier, valley, ridge upon ridge – the Matterhorn, Monte Rosa, the far-off Bernina, the still more distant Austrian Alps, shading away into a haze, somewhere near Vienna.

'Less than half an hour later, all of 130 miles had dropped smoothly away behind the tail-fin since that dazzling surge across Mont Blanc. And there, in rapidly receding miniature, but still crystal-clear, on the confines of the world, the great arc of the Alps swung through 300 miles, from Dauphiné to the Julians, into Jugoslavia and endlessly on, to the Dinarics far down towards Albania.'

This synoptic glimpse, at a given moment in time, may perhaps serve to pinpoint the mere geographical immensity of the task facing me; but the Alps are so much more than a simple feature of geography which might conceivably be dealt with by a comprehensive list of tables classifying peaks, valleys, lakes and main tourist centres. This great barrier of sky-raking peaks and ridges has written chapter after chapter in the history of Europe, ethnic, social and military. During the last two centuries it has increasingly brought health and happiness to countless millions, drawn to them from the far corners of the earth, in a multiplicity of activities, pursuits and enjoyments, indigenous and imported. It has given birth to and fostered one of man's most splendid and rewarding recreations – mountaineering; later to one of his best-loved sports – skiing. It has inspired a magnificent literature, in prose and verse; and to a much lesser degree – rather surprisingly – to a pictorial art of its own.

The great peaks themselves – Ruskin's 'Perpetual Hills' – stand changeless. If there were only their challenge and ineffable scenic beauty to describe, there would be little or no problem. The difficulty is that they have looked down, however impassively, on immense changes in the valleys at their feet during the 300 years since men ceased to regard them as the fearsome, hideous and inhospitable haunts of demons and dragons and come to find them beautiful, health-giving and increasingly accessible. Even during the more than 60 years since I first visited them as a child, instantly to fall in love with their ever-changing beauty of light and shade, sunshine and storm, dazzling snows and dark, marching forests, the Alpine 'scene', unlike its scenery, has changed out of all knowledge. No book about the Alps would be complete without a survey of the fantastic developments which the demands of modern tourism and the advent of the affluent society, with its inevitable transformation and exploitation of the local resources, have brought to the remotest corners of what were, even when I first knew them, quiet, sparsely-populated, poverty-stricken upland valleys. All this, and a good deal more, must be attempted within the compass set by editorial decree.

If I do not set out on this whistle-stop tour of the Alpine world with the bland confidence of a Phineas, it is because many years ago I wrote a book about a single aspect of its multifarious activities and delights, the driving of a car to and over the great passes. It ran to 120,000 words.

'The Alps in 80,000'? Well, one can but try.

1. The Structure of the Alps

The true Alpine watershed, the 'Backbone of Europe', rises from between Nice and Ventimiglia, with its coccyx bathed in the blue Mediterranean waters. It runs, before suffering from severe curvature, due north, forming the Franco-Italian frontier till, between Condamine and Borgo San Dalmazzo, 50 miles of the Alpes Maritimes give way to the Cottians, a sector of similar length and they in turn to a somewhat shorter group, the Graians, terminating at the Little St Bernard Pass, which links French Bourg St Maurice with Italian Aosta and Piedmont.

Due north of that pass rises the greatest complex of the whole Alpine spine, the Mont Blanc group in Savoy, 40 miles south of the Lake of Geneva – by far the largest of the Alpine lakes – the Monarch towering almost a thousand feet above its cluster of mighty satellites, the massif thrusting a wedge between the Franco-Italian and Franco-Swiss frontiers.

Here, some 150 miles north of the Mediterranean, the main crest of the Alps swings away, slightly north of east, into Switzerland, with 50 miles of the mighty Pennines separating the long, deep furrow of the Rhône Valley from the Piedmont and Lombardy plains to the south; while to the north the Bernese Oberland range runs almost parallel, forming a separate 'island' of high peaks and glaciers, divorced from the main range of the watershed by the early course of that great river. At the eastern end of the Pennines, which are deeply scored by five subsidiary valleys falling into the Rhône cleft from the south, rise the famous peaks of the Valais – the Mischabel, Monte Rosa, Breithorn, Weisshorn and, so famous as almost to merit by now the epithet 'notorious', the Matterhorn, dominating Swiss Zermatt on its north and Italian Valtournanche to its south.

A few miles farther east, the saddle of the Simplon Pass, crossing the frontier between Brigue and Domodossola, links the Valaisian Alps with the humbler Gotthard (Lepontine) Alps, running more sharply northeast for 25 miles to Andermatt, at the eastern end of the Urserental, a geographical phenomenon described in detail below.

Turning due east again the watershed now swings away from the upper valley of the young Rhine and, still revealing no summits of great altitude, runs for another 30 miles, separating the Rhine and southern Switzerland from the headwaters of Lago Maggiore and Lake Como and rising at its eastern end into the sizeable Rheinwald group.

The Rhaetian Alps, which follow, turn northeast again, embracing the spiky Bregaglia group and, to the east, the third highest cluster of peaks in Switzerland, the beautifully snowy Bernina, which for some 20 miles form the southern containing wall of the lofty valley of the Upper Engadine (Inn Valley), rising between its 6,000-foot level and the deep lowland trench of the Valtellina to the south in Italy. The Rhaetians then continue, diminished in stature, for another 20 miles on either side of the gradually descending Lower Engadine, the northern range rising to the relatively high summits of the small, isolated Silvretta group on the frontier with Austria's Arlberg, which here turns south through Nauders at the end of the long Engadine corridor, and down to Spondigna in the Adige Valley (Italy).

At Landeck (Austria), a few miles north of Nauders, the Inn, having carved a passage through deep and narrow gorges, emerges to turn due east on its journey along the wide, straight valley to Innsbruck, thence northwards, through the Limestone Alps, to fall into the Danube (see later). The Alpine backbone continues parallel with it but some miles to the south, at the head of three beautiful lateral valleys, presided over by the high glaciated Ötztal and Zillertal groups, whose southern slopes fall abruptly to Italy's South Tyrol. First to the lovely valley of the Upper Adige, later to the smiling Val Pusteria, which respectively sunder the main chain from two completely isolated groups well to the south – the splendid Ortler crescent and the 'rectangle' of the Dolomites, only 20 miles to its southeast, both on Italian soil.

Beyond the Zillertal crests, in this 100-mile stretch of the main watershed, comes the Hohe Tauern group, dominated by the Grossglockner's 12,460-foot spire, the last glaciated sector before the range gradually loses height through the Austrian ranges of savage but smaller rock-peaks – Niedere Tauern, Ennstaler Alpen and Gesäuse – to sink into the foothills and plains to the east. The main divide, however, diverges southeastwards through Carinthia to the great stony mass of Triglav just inside Jugoslavia (Carnic and Julian Alps), finally thrusting its foothills round to the south almost back to the shores of the Mediterranean again, near Trieste.

Such is the 600-mile-long main barrier of the Alps – the great divide between the Nordic and Mediterranean lands, races and cultures of Europe.

Of the great glaciated groups which lie to one side or other of its main axis, the Bernese Oberland and continuing ranges to the north contain the mightiest peaks and the loveliest scenery; the stony mountains of the Northern Limestone Range on the long borders between Germany (Bavaria) and Austria provide some impressively rugged mountain walls, and in North Tyrol (Salzkammergut) the most picturesque district of small gem-like lakes in the whole area; the Ortler massif and the Dolomites, already mentioned, house respectively a snowy diadem of majestic peaks and an area of sunny valleys liberally dotted with unique groups of shattered limestone castles, rather than mountains, as wonderful in their colouring as in their grotesque shapes, which distinguish them from the rest of the Alps and indeed from any other mountains.

So much for the mountains – of which an American, asked what he thought of Switzerland, replied, slowly: 'Well, take'm away and what's left?' Hearsay also has it that there was, many years ago, a guide-book on the area, which stated: 'It is almost completely filled with mountains. Those who go to the top of them are called mountaineers, those who come down again, survivors.'

In the context of the main watershed, reference is essential to the unparalleled phenomenon of the chief rivers which flow from its glaciers to debouch in far-distant and widely differing seas. Of these the most important are the Rhine, the Rhône, the Po and the Inn.

The fact is that the first two named and the most important tributary of the upper Po, as well as two major tributaries of the Rhine – five considerable rivers – are born within ten miles of each other in the comparatively low ganglion of ranges forming an oblong box, cradling Switzerland's deep Urserental, near Andermatt, a small traffic-junction and hotel-cluster, the only town within miles.

Here, at some time or other the granite substructure of the Alpine chain was heavily compressed and flung up to great heights, to be covered in primeval days by an immense layer of ice thousands of feet thick, whose base would appear to have been not lower than the 8,000-foot level. The peaks and glaciers of this upheaval have long since been worn away, and the chief mountain group of the area now contains no summits of more than 11,000 feet. The basic structure, however, from which the dividing ranges rise, remains the loftiest and largest solid core in Switzerland; and from its flanks those five important European rivers set out on their courses, to flow in different directions and eventually to empty their waters in seas as distant and diverse as the North Sea, the Adriatic and the Western Mediterranean. For it is here in this mountain nexus, without parallel in the whole length of the Alps, that in a space ten miles long and five broad we find the sources of the Rhine, the Rhône, the Aar, the Reuss and the Ticino.

Of these, those two great rivers, the Rhine and the Rhône, spring from watersheds just six miles apart, to turn their backs frigidly on one another and start out on courses running due east and due west respectively, rather as the Severn and the Wye rise in close proximity high among Plynlimmon's ridges, to flow at first in diametrically opposite directions. The two great European rivers, however, later on take a right-angled change of direction, the Rhine to flow almost due north on its 960-mile journey by way of Bâle and Holland to the North Sea; the 850-mile Rhône turning due south a little above Lyons, to traverse the breadth of southern France to its Mediterranean mouth.

Only five miles to the northwest from where the Rhône glacier gives birth to its grey foaming torrent, across the Grimsel watershed, in the glaciers of the Finsteraarhorn lies the source of the Aar. This considerable but brief river flows due north till, at Meiringen, it strikes the broad deep trench which cradles the lakes of Brienz and Thun and leads to the fertile Bernese plain. Traversing the lakes, between which lies Interlaken, and the 30-mile-long plain, the river swings back northeastwards at Bern, to find its way through a gap in the foothills beyond Aarau and join first the Reuss, then the Rhine, at a point where it is flowing due west between Chur and Bâle, before its final swing to the north.

The Reuss, the smallest and least important of the five is, in its early course, the most remarkable. Springing from a small glacier to the east of the Furka-Rhône watershed, only about two miles from the Rhône's source, it first flows east along the extraordinary Urserental. This elevated plainlet, at an altitude of 5,000 feet, frowned down upon from all sides by high, rocky combs, is truly the 'Navel of Switzerland' and indeed of all Europe. It forms a kind of bath-shaped basin between the Furka and Oberalp watersheds, with no normal outlet for the waters draining into it from the surrounding peaks. But for one circumstance it might indeed have provided one of the most remarkable lake-basins in the Alps. Nature, however, arranged otherwise; for at its northeastern corner she left a weakness in the containing walls of rock, through which the Reuss gratefully bored a most sensational passage, more fully described in a later chapter. Its waters are thus able to escape into the outer world through what almost amounts to a natural tunnel and find their way steeply down northwards to the foot of the mountain barrier beyond, and so to the head of Lake Lucerne. Passing through the lake, the Reuss continues northwards and eastwards to fall into the Rhine.

The other important arm of this star-shaped quintet of river basins is that of the Ticino, which again rises only a mile or two away, but on the south side of the main Alpine watershed, among the southern glaciers of the Gotthard Group. Draining the whole southern flank of that massif, this river brawls its way steeply down into the smiling, sub-Alpine trench of the Ticino Valley, which gives its name to Switzerland's Italianate canton. Along this broadening valley it then flows less tempestuously to reach the head of Lago Maggiore, through which its waters are carried on into the Po and are thus emptied into the Adriatic.

So, three of Europe's great river-systems – the Rhine, the Rhône and the Po – are nourished by streams rising in this extraordinary ten-mile area. The fourth – the Danube, rising in Germany far to the north of the Alps, to debouch 1,500 miles away into the Black Sea, is fed by Switzerland's other great river, the Inn.

Rising just to the east of the Bregaglia group, close to the Maloja Saddle at the head of the Engadine, and destined to traverse Upper Austria and part of East Germany before falling into the Danube at Passau, the Inn affords another curiosity in the way of 'near-misses'. For at Maloja it flows within a quarter of a mile of the strangest watershed in the Alps. This tiny neck, a few hundred yards long and certainly not more than 50 feet high, is all that here separates the infant stream from a 2,000-foot drop into the Val Bregaglia on the southern side of the main Alpine chain; by only this much is the great river-to-be diverted from a southward course by way of Lake Como into the great river basin of the Italian plain – a course actually taken by the Mera, whose waters originate only a few yards on the other side of this lowest and slenderest of Alpine divides.

The Po, one of the only two other major rivers to rise in the central Alpine chain, trickles gently from the soggy foot of Monte Viso, far to the west in the Cottian Alps, down to Turin, where it is joined by the Dora Riparia, coming from the heart of the Graians and the Dora Baltea from the southern ramparts of Mont Blanc. Fed again further eastwards by the Ticino, as explained above, and later still by the Adda, draining Lake Como, and the Oglio bringing down the waters of the Bergamasque and Adamello ranges through Lake Iseo, this great river fertilizes the whole Lombard-North Italian plain on its way to the Adriatic.

The other is the Adige, which rises on the southern Italian flank of the low Reschen-Scheideck watershed, separating Switzerland from Italy near Nauders. Flowing east through a wide and lovely valley to Merano and Bolzano, traversing the whole of South Tyrol, it turns abruptly southwards to enter the great plain at Verona and, resolutely refusing to merge with its mightier neighbour, empties its waters into the Adriatic only a mile or two to the north of the Po's several mouths.

These major geographical features seems to me essential to a better understanding of the extent and structure of the Alpine area; the minor ones should emerge more clearly in the development of the separate regional chapters.

2. The Playground of Europe

When in the mid-nineteenth century Leslie Stephen, mountaineer, philosopher and father of Virginia Woolf, coined the phrase and gave the title to his classic book about the Alps, he was being prophetic to a degree he cannot have begun to suspect.

At that time there was only a handful of resorts scattered about the region, most of them in Switzerland, the only sector which was at all well-known and had already become popular with the leisured and wealthy who could afford the luxury of foreign travel, as a holiday paradise. Those were the days of honest-to-goodness, comfortable, pinewood-floored, beeswax-smelling hotels; of the Swiss cuisine and the 'ascent' of the long dining-room table by virtue of length of residence. As late as 1899, A. D. Godley was writing :

'They will dine on mule and marmot and on mutton made from goats,
They will face the various horrors of Helvetian table d'hôtes;
But where'er the paths that lead them and the food whereon they fare,
They will taste the joy of living as you taste it only there.'

Yes, the joys of living were there for those who, having once sampled them, returned again, summer after summer, to their favourite haunts in the growing number of mountain- and climbing-centres. The best known and most frequented were Interlaken and Kandersteg in the Oberland; in the Valais Zermatt, sprung to world fame through the first ascent and tragedy of the 'unconquerable' Matterhorn in 1865, and Saas Fee; St Moritz and Pontresina in the high, lakelet-studded Engadine; and the lowland lake resorts – Lucerne and the villages fringing its many-armed waters, Lugano, a kind of cross between Switzerland and the traditional Italian holiday-lands, Lausanne and Montreux on Geneva's open, sunny shores.

They were simple joys in those days. Here, face to face with the world's most beautiful scenery of great snow-capped peaks, green, wooded valleys and turquoise lakes, the elderly and the middle-aged could indulge in gentle strolls on woodland paths, or take one of the puffing, panting rack-and-pinion railways to high view-points like the Rigi and Pilatus, Schynige Platte in the Oberland, the Gornergrat above Zermatt, Monte Generoso or Mottarone above the lakes of Lugano and Maggiore, to sit in the sun sipping their *kaffe* or *schokolade*, admiring the vast panorama unfolded of the distant or nearer Alps.

The younger members of the family holiday-party, scorning the assistance of steam, would spend the long day in walking up to similar vantage-points by steep zig-zag paths through the pine-scented woods, up the flower-starred slopes and across the high green alps where the cattle shook their melodious bells and, in low ramshackle huts, the milk was drawn and the cheese was made.

This may perhaps be the right point at which to explain to the few who have not already had the truism rammed down their throats, that 'The Alps', as generally applied to the high ranges of Europe's great mountain complex, is a misnomer. An 'alp' is, in fact, a high, sunny pasture, usually somewhere about the 5- to 7,000 feet level, at the foot of the mountains still dominating it, to which the cows and goats are driven up as soon as the last snows have melted in the spring, and where they crop and live through the summer months, till they are brought down again in late September or October to their shelters in the valley.

There are, incidentally two basically different types of alp: store-herd alps, concerned only with cattle rearing, though a few cows are mostly kept alongside the oxen and calves, simply to supply milk, butter and cheese for consumption on the spot. There is no difficulty in distinguishing one of these from a cow-alp, since it normally consists of only one hut or at the most two, in which the meat-herds live and the cows are sheltered. Whereas on the cow-alps there is usually a big main hut in which cowherds, cheese-makers and maybe their womenfolk live and the milk is prepared and processed, with up to 50 stalls and sheds surrounding it, according to the extent of the alp.

The more energetic members of our nineteenth-century holiday parties, who took their mountains more seriously, would hump their rucksacks and embark on walking-tours of some days' duration from valley to valley by the tracks and mule-paths across the high intervening saddles, or even by the famous Alpine carriage-roads, on which the only traffic-dangers were the occasional horse-drawn vehicle – tours over the passes in the iron-tyred open 'victorias' of the day were early popular – a hay-cart, or the postal '*Diligence*' clattering down at speed behind three steeds, but tact-fully heralding its advent by blasts blown by a postilion on the posthorn.

The most adventurous and hardy of all came in twos and threes for serious mountaineering, which by the second half of the century had reached and passed its 'golden age'. These tough men – mostly 'gentlemen' of the professional or leisured classes – had by the end of it found a way up almost every peak in the Alps. They climbed them mostly by the 'ordinary route' – the one by which the summit had first been won and could be most safely and directly ascended; and they came back season after season to repeat the climb of their favourite mountains and to extend the number of their triumphs, operating from small, much more spartan inns in the higher climbing centres, from draughty cow-huts on the lofty alps above, and from bivouacs where the night was spent at the foot of the projected climb. In this new 'sport' they found the joys of heavy exercise in clean revivifying air, of reliance in their own judgment, skill and physical powers, of com-panionships forged with friends on whose skills and courage they also relied at times for the safety of their lives, and the spice of danger which is good for the soul of a townsman and an 'office-wallah'. Above all it was a pursuit which kept them, all through the long day and often through the night, close to Nature, among her most glorious and varied scenery, where the dawn came up in blue and gold and the dusk lit the west with flame, staining the snows to red and orange, before the stars blazed out of an indigo night over the chalk-white slopes.

A century has passed since Stephen wrote his charming book in praise of the Alps and enthused over the mountain-prospects which most gladdened his eye. (He claimed that the most beautiful of all Alpine views was that from the Baths of Santa Caterina, in the Ortler Group above Bormio, onto the lovely pyramid of the humble Tresero – a claim which not everyone would support. How many, a century later, had gone there to look at it, or until its recent recrudescence as a skiing-centre, had even heard of the tiny mountain resort he failed signally to popularise?)

The mountains stand changeless and unchangeable. They still offer the same gifts they offered then – magnificent scenery, pure, health-giving air, strenuous exercise which sends you to sleep at night dog-tired, to wake next morning – because of the qualities of that air – fresh and hungry for more, be you promenader, hill-walker or dedicated climber on rock and ice.

But in the relatively short space of a century, and more particularly in the second half of it, everything around and about them has changed, and changed beyond belief, far beyond anything Leslie Stephen and his contemporaries could have imagined in their wildest dreams, almost beyond the belief of our watching eyes as the tide of nothing less than a revolution has swept the valleys and slopes during the last six decades. For the Playground of Europe has become one of the playgrounds of the world.

To start with, the Alps have become vastly more accessible. Less than forty years ago the voyage to them began at Charing Cross or Victoria, entailing a more or less uncomfortable journey across the Channel from Folkestone or Dover, followed by a long overnight journey of more than twelve hours from the French port, often jammed bolt-upright four a side if you were not in the income bracket which commanded a berth in the sleek *wagons-lits* farther up the train. Of course it was all worthwhile, and it had its own peculiar charm, that leisurely journey across the sea and the endless flatlands of France, with the same old but ever-new sights flitting smoothly past the carriage-windows: for to sleep, even if it were possible, would have been unthinkable – till at last the long night gave way to the enchantment of the dawn and the first fore-runners of the Hills, arriving simultaneously.

In his autobiography, *Switchback*, Brian Lunn captured some of the unforgettable flavour of those nights full of discomfort, excitement and expectancy: the giant express-engine at Boulogne, drawing long sobbing breaths; the slow amble through the streets of that seaport, before the speed of the night express traversing the plains acquired its authentic rhythm – vv-vv-vv-vv, and the hood was drawn over the gas jet in the compartment for the night. Small stations near the frontier, at which a mysterious gong sounded twice to speed the train on into Switzerland; the keen morning air, the first châlet in its close-cropped meadow, then the first point in the Jura from which there is a brief glimpse of the distant Ober-land peaks. There they always were, the same as in previous years. Breakfast at Bern, coffee, rolls and cherry-jam – Arnold's 'feast of the Gods'. Later, as the train skirted the Lake of Thun, the whole Oberland coming into permanent view. Eiger, Mönch and Jungfrau, pleasantly magnified since that momentary glimpse from the Jura . . .

Today we board the airport bus from the West London Air Terminal for the longest part of the journey, the drive to Heath-row and the subsequent boarding of the jet after all due formalities and delays; an hour and a half, shall we say – about the time the boat-train used to take to the coast.

A little more than an hour later you are stepping out of the aircraft on Swiss soil at Bâle, Zürich or Geneva, according to the sector for which you are bound. Another ride in an airport bus, a journey of an hour or two in a comfortable electric train and hey, presto! you are wherever you want to be among the High Hills.

Or you take your car across one of the half dozen sea or air ferries and, since the great French *autoroutes* were opened a few years ago, it is possible to be looking at the mountains seven or eight hours of mile-a-minute motoring after leaving the coast, even if you don't drive an E-type Jaguar. Every year 750,000 cars leave these islands for the continent, a large proportion of them bound either to or through some sector of the Alps. The mountains themselves are criss-crossed by first-class road systems, many of them motorways to rival anything in the lowlands, the passes have been continually widened, resurfaced and re-engineered to cope with the incessant stream of cars, caravans, 40-seater coaches and postal-motors – not to mention the huge articulated lorries – which in high summer crowd them almost bonnet to tail. It is possible – if this be seeing – to see something of the French, Swiss, Austrian and Italian Alps in a ten-day tour by luxury coach, on one of the innumerable package trips leaving these shores every day. See it all from an armchair – yes, the Alps have indeed become accessible !

If you prefer an extended holiday based on a single holiday-resort, the difficulty nowadays is to make up your mind which of several hundred to select with the aid of a veritable library of gaily-coloured brochures. Not that it matters a great deal, since all are set in delectable scenery, all are beginning to look very much alike, with their white hotels, villas and tall blocks of flats, and the pattern is almost identical in every one of them. A few luxury hotels, a larger number of less pretentious ones, a cinema, a swimming-pool, a golf-course (nine holes), if sufficient ground is available, a choice of overcrowded bars, cafés, *konditoreien* and *dancings* for the stuffy gaieties of the night life and *après-ski*. In short, everything you would expect to find in an equivalent resort of the plains or on the Costa Mucho, except, of course, the sea itself, which has so far defied importation. (Though I have this week read of one modern resort's claim, high in the hills, to have installed the first salt-water indoor pool in Switzerland. If you have ever swum in an indoor salt-water pool, this will probably *not* be the resort you finally decide to favour.) But if water, as well as wine and song, appeal to you, you choose a lake which, if of late likely to suffer to a greater or lesser degree from various forms of pollution and therefore be less agreeable to swim in (the sport is in fact forbidden, lest the sportsman be polluted, at least at one famous Swiss resort) will still offer speed-boating and water-skiing as good and expensive as that in any blue bay along the Riviera.

Altitude, once a problem, especially in a 'poor' winter, when the lower resorts were often bare of snow, is no longer of concern. It has been annihilated. Whether your holiday resort is in a deep valley or on a sunny shelf half-way up the slopes of a great range, there are chair lifts or cable-car ropeways to the local belvedères in summer or the plentiful snow-fields high up among the peaks in winter. This lavish elimination of the necessity for any uphill use of the limbs has led to the rapid development of summer skiing. Every week-end, the plainsmen and townsfolk drive their cars, skis projecting from the roof-rack like crazy antennae, hell-bent for the foot of the nearest lift, pack it with themselves and their gear and spend long days running (downhill – a ski or drag-lift will attend to the return to the top) and sunbathing among the high snows which never melt. Indeed, a new form of triple-package holiday has been made possible and is rapidly gaining in popularity – the *dolce vita* of a soft Swiss or Italian lakeside, with its sunbathing and water-pastimes, combined with the rigours of a dash by car to an Alpine centre only an hour or two away, a quarter of an hour in a cable-car and all the joys of a day's high-mountain skiing, before the headlighted dash back through the dusk to the strumming and thrumming of pop music in an over-heated bar till the early hours. Who shall say whether the energy, fitness and endurance shown by the hardy pioneers of mountain-eering a hundred years ago was any greater?

Till the turn of the century the mountains were regarded purely as a summer holiday playground. Then, suddenly they were in-vaded by a new element, originating and practised for centuries past in Scandinavia as an essential method of transport – the art and sport of ski-running. Fostered in all the central European countries and soon popularised for the British by the organisation of winter-sports hotels and holidays in Switzerland by the Lunn family and the public schools' initiatives – the Oberland resorts of Adelboden, Mürren, Grindelwald and Wengen leading the way, with Davos, St Moritz and Pontresina in the Engadine soon to follow – 'winter sports' had not only come to stay but, in half a century, to revolutionise men's attitudes towards the mountains. Now, in the second half of our twentieth century, millions of non-experts come every winter to literally hundreds of ski-resorts, scattered high and low over the length and breadth of the Alps, for a fortnight's package-tour holiday. There, aided and abetted by ropeways, ski-lifts, chair-lifts and drag-lifts sprouting like mush-rooms on every suitable hillside, by day they frequently queue up for the upward journey to the head of hard-beaten *pistes*, run down them briefly as many times as they can cram into a day or into the resources of their purse, and return in the evening to enjoy the sounds, germs and pleasures of revelry by night. As one packaged group moves out on the 'second Saturday', the next moves in almost before the rooms are tidied and the beds made.

Far away indeed are the days when you booked in at your chosen hotel for as long or short a stay as you liked, and skiing meant shouldering your 'boards', climbing the slopes of your mountain till forced to strap them on; then, 'herring-boning' your long weary way up it on 'skins' to the summit, enjoyed an hour or two of downhill cross-country running, involving every kind of terrain and more or less virgin snow conditions, through the blessed solitude and silence of the high places, to the valley, the evening meal and a blissful, very necessary night's rest.

Today's casualty-rate, in terms of minor and major injuries to limbs is (literally) staggering. At one small but well-known resort alone the hospitals dealt with 1,500 cases in a single winter season recently. The unhealthy atmosphere of the overcrowded indoor activities ensures constant epidemics of flu, throat and stomach troubles and almost everybody returns home with a raging *après-ski* cold.

Nonetheless everyone is happy as a snowboy – the individual

parcels in the package, the hoteliers and restaurateurs who house and feed them, the hospitals and doctors who plaster them together (woe betide you if you have not insured against medical expenses before you set out, for the healing hand in some of these parts is not always a benevolent one held out, readily if roughly, by the State, and knows how to exhibit a firm grasp at the close of its ministrations), the shopkeepers who sell the souvenirs of bliss-on-earth, the treasurer of the local commune totting up his *taxes de séjour* and, above all, the tour operator at home, who has found a gold-mine buried in the snows of this new and more accessible Klondyke.

This, indeed, is what the Alps have come to mean to a high proportion of their twentieth-century lovers, who thanks to the universal white blanket covering all, cannot even distinguish between the mighty peaks of eternal snow and the local rock-knob six or seven thousand feet high; and greet with a faintly superior air of incredulity the information that people come to these places – to do what? – in summer, when the valleys and slopes are starred with flowers, butterflies and birds, the forests sweep dark and serried to the bare rock bluffs and combs above, and, high over all, the glittering castles and palaces of trackless snow and blue-green ice, made visible by the scouring rays of the summer sun, point nature's most ravishing contrast.

Of course countless thousands still come in summer to enjoy what the Alps have always offered – the scenery, the champagne quality of the air, healthy exercise from those woodland promenades, through serious walking – the activity now known as 'hiking' – to mountaineering proper. They also come, nowadays, to bare their bodies to the sun and swim and water-ski, to motor over the passes by private car or by coach, to play tennis and golf, and dine and dance as well – 'international' *cordon bleu* cuisine please, nowadays; none of your goat dressed as mutton. And in recent years yet another exacting and exciting sport has been added to the Alpine calendar – canoeing of various degrees of difficulty and danger on the swiftly-flowing mountain-streams and torrents, and – for the very expert and daring – on the turbulent,

5 *Summer: climbers on the Matterhorn*

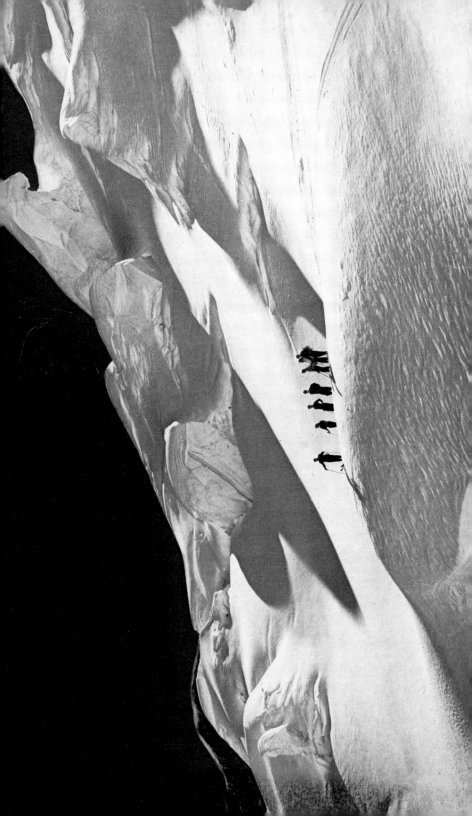

rock-strewn rapids which rage and foam headlong through the great gorges of Switzerland, Southern France and Austria.

Yes, the great snowy peaks which have looked down on the lakes and valleys of the Alps since time immemorial stand unchanged. It is the world at their feet which has undergone a kaleidoscopic metamorphosis.

If one utters a short sigh for the quiet days when the cowbells in the valley-meadows could still be heard above the roar of the traffic and smaller bells jingled merrily on the collars of the horses drawing landaus along almost deserted roads; when brown-planked, weathered châlets lined the village streets in picturesque confusion, and when there was room and safety to move in those streets without being jostled by hordes of souvenir-hunters or run over by juggernaut coaches and builders' lorries; when you were free to buy – for oh how unbelievably small a fee ! – your Alpine delights without being made conscious, from the hotel foyer to the luxury restaurant at the top of the rail- or rope-way on a high mountain-peak, that you are constantly having one thing or another sold to you; it is not that one is reactionary, merely sentimentally nostalgic.

There is no halting 'Progress'. Progress has come, during these years, in a big way to the Alps. It has come with and for the happiness of the millions who now swarm to them yearly from countries within a day's reach and from the remote corners of the earth by jet-flights across the oceans. There is no doubt that, in their own fashion, they find there their greatest happiness, just as we always found our (rather different) greatest happiness there, returning to it again and again.

John Stuart Mill would not have quarrelled with the developments.

6 *Winter: skiers at Eismeer, Bernese Oberland*

3. Alpine History

The Alps constitute the dividing line between the wide sub-temperate plains of northern Europe and the sunny more genial Mediterranean countries. They are, however, much more than a mere geographical feature on the face of the European map, the watershed distributing its rivers to one side or the other, the huge concatenation of mountain groups dictating different weather-systems and patterns on their northern and southern flanks. Though it should be noted in passing that the mountain belt, only at a few points more than 30 miles deep, tends throughout its length to build up to maximum elevation towards its southern fringe, then plunging steeply to the plains in an immense wall with only a short belt of foothills at its base. The prevailing south-westerly winds thus drive the moisture-laden air up from the Mediterranean to break first against the highest ridges of the barrier and the heavy precipitation resulting is responsible for the lush fertility of the Cisalpine area at its feet.

The ethnic, social and political influences of the Alps are as great as, or greater than their geographical aspect, though the two facets are obviously closely related and interdependent. Historically, they have since time immemorial formed the great racial and cultural divide between the Nordic and the Mediterranean peoples, sundering the dourer, tougher races of the more physically exacting north from the more voluble and mercurial strains of the softer, kindlier south.

With one exception, that of Rome's upward drive into Gaul and beyond – and even Rome suffered its eventual decay and decline, over a few centuries, under the softening and emasculating processes of sun and a superfluity of nature's abundance – all the great movements across the Alps have been from north to south. Time and again hordes of fierce and hardy tribesmen have swept down across the barrier to ravage the rich and luscious southlands, meeting with little resistance once the power of Rome weakened.

Five hundred years before the sack of Rome by Attila and his Huns, true, Julius Caesar had broken northwards out of the Italian plain to overrun the Gallic tribes, the Germanni, Teutoni and Helvetii beyond the mountains, and build the system of camps, forts and roads which enabled the Pax Romana to establish itself securely in thrice-divided Gaul and on into these inhospitable islands beyond the northern sea. Half a century later, in A.D. 13, Augustus extended the empire by crossing the Brenner to subdue and civilise Tyrol, its capital thenceforward Oenopontum (Innsbruck).

Two hundred years earlier, another great power had moved northwards from African Carthage to dispute the mastery of the Mediterranean basin with youthful Rome. Hannibal, starting from his base in conquered Spain, achieved the first crossing of the Alps by a sizeable army, some 30,000 men and 50 elephants (the tank corps of the day). His truly remarkable feat was achieved from west to east through the less elevated sector of the Provençal Alps and the formidable Cottians, and to this day, in spite of detailed accounts, not always in full agreement, by Polybius and Livy, conflict rages among the pundits as to the actual pass over which his troops, decimated by the resistance of the local tribes and the rigours of an icy transit, finally descended into the Piedmont plain. The latest expert opinion, dismissing at least two comparatively easy cols traditionally associated through the centuries with his passage and with some supporting evidence still *in situ* on one of them, have decided that he chose the highest, bleakest and most inaccessible narrow nick in the whole range – to and over which, to this day, it has proved, owing to the narrow, vertical-sided gorges on its approaches, impossible to construct anything better than a mule-track: and even that has to tunnel under the saddle to get through – the 10,000-foot Col de la Traversette. At the point where Polybius and Livy are unanimous that he, with his 30,000 men – including cavalry and with 50 war elephants – encamped for the night before the actual crossing into Italy, there is not room to house a troop of boy-scouts comfortably. Had I been Hannibal, I would have settled for the broad and relatively easy Petit St Bernard, 2,500 feet lower, where there remains to this day a vast perimeter of mighty stones, which could only have been set in place by an army or an elephant, and which has been known through the ages to the natives as the *Cirque d'Annibal*. There is, of course, nothing like doing things the hard way. But, as Mark Twain once said: 'The researches of many antiquarians have already thrown much darkness on the subject, and it is probable that if they continue, we shall soon know nothing at all.'

Apart from those three pushes from below the main west–east axis of the barrier, all subsequent drives have been from north to south, in search of plunder and rapine.

In the early part of the third century the Allemanni and the Goths, using Augustus' easy Brenner route in the reverse direction, descended upon Rome; the Romans, already degenerate, having survived an earlier 12 years' invasion by the Marcomanni, bought them off and they withdrew to their own lands. In A.D. 452 Attila and his Huns poured southwards over the same road, and this time the Roman Empire of the West was finally destroyed. Fourteen years later Odoacer followed, leading the Rugii, and established himself as King of Pavia: but in 489 Theodoric, again using the Brenner, evicted him and founded an empire stretching from the St Gotthard to the Black Sea. By 550 it had been disrupted owing to internal dissensions, leaving the Lombard kings masters of the Italian part.

There followed the wars of the Lombards and the Ostrogoths and the Franks, the wars of Charlemagne and the Lombards and, after the demise of the Carlovingian line, endless wars on behalf of the dukes of Bavaria, who then annexed the Tyrol, till Maximilian's advent in 1496.

Through the succeeding centuries the Alps, whose terrain one might have thought the least suitable for military activities, have been the site of continual wars. Swiss, Bavarian, Austrian, French and even Russian armies have fought and refought incredible and bloody campaigns in their valleys, through their ravines and gorges and on their heights. This book is no place for a detailed account of them; it is all to be found in the histories.

There is however one aspect of the Napoleonic campaigns, in which he conquered Italy, Switzerland and Austria between 1790 and 1805, only to lose them again in his final defeat and overthrow ten years later, which is of relevance to any non-military history of the Alps. This is the construction, at his command, purely for his strategic purposes, of the great Napoleonic military roads across the barrier, converting what had been rough tracks into carriageways suitable for the passage of great armies and their artillery and supply-trains. These are today the great motorable passes of the Alps – among them the Mont Genèvre, Mont Cenis, Great St Bernard and Simplon.

In both world wars of the present century, fierce fighting took place among the snows and rocks of the high Alps, even on the craggiest peaks of the Dolomites, which are honeycombed with trench-systems and tunnels, and festooned with rusty barbed wire to this day. In both these conflicts, however, little Switzerland alone of all the European nations contrived to maintain at least a semblance of neutrality, for the road and rail links across her territory were too important to be destroyed by the combatants and they provided Hitler with such a vital link with his Italian ally to the south that even he was compelled to leave Switzerland unmolested. The tremendous wartime traffic rolling and rumbling day and night to and through the great Alpine railway-tunnels and over the main road-passes thus became a great contributing factor in Switzerland's postwar wealth and prosperity.

In a small book such as this the main historic aspect must, apart from the social and touristic aspects already touched on, be that of the mountains themselves: some account of men's attitude towards them and the chief activity associated with them – mountaineering.

Through the middle ages and down to the end of the eighteenth century, the general attitude of civilized men towards the high-mountain regions and the lofty valleys at their feet was one of abhorrence, revulsion and genuine fear. They were looked upon not only as cold, bleak, savage and inhospitable but positively hideous to the eye. Moreover, superstition and unfamiliarity peopled them with malevolent spirits, mythical dragons and races of bloodthirsty, evil men. The main reaction expressed by writers before the dawn of the Romantic era, only some two hundred years ago, was one of desolation and horror.

John de Bremble, a twelfth-century monk, returning from a journey to the Great St Bernard wrote, ' "Lord", I said, "restore me to my brethren, that I may tell them, that they come not into this place of torment" '.

John Dryden: 'High objects, it is true, attract the sight, but it looks up with pain on craggy rocks and barren mountains, and continues not intent on any object which is wanting in shades of green to entertain it.'

John Evelyn, in his diary, recorded his impressions of a crossing of the Simplon Pass, in 1646: 'The next morning we mounted again through strange, horrid and fearful crags and tracks, abounding in pine-trees, and only inhabited by bears, wolves and wild goats . . . This night, through almost inaccessible heights, we came in prospect of the Mons Sempronius, now Mount Sampion, which has on its summit a few huts and a chapel . . . From this uncomfortable place, we prepared to hasten away next morning.'

Horace Walpole, writing from Italy in his turn, did not like it any better. A passage from a letter to a friend runs: 'We were eight days in coming hither from Lyons, the four last in crossing the Alps. Such uncouth rocks and such uncomely inhabitants! My dear West, I hope I shall never see them again!'

The most amusing passage in dispraise of the Alps appeared in a geological textbook written in 1684 by Thomas Burnet, and is, I think worth quoting in full:

Tis prodigious to see and to consider of what Extent these Heaps of Stones and Rubbish are ! . . . in what Confusion they lie ! They have neither Form nor Beauty, nor Shape nor Orders, no more than the Clouds of the Air. Then how barren, how desolate how naked are they? How they stand neglected by Nature? Neither the Rains can soften them, nor the Dews from Heaven make them fruitful . . . These mountains are placed in no Order one with another, that can respect either Use or Beauty; and if you consider them singly, they do not consist of any Proportion of Parts that is referable to any Design, or that hath the least Footsteps of Art or Counsel. There is nothing in Nature more shapeless or ill-figured than an old Rock or Mountain, and all the Variety that is among them, is but the Various Modes of Irregularity.

There were, of course, exceptions. As early as 1611 Hermann Kirchner of Marburg was uttering the earliest known enthusiastic appreciation of mountain scenery and mountain delights in his *Coryats Crudities:*

The Heigth of Hilles

What I pray you is more pleasant, more delectable, and more acceptable unto a man than to behold the heigth of hilles, as it were the very Atlantes themselves of heaven? to Admire Hercules his pillers? to see the mountaines of *Jupiter?* to pass over the Alpes that were broken by Anibals Vineger? to climb up the Appenine promontory of Italy? from the hill Ida to behold the rising of the Sunne before the Sunne appears? to visit Pernassus and Helicon, the most celebrated seates of the Muses? Neither indeed is there any hill or hillocke, which doth not containe in it the most sweete memory of worthy matters.

But broadly speaking, mountains remained objects of terror and discomfort, unpleasing to the eye, till well into the nineteenth century. Even Shelley, Wordsworth and Coleridge in their rare poems describing Mont Blanc and other mountains gave vent to sentiments of awe and amazement, though they were among the first to reflect a sense of the beauty of the mountain scene in all its varied moods as they affected the poet's mind.

All those mentioned were of course writing before men began to climb regularly and so discovered that they were fully equipped to grapple successfully with the terrors which had seemed so much more daunting when viewed from afar and still not properly understood.

Exceptionally, there had been a few early isolated ascents of reasonably high and quite difficult mountains, ever since in the fourteenth century Bonifacio Rotario, a hermit, carried a heavy brass triptych dedicated to the Virgin to the top of the 11,605-foot Roccamelone, above Susa. Again, in 1492 the formidable cliffs of Mont Aiguille (6,880 feet) south of Grenoble were somehow scaled by Antoine de Ville de Beaupré and his men, using ladders, iron stanchions and ropes (a prophetic touch!); not because anyone was anxious to climb a mountain, but because Charles VIII of France had issued a somewhat capricious order to that effect. In 1770 the brothers Deluc, of Geneva, climbed the Buet, and nine years later the Abbé Murth reached the summit of Mont Vélan (12,333 feet), a much more difficult assignment and really the first ascent of a high snowpeak. These early climbs, like the long series of attempts on Mont Blanc which began at about that date, were undertaken more in the interests of science and a spirit of discovery than from any feeling that there could be actual pleasure in climbing a mountain.

The breakthrough came on a June afternoon in 1786, when Michel-Gabriel Paccard, a son of the Chamonix notary, taking with him Jacques Balmat as a porter – Balmat was a local hunter of chamois and crystals – succeeded in reaching the 15,782-foot summit of Mont Blanc. A few weeks later, the distinguished Genevese scientist Horace Benedict de Saussure repeated the feat.

Not only had it been proved that man could live in such rarefied air and even survive the cold and the elements of a night out at such great altitudes, but that men of sophistication and refinement, used to the comforts of city-life could cope with the rigours of such uncivilized surroundings and enjoy the triumph of reaching their desired goal. The age of mountaineering had begun.

A little before this date a new feeling was already springing up in men's minds about mountains, as a manifestation of Nature, and about the simple peasants who lived a 'natural', and therefore a virtuous, life among them. This was greatly fostered by the publication of *La Nouvelle Héloïse*, a novel by the great Genevese philosopher Jean-Jacques Rousseau, in 1761. The book became a bestseller and Rousseau's devotees flocked to the places immortalised by their idol in those passages of the story which dealt with the hero's journey through the Valais, to worship and admire. Travellers began to flock to the Lake of Geneva, and increasing numbers visited such Alpine villages as Chamonix and Grindelwald. The Romantic era dawning in literature, with Ossian, Lamartine and others, conscious of the beauty of antiquity and ancient ruins, embraced the mountain scene in due course and within half a century the Alpine landscape was stripped of its aura of fearsome austerity and terror, its beauty and sublimity gradually realised.

For many years to come, a scientific label was still to be tagged to the rucksacks of the men who began to scale the peaks themselves in growing numbers – the study of snow-structures, temperatures, the movement of glacier-ice, geology and cartography. During the first decades of the nineteenth century, a succession of Swiss scientists, followed later by other eminent figures from England and elsewhere, moved about and lived among the high peaks, climbing any convenient and not too exacting summit at hand. By 1850 a new era was dawning and the publication of two books by the British scientist J. D. Forbes, *Travels through the Alps* (1844) and *A Tour of Mont Blanc and Monte Rosa* (1855) did much to enhance and stimulate a completely new attitude of mind towards mountains – a wish to visit them for their own sake and to climb them in a spirit of joyous exploration and adventure in a new realm.

At this moment, in September 1855, Alfred Wills (Mr Justice Wills) lawyer and naturalist, climbed the Wetterhorn above Grindelwald – actually, it had been climbed five times before – but his was the first ascent of any mountain to result in a well-written description of the climbing of a high peak for the sheer pleasure of the thing. Wills settled in Switzerland, making continual high-level tours and climbing other peaks, among them Mont Blanc and Monte Rosa.

Others from Britain, the central European countries and, naturally, from Switzerland itself, came to follow in the footsteps of the first truly 'amateur' mountaineers. One by one all the peaks of the Alps, smaller and greater, were climbed by parties which always employed local guides, coming out year after year for a climbing holiday and to enjoy what were at last recognised as the beauties and pleasures of the Alpine scene.

In those days and for decades to come it would have been unthinkable to embark on a major tour or climb without the inclusion of one or more local guides in the party. Even the most experienced and skilled amateurs – Whymper and others showed themselves perfectly capable of climbing by themselves and when so minded – relied on these strong, trustworthy men for their support, their knowledge of local routes and weather conditions and their companionship; indeed, numerous deep and memorable friendships developed between a 'Herr' and his favourite and trusted guide – to quote only Geoffrey Winthrop Young and Josef Knubel in the present century as an example. Every climbing centre boasted its corps of guides – Zermatt, Saas Fee, Chamonix, Grindelwald among the more prominent – and a list of the great individual names would be a formidable one, from the Burgeners, Laueners Supersaxos, Devouassouds of those days (many of those names persist on today's rotas at the various Bureaux des Guides) to the giants of the modern era of climbing, Rébuffat, Bonatti Diemberger and a dozen others.

Guideless climbing was a comparatively late development, born of the experience of great amateurs like Mummery towards the end of the century, perfectly capable of undertaking the greatest climbs of their day without professional assistance. With the wider extension of skill, technique and experience over the years, the practice has become pretty general, and the greatest and most difficult ascents are competently undertaken without professional assistance. Another factor which has contributed to this development is the economic one : most of those who now come to climb in the Alps do so on a shoestring budget, and the guides' tariff, like everything else in the world, has soared to prohibitive heights, far beyond their means. Unfortunately, not all of these countless thousands command the knowledge and experience demanded by Alpine climbs and conditions, and tragedies and fatalities are the result. By the rules of the game written and unwritten it is still the professionals who have the thankless task of going to their rescue or, in the last resort, bringing down their bodies.

The 'Golden Age' in the mid-nineteenth century, lasting some 25 years during which all the great peaks were mastered, suffered a brief set-back by an affront to world opinion which momentarily brought the new 'sport' into disrepute and even caused Queen Victoria – even less amused than usual – to consider issuing a royal ban on it.

In July 1865 a young artist and engraver, Edward Whymper, who had long fallen under the spell of the Alps and proved himself a born and fearless mountaineer, led a party of prominent British climbers up the 'unconquerable' Matterhorn, on which he had been making attempts by a variety of routes for some years past, triumphantly to set the shirt of one of his guides (the party carried no flag) waving on its proud summit. Owing to circumstances described elsewhere a hundred times – the best reconstruction, a semi-fictional one, can be found in Ronald Clark's *The Day the Rope Broke* (1965) – disaster struck and four of the party fell to a tragic death. The world was stunned; it remains the most notorious of the many inevitable accidents in the long history of mountaineering.

The setback was only temporary and the spoliation of the great Alpine summits was soon resumed. A few recalcitrant peaks resisted till the 80s. By the turn of the century there was not a crest in the Alps which had not been climbed, cairned and furnished with a bottle containing the names of its first visitors.

Mountaineers are an ingenious and fortunate breed. Unlike Alexander, they never run out of worlds to conquer. This is not only because when you have climbed every knob in the Alps worthy to have the description of Horn, Spitze, Mont, Pic, Aiguille or Punta bestowed on it, there are still the Caucasus, the Himalaya, the Andes of Bolivia, Peru, Chile and Argentina, the New Zealand Alps, the Rocky Mountains, Greenland's icy ones, the Russian Pamirs, Kuen Lun and Tien Shan, and Afghanistan's Hindu Kush, all awaiting your devoted attentions. True, after the subjugation of the Alps, a small number of eminent Alpinists were soon sampling the first five ranges named; though it was to be another half-century before a new 'Golden Age' began in the Himalaya – the world's 14 'Eight-Thousander'* giants all falling within a decade, starting with Annapurna in 1950 – the Andes and the Russian ranges suffering their heaviest onslaught about the same time, with the Hindu Kush still being explored and opened up as a climbers' paradise during the last ten years.

Not a bit of it. The surface of the Alps had only been scratched. With every summit climbed by the route which finally yielded success, somewhat naturally the most obvious, least difficult and hazardous to be found on it – now known as the normal or 'ordinary' route – climbers switched their attention to a new idea, born and largely depending on the great advances in skill, technique and experience undergone by the craft during those years of arduous conquest.

Every Alpine peak, like every other mountain, has a number of ridges, containing a number of 'faces', some consisting of solid walls of rock, others of vertical shields of plastered ice. All of them were likely to be more difficult, exacting and exciting than the 'ordinary' route. Until each and every one of these, roughly quadrupling the objectives available, had been ascended, the 'last problem of the Alps' would not have been exhausted. Eventually

* The 'Eight-Thousanders' are the 14 peaks of 8,000 metres or over (26,205 feet) – all in the Himalaya.

even this enormous bonus was absorbed, so far as it lay within the limits of what had up till then been understood by the term 'climbing' – of the possible techniques and means of what is now – does one detect a slight air of denigration? – referred to as 'free' climbing.

Mountaineering stopped a moment to scratch its head and then, in the 30s and again as soon as the sport could be resumed after 1945, overcame the difficulty with the resourcefulness one would expect of the hardy (and rapidly-increasing) tribe which scorns other delights and lives laborious Alpine days. 'Free' climbing had mastered everything hitherto considered possible. A method must be evolved which would provide an infinite number of climbs on Alpine ridges, walls, towers and pinnacles, on rock and in the ice, by making it possible to climb the impossible. No sooner said than done.

With remarkable speed, a totally new concept of mountaineering, implemented by the appropriate advances in techniques, clothing and equipment, sprang into being. Throughout the long history of the sport no respectable mountaineer would have dreamed of relying on 'adventitious aids' – indeed for many years it was laid down that the rope connecting the members of a party was there to lend only 'moral' assistance, a theory sometimes a little difficult to maintain when one of them inconsiderately 'came off'. To resort to any mechanical aid, apart from the occasional ladder in the unschooled days of the earliest ascents and of course, the axe, the rope, tricouni-nails in boot soles, and – thin end of the wedge? – the crunching of crampons, sets of steel spikes to strap on for work on ice; to chip a hold in rock, where nature had neglected to provide one (an action which, on a certain Lakeland climb sparked off a bitter controversy among British climbers); to safeguard oneself or one's partners by anything but the accepted 'belay' of rope round rock or, on snow, round the deeply-embedded axe; such crimes and contrivances had been looked upon as savouring of sacrilege and moral turpitude.

Now, with a remarkably swift reflection of that 'permissiveness' which has swept the world since the end of its second great war, the technique of climbing was evolved and extended to embrace every form of mechanical and material aid which could be invented or devised to facilitate the mastery of the impossible, and so extend the (vertical) horizons of the mountaineers indefinitely. The simple basis of this revolution was the *piton*, an iron spike hammered into rock or ice, with a ring in its head through which to thread a rope or, later, a multiplicity of ropes, thus providing an artificial belay and a source of additional leverage on vertical, holdless faces of whatever consistency.

The first protagonists of the new methods, on climbs previously held to be unthinkable, were the Germans and Austrians of the Munich and other schools, who, it was alleged and not without good grounds, came to the murderous rock-faces of their own stony ranges to risk death for the greater glory of a symbol, an ideology and a nationalism since discredited. After the war, defeated and disillusioned, they returned to even more hazardous undertakings to prove their mettle and re-establish their self-respect. In this they were joined by a new generation of French and Italian climbers, highly trained during the past few years in the techniques of Alpine warfare and extremely daring and efficient. British climbers, not burdened with guilt and other complexes, were slow to take to the 'new mountaineering', but when they did they were not long in establishing themselves among its top-ranking exponents.

With the improvements in equipment, its proliferation into a vast armoury of ironmongery, and the elaboration of rope techniques into a veritable cat's cradle, a stage was in due course reached where it was simply a question of choosing another 'impossibility' on rock and ice and hammering, slinging, stirruping and block-and-tackling a way up it, always supposing you had the courage, strength, patience and endurance, allied to a vital command of techniques – all requisite to the highest degree – to face such exacting, exhausting, nerve-racking labours and perils. Countless routes in the Dolomites, on the huge Karwendel faces, on smooth Savoy granite and on our coastal cliffs and rickety pinnacles have been mastered in this way, which three decades ago would simply not have been contemplated as within the realms of safe and sound mountaineering possibilities. The new techniques have made it possible to defeat not only the vertical and the slightly outward leaning but also the great bulging overhangs, jutting out above hundreds of feet of thin air, where the modern climber, hammering and stringing his protective network of pegs and ropes close above his face, is poised horizontally with his back to the abyss. This way there are no limitations. If it were felt desirable, the exterior of the Post Office tower's sleek column or the massive 1,250-foot face of the Rockefeller Center could be scaled using these methods: indeed, not long ago television regaled us with a climb of the iron structure of the Eiffel Tower.

Many of these long and fearsome routes require several days of strenuous toil. The new techniques have made even this possible, for at the end of the day's labours, the climbers hang themselves and their protective 'tent-sack' covering from pitons driven into the wall and spend night after night in greater or lesser discomfort. Let there be no doubt that the climbing of the second half of this century demands 'guts' . . .

On the mighty peaks of 'mixed' rock, snow and ice, the breakthrough came as early as 1938 when, after some years of abortive attempts and numerous fatalities, Heinrich Harrer's Austrian foursome finally defeated the notorious north face of the Eiger and returned alive to tell the tale.

No account of recent Alpinism can avoid some reference to this odious 'killer' face which, because it happens to stand in full view of the masses of Oberland tourists, has unfortunately captured the imagination of the world, as the Matterhorn did a hundred years ago. Seen through their eyes, those of a Press greedy for sensation and woefully ill-informed about mountain matters and the compelling influence of radio and television, this monstrous death-trap has become a legend. I say 'unfortunately' because it cannot and should not be regarded as in any way representative of mountaineering as a sport or a recreation.

This tallest of all the Alpine north faces, 6,000 feet high from base to summit, is not only a vast combination of sheer rock and ice; it is incessantly raked by the stone-fire of its own disintegration and subject to its own freakish weather-system, which can turn it in a matter of minutes into an icy shroud for those trapped high up in its sombre recesses. As Harrer has made crystal clear in his famous Eiger history, which I had the honour of putting into English as *The White Spider*, it is a place only for the most hardy, skilled and experienced, if they must pit their very existence against its perils: all others should give it a wide berth. Sadly, a whole regiment of young men, totally unequipped, either humanly or materially for a challenge of this magnitude, has nonetheless been drawn by its siren lure and come, over the years, to match their inadequacy with its stacked cards, and to die. It has now been climbed innumerable times in summer; for the first time in winter by Tony Hiebeler's rope of four in 1960 – when it was established that the face is less difficult and dangerous in winter conditions (provided you do not succumb to the cold) because its fragmentation bombardment is then frozen into virtual quiescence.

In 1970 it was climbed by a *direttissima*, a perpendicular route up the central fall-line, far more exacting than even the established one. This feat of sheer virtuosity was accomplished over a period of weeks by relays of climbers, inching their way up and planting fixed ropes all the way, returning when exhausted to the Scheidegg Hotel at the foot of the face, to revive themselves with the recreations of good food and drink, the pleasures of the dance with their girl friends and nights of sleep in a comfortable bed; then reascending by the fixed rope stairway to fight their way forward a few more feet towards the top. Even so that fine American climber James Harlin lost his life during the long, perilous campaign. I do not pretend to know what pioneers like Wills and Whymper would have thought of these commercially sponsored goings-on, but then men of their ilk might anyway have felt themselves somewhat adrift in all the parallel manifestations of our permissive era.

Since the development of winter sport among the Alps has already been dealt with in an earlier chapter, this latest and, I suppose, greatest of Alpine achievements must bring to an end my

7 *Nineteenth-century Zermatt; a Whymper engraving*

8   *Gornergrat Station, with the Matterhorn and Dent Blanche*

9   *Monte Rosa from Gornergrat*

brief sketch of the history of Alpinism, woefully lacking though it is in famous names of men and mountains alike, in details of first ascents and landmarks, whether on peak, ridge or face. If it may seem that the 'last problem of the Alps' has now finally been solved and almost everything worth climbing there has been climbed, one thing remains beyond doubt.

Summer after summer, and even in winter, thousands of keen and energetic young men – and the army is steadily growing – will come back to pit their skill, resource and courage against the challenge of the great routes and the lesser ones already climbed. Even the 'ordinary' way will charm the novice and the less experienced, and for two or three weeks, each year, they will all find there their heaven on earth.

4. Literature and Art

The laterature of the Alps is rich indeed. Their history and the story of their development, exploration and conquest by the strenuous, heroic men who during the last 200 years have been inspired by their irresistible call and their own skill and courage to wrestle with the unimaginable and surmount the insurmountable have been charted in writings of an extraordinarily high standard. Or is it, after all, so surprising that some of these men of imagination and character, a large proportion of them highly educated, should have known how to dip their pens in the gold of the Alpine sunrise itself?

As already said, early accounts of journeys and minor ascents among the Alps dwelt for the most part on their horrific and repellent aspects. Some rare exceptions have already been quoted, and Shakespeare's sonnet, which starts –

> Full many a glorious morning have I seen
> Flatter the mountain tops with sovereign eye,
> Kissing with golden face the meadows green,
> Gilding pale streams with heavenly alchemy –

must surely qualify, even if his mountain-tops were not Alpine.

It was however not till well into the nineteenth century, when the simultaneous influence of the great romantic writers and poets, recognising at last the majesty and beauty of mountains, and of the pioneer climbers who found that it was not only possible and safe but actually enjoyable to move about among them, that a separate literature of the Alps was born.

When Rousseau in the mid-eighteenth century was waxing enthusiastic and poetic about the mountain scene as viewed from the lakes and valleys at their feet and setting the new fashion for travellers to visit them, the first epoch-making ascent of Mont Blanc still lay 25 years ahead. The true literature of the Alps, though foreshadowed and fostered by the tardy acceptance of the idea that there is beauty in mountain scenery, did not come into being till half a century after Paccard's breaking of the height-barrier when, following the years of scientific data and reports, the sport of mountaineering was born and its devotees began to relate their struggles, adventures and experiences, as well as to attempt descriptions of scenic magnificence and beauty at its most diverse, in an intense desire to share them with others.

Since these pioneers were mainly scientists and professional men of good education, they were well able to express their reactions and describe, in good, readable prose, what they felt and saw. The resulting literature of the Golden Age and the succeeding decades up to the First War was considerable and often reached a very high standard of documentation and description. Times and fashions have changed markedly since then and, if they have inevitably adopted a less sentimental and more technical approach, the many articulate men of high intellectual attainments who still contribute a strong leavening to the wider and more mixed sector of the community which can now afford to travel and climb, have continued to ensure that the first-class treatment of their subject continues. (And for those not quite so articulate, has it not already been shown that the mountains have always been the home of ghosts?)

This wealth of well-written books has been almost entirely factual or historical; for flights into the realms of mountaineering fiction have been notably less successful. The truth seems to be that great climbers are on the whole not by nature good novelists, while good novelists – a number of whom have none the less ventured to tread the slippery slopes of fictitious mountaineering – seem to know too little about climbing, or even about mountains, with frequently disastrous results.

In the factual realm, mention has already been made of Alfred Wills's account of his Wetterhorn climb as sparking off the essential literature of mountaineering, and J. D. Forbes's books are fine early examples, which stimulated the public interest and a demand for more accounts of this kind. They were followed by numerous books about the Alps and climbs among them which have become classics not only in the narrower mountaineering field but in the wider context of exploration, adventure and travel generally.

The one which achieved the widest acclaim and influenced more people than any other to turn their attention or, in many cases, their active lives to mountaineering was Whymper's *Scrambles in the Alps* (1871) and later his *Conquest of the Matterhorn* (1880).

Other important publications were *Peaks, Passes and Glaciers* (1859), Tyndall's *Glaciers of the Alps* (1860), Ball's *Guide to the Western Alps* (1863) and in 1877, A. W. Moore's *The Alps in 1864.* At this time, too, Ruskin, who had a passion for the Alps though he lacked the courage to climb them, was hymning their aesthetic joys in his series *Modern Painters, The Stones of Venice* and *Sesame and Lilies,* which had a widespread influence. Leslie Stephen's *Playground of Europe* (1871) followed two earlier accounts of individual climbs; and A. L. Mummery's classic, *My Climbs in the Alps and Caucasus* followed, with great effect, in 1880. W. A. B. Coolidge's first book appeared in 1889 and his immense output continued to cover the next 30 years, his most famous book *The Alps in Nature and History* appearing in 1913. From 1881 to 1932 that great climber and explorer Martin Conway (later Sir, then Lord) issued a number of important books, the best-known of which probably remains *The Alps from End to End* (1895). In 1909 R. L. G. Irving, who far into a ripe old age remained the mentor of numerous great climbers (G. L. Mallory of Everest fame among them) published his first book *Five Years with Recruits; The Romance of Mountaineering* (1933), *The Mountain Way* (1938) and *The Alps* (1939) all became classics. Geoffrey Winthrop Young's *Mountain Craft* appeared in 1910, to be followed by one of the finest Alpine books ever written, *On High Hills* in 1924. The year 1910 saw the publication of C. E. Matthews' *The Annals of Mont Blanc*, and in 1914 Mallory appeared on the scene, though only as a contributor to the journals of the Alpine and Climbers' Clubs.

It is impossible to do justice to all those who have written first-class books on the subject since the twenties. Outstanding among them are the names of F. S. Smythe, G. I. Finch, Lord Schuster, Dorothy Pilley and her husband G. J. Richards, Arnold (later Sir Arnold) Lunn, L. S. Amery (the statesman), C. F. Meade, Douglas (later Sir Douglas) Busk, Wilfrid Noyce, Eric Shipton, H. W. Tilman and a host of others. I can only apologise to those omitted for sheer lack of space.

For reasons which are obvious, the largest output of mountaineering literature during the nineteenth century came from British pens. The number of mountain classics contributed by continental authors is, even so, surprisingly small.

As early as 1830 Victor Hugo wrote an account of an Alpine journey in the *Revue des deux Mondes*, Dumas a book of Alpine impressions two years later. R. Töppfer published two volumes of his amusing *Voyages en Zig-Zag* in 1844 and 1854. In 1878 Boileau de Castelnau wrote an account of his late conquest of the Meije in the journal of the Club Alpin Français. Eight years later the great Austrian alpinist Emil Zsigmondy published his *Dangers de l'Alpinisme* and in 1888 *Im Hochgebirge*. 1892 saw Emil Javelle's somewhat heavy *Souvenirs d'un Alpiniste* and in 1900 Guido Rey, 'the King of the Matterhorn', enshrined his lifelong passion for that peak in *Il Monte Cervino*, followed 20 years later by his *Ascensions*. 1924 was marked by P. Dalloz's *La Pointe Lagarde*, 1926 by J. Estaunié's *Le Silence dans la Campagne (Le Cas de Jean Bunant)*. In 1931 Claire Eliane Engel published her comprehensive two-volume study of Alpine Literature (in French), the first of many Alpine books of great value, culminating in 1950 in her *History of Mountaineering*, published here in her own English version. 1932 saw Dalloz's *Haute Montagne* and two books by famous professional guides, one Swiss, one Austrian : Christian

Klucker's *An Alpine Guide* and Luis Trenker's *Kameraden der Berge*. Another guide, J. Kugy, wrote *Alpine Pilgrimage* (1933) and *Son of the Mountains* (1938). Charles Gos's *Alpine Tragedy* appeared in its English translation by Malcolm Barnes in 1948. Samivel's *L'Amateur d'Abîmes* came in 1941; André Roch's *Les Conquêtes de ma Jeunesse* in 1943, Jacques Boell's *S.E.S.* and G. Sonnier's *Où règne la Lumière* in 1946.

On the continent, as in Britain, there have been many remarkable books written in recent years dealing with the postwar era in the Alps by such great professional climbers as Gaston Rébuffat, Lionel Terray, Walter Bonatti, Kurt Diemberger, Tony Hiebeler and other prominent climbers and gifted authors. Once again lack of space dictates my apologies to those not included in this sketchy list.

It has been stressed that this wealth of well-written books is almost entirely factual. When it comes to the sphere of fiction the story is very different. The reasons are not difficult to assess.

The factual details of mountaineering, in the hands of a good writer, will always be so much more evocative and thrilling than any invented happenings revolving around imaginary characters; and, in the end, the mountains themselves are so immense and dominant that, if justice is done to them, they will almost certainly finish up as the heroes of the story, dwarfing the toy figures jerking feebly like puppets as the author frantically manipulates the strings. The most that can be hoped for is, I think, the interpolation of climbing passages into a novel dealing with some other theme, as in A. E. W. Mason's *Running Water*, the Chamonix sequences of which can surely never be bettered, and the occasional trenchant success achieved in a short-story, as in C. E. Montague's 'Action' and 'In Hanging-Garden Gully' or, in a quite different way, in Wells's *Little Mother of the Morderberg*. Alphonse Daudet's delightful and frankly farcical *Tartarin sur les Alpes* (1885) is of course a novel, but its success lies in another genre altogether, that of light-hearted satire.

I can sympathise with the failures, having tried my hand many years ago in five Alpine novels and, while perfectly competent to produce a story in which the situations and details are authentic and free from the howlers of the non-mountaineering novelist, failed signally, for one of the reasons given earlier, to write the 'great' mountaineering novel of my aspirations. I no longer believe in its possibility.

So many novelists of fame and repute have fallen by the way-side. Galsworthy wrote a sadly symbolic and metaphysical play about climbing, *The Little Dream*. A. J. Cronin, blinded by the dazzling marvels of a winter holiday published a thriller, *Enchanted Snow*, in which the hero, a champion ski-runner, pursues the heroine, apparently another, at high speed through an 'arrow-swift flight' for a period which, by comparison with the championship time for the Parsenn run, would have achieved twice the 16,000-foot descent from Mont Blanc's summit to sea-level. Later on an aged professor finds himself – not surprisingly – in some difficulty with his ski on a glacier's 'blue ice'.

So knowledgeable a student of things mountainous as the American writer, the late J. Ramsey Ullmann, in his well-written and enormously successful novel, *The White Tower*, fell into an avalanche of error. For the purposes of his story he collects, to climb an 'impossible' killer of a peak, six people whom nobody in their senses would have for one moment dreamed of tying onto the same rope. He then confronts us with an *unclimbed* Swiss peak, a commodity which went out of supply half a century ago. And such a Swiss peak at that! For it has to be scaled by Himalayan methods with a string of camps established and provisioned up the endless weeks of its ridge. A rough calculation, taking the total time apparently involved in the ascent, and applying an average rate of feet per hour for normal Alpine climbs of some difficulty, reveals that this odd Swiss virgin was something over 30,000 feet tall (from the valley). Poor old Everest! Notwithstanding, two of the party succeed in making passionate love all the way up – 'love in a cold climate', indeed!

That author of splendid best-selling novels, John Masters, crammed almost every kind of mountain solecism into his stirring tale of Alpine and Himalayan adventure, *Far, Far the Mountain*

Peak. The hero, in the process of turning himself into the greatest climber of the age by a praiseworthy training programme of 'twenty-three major Alpine peaks in fifty-three days – sometimes two a day', suddenly realises that he loves the heroine, an Alpinist of only modest attainments. So he takes his novice with him and they climb the Zmutt Ridge of the Matterhorn, one of the major ridge-climbs in the Alps, for which eight to ten hours would be good going for a strong party, by night, carrying a lantern in his teeth, in a mere six. However these are evidently no ordinary mortals. For, apparently feeling no adverse effects from six hours of tough climbing plus four more of the long knee-jarring descent by the Hörnli ridge and Schwarzsee path, they enact a mutually enthusiastic seduction scene in the woods before reaching Zermatt. Truly 'the great climbs of yesterday are become an easy day for a (?) lady !'

There are many Alpine disasters of this kind. Even the ex-guide turned novelist, Frison-Roche, whose first novel of the Chamonix valley 'First on the Rope', abounded in (too many) fine climbing descriptions, failed in his novelettish story; the sequel *La dernière crevasse* was frankly ridiculous in the impossibilities it demanded of one's belief. I believe there was a 'third helping', but not having felt strong enough to read it, I cannot comment on it.

Strangely the lack of great Alpine fiction also applies, very largely and more surprisingly, to the field of poetry. Great poems about mountains from the hands of our recognised major poets are singularly few, and while some of them reveal flashes of rare beauty, on the whole they fail disappointingly to reflect the magnificence of their subject. Major poets have not normally climbed major mountains, and the resulting fundamental lack of real knowledge has tended to produce ethereal mountains of the mind rather than the massive upheavals of stone, ice and snow they really are. Oddly, it is the minor poets who have most often most successfully caught – in vignettes – the essential mood of the mountains.

Shelley, Wordsworth and Coleridge, visiting the Chamonix Valley and each apostrophising Mont Blanc in a paean of praise, all struck a note of awe mingled with a triumphant feeling of joy. Shelley's solitary poem addressed directly to the mountains, 'Lines written in the Vale of Chamouni' is a fine one, abounding in touches of admiration for the magnificence of the scene and its message for puny men, looking upward to the heights. His finest lines, reflecting the beauty of the mountain scene are, however, reserved for the passage in 'Prometheus Unbound' which starts –

> The point of one white star is quivering still
> Deep in the orange light of widening morn
> Beyond the purple mountains . . .

Wordsworth, in his 'Freedom', voices the old feeling of awe –

> Great joy by horror tamed dilates his heart

Coleridge's 'Hymn before sunrise in the Vale of Chamouni' bows in worship before the mighty peak –

> Of, dread and silent mount . . . most awful form!

and leaves no doubt as to the message of its origin :

> Who sunk thy sunless pillars deep in Earth,
> Who filled thy countenance with rosy light,
> Who made thee parent of perpetual streams? . . .
>   . . . who bade the sun
> Clothe thee with rainbows? Who with living flowers
> Of loveliest blue, spread garlands at your feet? –
> GOD! Let the torrents, like a shout of nations,
> Answer! and let the ice-plains echo, GOD!

Byron, not always at his best in mountain poetry, excellent often in his letters from among them, loved them in a much more modern manner, as the following undoubtedly personal revelation from *Childe Harold's Pilgrimage* confirms –

> I live not in myself, but I become
> Portion of that around me; and to me
> High mountains are a feeling, but the hum
> Of human cities torture . . .

Few other major poets have left us anything Alpine, though Swinburne, in a well-known passage from 'Atalanta in Calydon' affirmed the spell with which the mountain-scene bound him:

> ... Me the snows,
> That face the first of the morning, and cold hills
> Full of the land-wind and sea-travelling storms ...
> Me these allure, and know me ...

There are a number of short, charming poems and pieces of light verse from minor Victorian poets such as John Addington Symons, F. W. Bourdillon, A. D. Godley, whose delightful 'Switzerland' was written in 1899, W. J. Turner and F. W. H. Myers the Yorkshire poet, who left a little poem forming the mountaineer's perfect epitaph, which adorns the headstone of two famous mountain graves:

> Here let us leave him; for his shroud the snow,
> For funeral-lamps he has the planets seven,
> For a great sign the icy stair shall go
> Between the heights to heaven.
>
> One moment stood he as the angels stand,
> High in the stainless eminence of air;
> The next, he was not, to his fatherland
> Translated unaware.

Later Geoffrey Winthrop Young, crippled in 1917 by a war wound and returning to the Alps in spite of it to climb peaks a few years afterwards, wrote several books of poems – among them *April and Rain* and *Wind and Hill* – in which the climber's attitude of mind and communion with his surroundings are better expressed, in verse of a very high standard, than in any other mountain-poetry I have read. More recently, Wilfrid Noyce, killed during a joint Russo-British expedition in the Pamirs in 1962, left us some lovely verse.

Reverting for a moment to prose, there is one specialised aspect – mountain humour – which deserves a passing mention. Fortunately, mountain days are not an unbroken sequence of serious thoughts, of terror, disaster and death; the pursuit or even the contemplation of a strenuous and sometimes dangerous activity would be intolerable if it were not liberally salted with fun and laughter. It is not surprising that the literature of mountaineering, skiing and of mountain travel is rich in humour, from the early slightly ponderous attempts to provide comic relief with details introduced in serious accounts of a climb to very amusing set-pieces written in a purely humorous vein.

Undoubtedly the greatest fun-maker ever to deal extensively with the Alps and mountaineering remains that master-humourist Mark Twain, who visited Switzerland a hundred years ago. Writing not long after the Golden Age of mountaineering in the Alps, he had read and been deeply impressed by the accounts the pioneers had left of triumph and disaster. He quotes freely and in obvious admiration from these sources. Nevertheless, his keen feeling for the foibles of natives and tourists alike prompted some of his best passages of amiable satire, in which the scientists also took a drubbing, nor did the absurdities of the more flamboyant Alpine sagas escape his acute perception.

The most masterly passages are to be found in chapters xxxvii–xlvi of *A Tramp Abroad*, where he describes an imaginary mountaineering venture of his own in hilarious terms. These passages are an extraordinary mixture of the sublime and ridiculous; they include, verbatim, Whymper's own account of the Matterhorn disaster and spring from the effect great mountains had on an immense intellect.

Perhaps the finest piece of foolery comes in the Chamonix chapter, this time directly after quotations from some of the most grim and tragic passages in the annals of Mont Blanc's fatal history. It consists of a description of a 'climb' of the mountain, made through a telescope in the main-street of the climbing centre. The descriptive passage of the summit view combines inextricably his own great skill in Alpine picture-painting with a fantastic sense of the ludicrous and the incongruous. This spoof account of the prospect from a summit on which the author never stood must have aroused the envy of many a mountaineer anxious to depict the scene from a peak actually attained. I could name at least one.

On a smaller scale, d'Egville contributed an immortal account of a downhill ski-race in the British Ski Yearbook of 1925 and Air Chief Marshal Dowding's report, in vol. I of the same journal, of a visit to Monte Leone in May with intent to ski, is also very funny indeed. The French author Samivel also developed a very personal brand of humour in his serious Alpine writings. The many other mountain humorists must forgive my neglect, for the usual reason.

The Graphic Arts

If the dearth of great mountain poems is a little surprising, the relatively small number of truly great mountain paintings seems even more so. The number of painters at all times vastly outstrips that of poets. There, on the doorsteps of all the artists in France, Germany, Austria, Switzerland and Italy, in three of which the visual arts have at various epochs attained the greatest fulfilment, rise the foothill ranges, forests and torrents behind which soar, in all their sublimity, Ruskin's 'Cathedrals of the Earth' demanding worship of the eye and spirit. Yet, for some strange reason, only a handful of the world's greatest painters have made the mountain scene their central subject for its own sake, often as they may have included it for fringe benefits.

It is understandable that the rocks and snows were kept in the background during the long years while they were regarded as bare, bleak and horrific and while men did not frequent them with any sense of pleasure, confining their contact with them to the occasional unavoidable journey through the barren, discomforting realms traversed by the rough tracks between one comfortable lowland country to the north and another to the south.

Moreover, landscape painting of any kind was a very late development in European art of the middle ages, and the Alpine landscape did not feature until the last stages of that development. It appears for the first time in the paintings of the great fourteenth-century Italian painters, Duccio and Giotto; and in the next century it was used by Bellini, Raphael and Mantegna – and, oddly enough, by some of the early Flemish masters, such as Jan van Eyck and Hans Memling – as a background contrast seen through arches and between pillars of the religious paintings.

As might be expected, about the same time German, Swiss and Austrian painters began to bring the scenes among which they lived more into the middle-ground of their pictures. Such were Konrad Witz (d. 1444), Michael Pacher (c. 1481), Albrecht Altdorfer (d. 1538) and Wolf Huber (d. 1553), at the turn of the century. Albrecht Dürer (1471–1528) is often held to be the pioneer of Alpine painting. A far greater master, and the first to render the structure of rocks with true perception and realism, he exercised a considerable influence on later scenic painters; but, for the most part, landscape still remained a background to the main subject of a picture.

This is strangely true of the two truly great Italian giants of the day. Titian, a native of the Dolomites, painted distant mountain scenes behind his saints and mythological figures, confining his real mastery of rock and crag to woodcuts and engravings. Leonardo da Vinci, who actually climbed an 8,000-foot summit of the Monte Rosa group in 1511, while invariably introducing a distant blue range of lofty peaks in his best-known masterpieces, left only one great mountain subject, the remarkable drawing 'Great Alpine landscape in storm'.

During the sixteenth century scientific and topographical publications about the Alps gave rise to a spate of engravings to illustrate them, mostly of a very fanciful nature, but landscape painting, developing more rapidly in the seventeenth in the low-lands, with Ruysdael and Hobbema in Holland and Claude Lorraine in France, still eschewed the steep, savage shapes of the Alpine scene.

As in literature, the first stirring of the Romantic movement in the eighteenth century, with Haller's poem 'Die Alpen' and Rousseau's popularisation of the Alpine scene, was to trigger off the more extensive representation in the visual arts.

Suddenly, it became fashionable to decorate the walls of one's *salon* with small, attractive engravings in black and white and colour of the beauty-spots so recently discovered, from the hands of such miniaturists as Aberli, Herrliberger, the Lorys, von Mechel, Zingg and Johann Caspar Wolf. Large paintings of purely Alpine landscapes were still few and far between, though after the ascent of Mont Blanc in 1786 a number of water-colourists began to produce wildly fantastic representations of crevassed glaciers and grotesquely shattered rock-pinnacles.

It was not until the early nineteenth century that mountain landscape painting including the specialised art of portraying actual mountain peaks in a realistic and accurate manner came into its own.

The first in this field was a Tyrolese peasant who found his way to Vienna and Rome, Joseph Anton Koch, whose large and beautiful oil paintings 'The Schmadribach Falls' (1814) and later 'The Bernese Oberland' were landmarks in the history of moun-tain painting. A contemporary, Casper David Friedrich, left two great, if somewhat over-idealised, mountain canvases of the Watz-mann and Mont Blanc; and a school of numerous Romantics, among them Ferdinand Waldmüller and Carl Rottmann, painted faithful, lively pictures of the German and Austrian mountain scene during the following decades. In 1825 Meuron painted one of the first 'mountain portraits', a splendid picture of the Eiger reflected in a tarn.

Partly inspired by Meuron, Alexandre Calame (1810–64) came to be considered the greatest Alpine painter of the century, regu-larly exhibiting his large Swiss landscapes in Paris year after year, till they were jokingly referred to as '*Calamités*'. In 1844 he did the illustrations to Töppfer's *Voyages en Zig-Zag*.

In England, rather earlier, that considerable artist J. R. Cozens had painted large watercolours of Alpine scenes, the best-known probably being that of the Chamonix Aiguilles and Mont Blanc, now in the Tate Gallery; while, round the turn of the century a lesser landscape painter, John Varley, handled Welsh mountain-scenes with great skill in the same medium.

Of the great masters, Richard Wilson, though he never painted the Alps, is famous for magnificent Welsh mountain paintings in oils, particularly his 'Snowdon' and 'Cader Idris' canvases. On the other hand, Turner (1775–1851) was one of the few giants to turn his attention specifically to the Alpine landscape. In oils and in a very large number of inimitable watercolour sketches he depicted every mood and changing light effect of the Alps, which he knew intimately. He must be reckoned among the greatest of mountain-painters and his influence on nineteenth-century mountain painting was marked.

In spite of their pre-eminence in nineteenth-century landscape painting, the French never devoted their attention to mountain painting for its own sake. It was left to the Austrians and Germans to proliferate in this field, as a large and active but on the whole not very distinguished school grew up in Munich. Few of its members reached the highest standards, though competent work was contributed by Thomas Ender, Albin Egger-Lienz, Franz Defregger, Wilhelm von Kobell and a number of others. Among the finest paintings to emerge from the Munich school were the late ones of Fritz Baer (1850–1919), whose Eiger pictures earned him wide acclaim and a gold medal.

It was left to the later years of the century to produce two truly great masters in this field, Giovanni Segantini (1858–99) and Ferdinand Hodler. Segantini, of Italian birth, migrated to the Engadine, where he found his mountain dreamland and spent the rest of his life capturing the colour, light and atmosphere of his beloved valley and snows. He specialised in large canvases depicting the life and toil of the peasants, eking out their meagre existence at the foot of the snowy ranges rising behind them. Many consider him the greatest of all purely mountain painters and thousands visit the Segantini museum in St Moritz every year.

Hodler (1853–1918), a Swiss, painted other subjects as well, but by 1900 his mountain paintings, especially of the Lake of Geneva, the Valais and the Bernese Oberland were recognised as being his finest work and among the greatest of their kind, rivalling Segantini's. Most of them can be seen in the various Swiss national galleries and museums.

These two outstanding talents were followed by a number of artists influenced by Cézanne's impressionism in his 'Mont Sainte-Victoire' canvases, though they were not mountain paintings in the true sense. Lovis Corinth (1858–1925), a German, came to live among the mountains and catch their light effects in impressionistic and later expressionist paintings. Ernst Ludwig Kirchner (1880–1938) came from Germany to Davos where he painted a great number of expressionist canvases of the Grisons landscapes in a somewhat exaggerated manner. A more naturalistic worker during the early twentieth century, mainly in water colours, was Erich Heckel.

From 1908 onwards the Swiss painter Ernst Hodel (not to be confused with Hodler) became one of the outstanding purely mountain painters of this century. Apart from huge murals decorating public buildings, he painted beautiful and faithful mountain canvases, which can be seen in the museums and art galleries of Geneva, Bern, Bâle and Lucerne. Many believe these to be the truest renderings of the high mountain scene any painter has achieved.

At this time there was also a Russian school which specialised in light effects on mountains and forests under snow – particularly the sunset or sunlight 'glow' on the peaks – of whom the best were Gourmatchev, Bessonov and outstanding among them Schultzé; but in the hands of numerous less talented imitators the cult became stylised and debased into a cliché.

In contemporary mountain painting a widely-acclaimed name is that of Oskar Kokoschka, the Austrian painter who has included a few famous mountain scenes, always in a turmoil of the elements, among his vast output of large oil paintings – the Dents du Midi, Dolomite scenes, Mont Blanc and his well-known Matterhorn, seen in stormy conditions. Unfortunately, vividly and colourfully as he portrays nature in torment, the true structure of the familiar peaks completely eludes him, thereby vitiating the effect for the true mountain-lover.

Other painters of today, too numerous to include in this brief survey, have mostly been lesser lights, though among present day

10   A Segantini subject: haymakers on an Alp

11   *The Lake of Lugano*

12   *The Wetterhorn from the main street of Grindelwald*

British Alpine painters, Dr Howard Somervell, of Everest and Alpine Club fame, is extremely effective in both watercolours and oils; and the snow and mountain oil paintings of E. Holroyd Pearce display a charming talent.

It remains only to revert to an entirely distinct breed of recorders of the mountain scene, the painter-mountaineers – climbers who were painters as well, as distinct from artists who loved their mountains from afar. These men worked from their local knowledge and experience instead of from remote observation; they drew or painted exact and authentic portraits of the mountains they climbed, many of them very beautiful – so that any mountaineer could recognise and enjoy the rock and ice by which he could climb, or had climbed, the peak portrayed.

Whymper himself was a first-rate pencil artist and engraver, as witness the illustrations to his books; as was Payer, another famous climber. The brothers Schlagintweit painted records of their Himalayan journeys, some of them executed at great altitudes. McCormick, whom Conway taught to climb so that he could accompany him on his expeditions and illustrate his books, worked at even greater heights.

Nobody in this field equalled the mastery of Edward Theodore Compton (1849–1921), who eventually established himself as the unrivalled master among the altitudes of the high peaks and glaciers, painting the high mountain scene with a marvellous faithfulness to structural form, allied to a superb handling of the atmospheric effects of light and clouds and mist. He lived, climbed, sketched and painted among the Alps, and at his request his ashes were buried at the foot of the Zugspitze. Mountaineers will always regard him as the greatest Alpine artist. When he died his son, Harrison Compton, carried on his father's tradition with highly attractive paintings of the Dolomites and other ranges.

Names of other great climbers who sketched and painted, several of whom lost their lives in difficult and dangerous climbs, are Ernst Platz (1867–1940); Rudolf Reschreiter, who meticulously reproduced the features of the Austrian Alps and climbed the Andean peaks of Chimborazo and Cotopaxi in 1903, portraying them as he went; Zeno Diemer, who made the first ascent of the Fernerkogel in the Ötzal Alps; Hans Beat Wieland, lured away from mountaineering to skiing as early as 1896; Gustav Jahn (1879–1919) killed on the north arête of the Oedstein, after a fantastic record of great climbs, who rendered the reddish glow of Dolomite rock and the burning gold of the larch woods in autumn; his Viennese friend, Otto Barth (1876–1916), a highly individual painter of figures and landscapes; Otto Bauriedl of Munich; Adalbert Holzer (1881–1966) who climbed all his life and painted the Lechtal mountains; Otto Opel (1881–1964); Julius Engelhard, who also drove racing-cars and flew planes over the Alps; Erwin Merlet of Meran, whose painting of Dolomite scenes was cut short by an early death at 35; Gustl Kröner, who showed great early promise in the pointilliste style, but gave up painting to concentrate on serious climbing of the 'extreme' kind and was killed by a stone at the foot of the Matterhorn in 1932; and that great climber Georg Maier of Ulm, whose ascents included the Walker Buttress of the Grandes Jorasses and the Brenva face of Mont Blanc, and who fell to his death when a cornice broke away on the Wildspitze in 1959.

This short history of Alpine painting reflects the truth that only a few truly great artists have painted immortal mountain paintings, but has, I hope, revealed the great numbers of affectionate and highly competent pictures produced by a host of fine craftsmen on a slightly lower level of talent.

Photography

The controversy whether photography is an art or not is long-standing. In the Alpine field the medium can hardly go unmentioned since it might be argued that it has been at least as successful as the artist's pencil or brush in portraying nature's true magnificence and beauty.

The early photographers of the mountain scene were severely handicapped by the bulk and weight of their equipment, which exacted prodigious feats of carrying either by the climber-photographer himself or by the team of porters frequently employed. Nonetheless some of the finest mountain photographs ever taken came from the cameras of such pioneers as Vittorio Sella (1859–1943) and W. F. Donkin (1845–88).

Sella, a native of Biella in the Italian foothills, established himself by a superb series of pictures taken in the Alps, the Caucasus, Ruwenzori in Africa, the Himalaya and the Karakorum, as the king of mountain photographers. His pictures can be seen today in the museum devoted to his prodigious achievements at his birthplace. Donkin, an 'amateur', who climbed extensively in the Alps and Caucasus, and died during an expedition to that range, left pictures which have not been improved on to this day, in spite of the immense improvement in cameras and equipment.

Other pioneers in the field were Dr Fritz Benesch (1868–1949), who at very great risk photographed the great climbs in the Dolomites and Eastern Alps; Professor Friedrich Simony (1813–96), whose splendid photographs are preserved in the museum at Halstatt; Emil Terschak (1858–1918), one of the first to record actual climbing scenes on steep rock-climbs; Willi Rickmer Rickmers (1873–1965), the founder of the Alpine Association's library in Munich and leader of its first expedition to the Pamirs, whose fine photography ranges far beyond the Alps.

General Theodor von Wundt (d. 1919), one of the first winter alpinists, published some of the earliest pictures taken on difficult climbs; and Otto Melzer of Innsbruck, who fell to his death while climbing in the Karwendel in 1901, besides trying to capture the natural beauty of the Alps, took photographs on the most difficult pitches of his climbs.

About 1880 the Alpine Club journal in London, followed by those of the Austrian, German and Swiss clubs, began to publish photographs and from then on, progressively, many of the finest mountain pictures have appeared in the pages of these publications and, later, those of periodicals like *Alpinismus* and numerous others devoted exclusively to mountaineering.

Colour photography came relatively late but spread rapidly with the setting up in 1908 of an Alpine centre for the collection

of lantern-slides at Leipzig. Colour will always remain a contro-
versial subject and, in spite of the multitude of splendid colour
photographs being taken today, many of the finest pictures of
snow-peaks ever taken are in black and white, which seems to suit
the subject ideally.

In 1925 mountain photography was revolutionised by the
arrival of the Leica camera, invented by Oskar Barrack, using
ciné-film, which could be 'blown-up' into enlargements of considerable size. Its extreme portability and that of the host of
miniature-cameras which followed in its wake enabled mountaineers who would never have thought of allowing themselves to
climb encumbered by the old ponderous equipment to bring back
pictures from their walking and climbing tours. Suddenly, everyone could be an Alpine photographer.

Between the two world wars Frank Smythe proved himself one
of the outstanding mountain photographers of our time. He was
of course one of the greatest climbers of the day and published, as
well as narratives, a number of magnificent picture-books of the
Alps, the Rockies and, eventually, of scenes up to 28,000 feet on
Everest. C. Douglas Milner of the Alpine Club is another eminent
photographer of the Alps, the Dolomites, rock-climbing and the
general scene; while W. F. Poucher, who has spent a life-time in
photographing British hills (where his picture-books have never
had a rival) has also produced fine photographs of the Alps.

The great Swiss climber, André Roch, active between the wars,
published remarkable books of photographs taken during his
Alpine climbs on 'severe' ice and rock, concentrating particularly
on the great peaks of the Western Alps. He was also partly
responsible with Raymond Lambert and Norman Dyhrenfurth
for an extraordinary book of Everest photography during the two
unsuccessful Swiss attempts in 1952. The last-named will always
be remembered for the production of the wonderful picture-book
of the American expedition which made the first traverse in 1963;
he also shot a magnificent film of that venture.

Heinz Müller-Bruncke, whose book *Mountain Photography*
appeared in 1958, has consistently produced fine photographs of

the Alps over a long period; while other prominent exponents have been Robert Löbl of Bad Tolz, whose lovely book *The Alps in Colour* was published here in 1970; Risch-Lau of Bregenz and Vilem Heckel, one of the leading eastern European Alpine photographers.

Kurt Diemberger of Salzburg, the only man living to have climbed two of the world's 'Eight-Thousanders', has photographed superbly in the Alps, Himalaya, Karakorum, Hindu Kush and Corsica. His sunset colour-photograph from the summit of 26,600-foot Broad Peak is world famous and probably the finest mountain photograph ever taken. His colour film *The Peuterey Ridge of Mont Blanc* is a valuable record of that huge six-day climb.

The German climber, Erwin Schneider, compiled an enormous collection of photographs of mountains all over the world, on which almost every author of mountaineering books has relied for illustrations. He must rank as the most comprehensive and prolific of this century's great climber-photographers.

In very recent years Dr Walter Kirstein, a fine mountaineer and member of the Alpine Club, has been prominent in colour and black-and-white. Among others of note are the late Basil Goodfellow and Christian Bonington. (Some of the author's own photographs will be found illustrating this volume.)

Films

A number of mountaineering films have been appearing at intervals since the twenties. Those intended for the commercial film circuits have mostly suffered from the same defect as mountaineering novels – novelettish and sometimes ludicrous scripts.

Dr Arnold Fanck (born 1889) set the fashion with a series of screen-dramas in the twenties, the best known of which were *The White Hell of Piz Palü* (1929) and *Storms over Mont Blanc* (1930). In making his later films he converted the Austrian guide Luis Trenker into first a film-star and then a director; the great Arlberg ski-instructor Hannes Schneider was also a pupil of his. On the whole, his instructional documentaries, such as *Snowshoe*

Marvels (1919–22) were the more acceptable, though the photo-graphy of the Alpine scene and especially of the grace and move-ment of the ski-runner were always of the highest class in his dramas.

In 1932 Leni Riefenstahl, of Olympic film fame, produced a drama of the Dolomites, based on an old legend of Monte Cristallo – *The Blue Light*. The settings were splendidly realised and the peasants of the locality represented with great truth and understanding but the story lacked pace and, apart from a few studio climbing sequences, action.

In 1928 Luis Trenker had appeared in the melodramatic *Flags on the Matterhorn*, which has had its remakes and sequels over the years, for the mountain is distinctly photogenic and has its box-office appeal. The stories and scripts have for the most part been sad travesties of the original ascent and the rivalry – not over a member of the opposite sex – between Whymper and Carrel. Trenker's first film in his own right was the very successful *Son of the White Mountains* (1930). In the following year he made *Mountains in Flames*, a highly exciting story of mountain warfare among the high Dolomite spires and crags, wonderfully photo-graphed.

More recently the cinemas have featured *The White Tower*, the film of J. R. Ullman's novel (see p. 63) in which the more ludicrous aspects of the story were greatly enhanced by some incredibly inept filming; as, for instance, the sequence where the party masters a vertical rock-face by the most 'extreme' rope and piton techniques (after the guide has declared it 'impossible') and then walks into a hut at its top to spend the night before grappling with the further 'impossibilities' of the unclimbed killer-peak.

Even more hilarious was *The Mountain*, also filmed in the Mont Blanc group, in which Spencer Tracy took the part of an aged guide, who consents to emerge from retirement to lead a rescue attempt to an aircraft which has crashed high on the snows of the local killer-mountain. By incredible efforts, well lubricated by tomato-juice when the rope runs out through his lacerated hands, he scales the hitherto unclimbed (what again?) North face of the peak (which has killed all who have attempted it before) and reaches the wrecked plane. There he finds one survivor, a gorgeous Indian girl in a sari and a mink coat. So what does he do? Constructing a crude sledge out of fragments of wreckage, he lashes her firmly to it and, like the good guide he is – tows her down an *easy glacier on the other side of the mountain*. . . .

In 1972 *Ski-Raiders*, featuring Jean-Claude Killy the Olympic ski-champion, contained some marvellous skiing sequences against a beautifully photographed background of the Valtournanche and Zermatt peaks.

For the same reasons as have already been suggested governing the factual and fictitious in Alpine literature, the finest mountain films have usually been documentaries, where there was little or no 'story' to distract one's attention from the true beauties of the mountains, skiing and climbing.

Outstanding examples are *Starlight and Storm* (1955) and *Between Earth and Sky* (1961) joint-products of the skill and expertise of Gaston Rébuffat and Georges Tairraz, of the family of Chamonix photographers. Marcel Ichac, of Annapurna fame, made *4100* (1934), *Karakorum* (1936), *The Assault on the Aiguilles du Diable* (1942), *Annapurna* (1952) and *Starlight at Noon* (1959).

Tom Stobart's epoch-making film of the successful British ascent of Everest (1953) was as magnificent as its subject. Almost every great expedition or climb nowadays produces its film, if only for financial reasons, and some of these have already been mentioned. Memorable ones have been shot on the Eiger north face, both on climbs by the 'normal' route and during the highly-commercialised *direttissima* (1966), and in late 1972 Chris Bonington's attempt on Everest's southwest face resulted in a marvellous, if brief, account of a splendid failure in face of impossible weather conditions, taken by members of the climbing party up to 27,000 feet, with a background of fantastic shots of the snow-plastered high Himalaya.

5. Alpes Maritimes and the Alps of Provence

As has already been said, for a short distance between Nice and Menton the Alps actually bathe their feet in the blue waters of the Mediterranean. Farther west, only a few miles inland behind the glittering coastal strip of lushness and luxury, along which all the well-to-do idlers of the world congregate to enjoy the holiday delights a little puzzling to the true lover of mountain paths and the peace and solitude of the high peaks, the green foothill mounds leap sheer up into the first frontal barrier of the mountain world in abrupt limestone faces or great wooded slopes, immediately reaching altitudes of from three to seven thousand feet.

This great area of the lower French Alps stretches away almost due north for a hundred miles from the coast to a line one can conveniently draw from Grenoble at its western fringe to Italian Turin at the foot of its eastern spurs; at its broadest point, a little below that horizontal, it is also a hundred wide. It embraces the Alpes Maritimes and the Alpes de Haute Provence (formerly known as the 'Basses Alpes' but recently renamed apparently through jealousy of their taller brothers) as well as Dauphiné, which for the purposes of this study merits a chapter to itself.

It is an area of bare, stony ranges for the most part, their highest summits running up to not much more than 10,000 feet, through which a number of sizeable rivers have carved deep, sheltered valleys, picturesque ravines and at least one stupendous chain of gorges. The two largest rivers are the Durance, rising in the Franco-Italian watershed near Briançon and carving a tortuous course down a narrow, steep-sided valley past Guillestre, Embrun, Gap and Manosque, eventually to join the Rhône near Avignon; and the Isère, whose source in the watershed is close to Mont Iseran and whose contrastingly broad and smiling valley leads it to Grenoble and on for another 50 miles, to fall into the Rhône just above Valence. The courses of these two major rivers are the only breaches in the mountain mass offering main valley highway approaches from the plains of the Rhône basin to its west to the Italian frontier on its east, though there are several hilly subsidiary links of no great altitude between them. It is a matter of consent that it was by one or other of these great valley-routes that Hannibal's army approached the final passage into Italy, however much conflict there is as to the actual saddle by which he crossed the high watershed.

Even at its coastal fringe, though it may all be sub-alpine in atmosphere, you cannot help knowing that you are where the Alps begin. Between Nice and Menton, where they actually rise out of the sea, you have the choice of two roads sufficiently mountainous in character to convince you of that fact climbing high above the traffic-jammed highway which skirts the shore. The Upper Corniche contours 1,800 feet above the sea to the Roman ruins at La Turbie (Tropeia), looking down as you go on the marvellously perched medieval village of Èze, where on a little eyrie overhanging space it is pleasant to eat a meal. The Lower Corniche, on the level of Èze itself, is picturesque enough, with the blue-green sweep of the bay steep and far below.

Incidentally, this balmy sun-kissed garden of the Hesperides, the Côte d'Azur, owes everything it stands for to the Alps, rising so close behind its narrow strip; for it is the first near outliers of the great mountain tract which shelter it so securely from the northerly winds and give it its superb climate.

Close behind Nice, beyond slopes dotted with villas, stand those charming old towns, unspoiled St Paul de Vence, with its ancient ramparts, and more modernised Vence itself, on the twisting road which contours the slopes at the foot of the 3,000-foot barrier of limestone crags behind them, through Pont de Loup, at the mouth of the spectacular Gorges du Loup, and on to Grasse. If you bear right at Le Loup, soon after leaving Vence, you find yourself on a mountain road which attacks the barrier itself and snakes its way up to its very top at tiny Gourdon, where two charming open-air restaurants hang like little balconies high above the ten-mile vista back to the sea. Here there can be no moment's doubt that you are already among the High Hills.

If you can at last tear yourself away from the Riviera fleshpots heading north by the highway from Cannes (the valley road from Nice through Puget-Théniers and Annot joins it at Barrême), bound for Grenoble and the high Alps, you come in a very few miles to Grasse, home of the perfume trade, sprawling among its acres of rose gardens up the wooded heights in a series of terraces. One of the most entrancing sights imaginable is the vista, in the indigo stillness of the heavily scented night, back across those few miles of darkness to the myriad points of light starring the coastal fringe of Cannes and its diamond necklace strung along the night-dark sea. A fitting au revoir to the luscious South.

From Grasse the highway climbs in a series of steep curves to the first minor col, and you are at once in mountain country. The road continues by a chain of small cols through Le Logis des Pins across a kind of high, ridged plateau, with the more rugged, barer ranges to the north and northeast, till it dips down to Castellane in a deep rift. On the descent there are fine wide views of the deep valleys and gorges biting into the tall hills on all sides.

Here you should not fail to turn aside, westwards from the main road, to visit one of the wonders of the Alps, the great gorges which the Verdon (whose foaming rapids are beloved by 'extreme' canoeists) has carved on its way to join the Durance. There is nothing comparable in Europe. The gorges, sometimes known as the Verdon Canyons, for they are at places more than 2,000 feet deep and offer a mini-challenge to their great American counterparts, can be enjoyed alike by motorists from a comfortable and scenically exceptional road and by hikers from a perfectly safe path, which bears the name of the geologist and pot-holer who first discovered this marvel of nature, E. A. Martel. Motorists can equally well approach the gorges from Moustiers Sainte Marie to their north or Draguignan to the south.

Beyond Castellane the main road climbs over the 4,500-foot Col de Lecques between stony slopes with beautiful colours and stratifications in their rock-faces, to drop steeply down to Digne and thence to follow the Durance valley to Sisteron. Leaving the valley, it climbs again through rocky defiles to the little township of Serres, which boasts a charming hostelry with a charming name – Fifi Moulin. On, unexcitingly through Aspres, St Julien and Lus, the road climbs to the low, bare Col de la Croix Haute (3,850 feet), soon after which the completely isolated table-topped Mont Aiguille (6,880 feet, climbed as early as 1492) is seen rising sheer on the left. This is the fringe of the Vercors country, the valley of the Gresse, through which you proceed with provocative distant views of the great Dauphiné snows lifting over the stark intervening Devolouy ranges to the right, through the little resort of Monestier de Glermont, dropping gradually down for 40 miles to Grenoble.

The parallel road from Sisteron to Grenoble through Gap, over the 4,117-feet Col Bayard and by way of Corps and La Mure in the Drac Valley, traverses the grim and barren Devolouy country and is altogether more austere and viewless.

Returning for a moment to Lus, at the southern foot of Croix Haute: here an interesting road branches off to the west. This is the Col de Grimone, another pass associated with the Hannibal controversy, which leads through a bare and rocky defile to Die and so on into the Rhône Valley south of Valence. At Die there is a remarkable natural phenomenon, for the limestone cliffs nearly 700 feet high have been moulded by erosion into what look like the pipes of a titanic church organ; and for all the air of tottering imbalance of these huge 'earth-pyramids', they are in fact remarkably solid and stable.

All this mountain country of Eastern Provence abounds in wooded ranges of no great height rising to the east of the great Rhône Valley plain, but continually gaining in altitude as they approach the main north-south axis of the Alpine watershed on the

Franco-Italian frontier, more than 50 miles to the east of the route described above. The highest point in the ranges overlooking the Rhône valley is Mont Ventoux (6,270 feet) visible for miles from the plain, and ascended by the poet Petrarch in the fourteenth century.

If on leaving the Riviera you intend to travel eastwards into Piedmont, the picturesque mountain-road of linked minor passes runs from Nice, through Sospel, with wonderfully colourful rocky ravines on the way, to La Giandola, where the main Col de Tende (Tenda) ascent begins, and Tende itself, whence the narrow $2\frac{1}{2}$-mile long road tunnel burrows under the actual col at a height of 4,331 feet. The road then winds steeply down on the Italian side to Borgo S. Dalmazzo and on to Cuneo in the plain 60 miles south of Turin. This is the lowest and most southerly of the passes crossing the true Alpine backbone (see chapter 15).

This region of the southeastern and Ligurian Alps contains a wealth of lovely scenery. To mention only a few of its delights, the road from Borgo S Dalmazzo at the Italian foot of the Colle di Tenda, in the upper Gesso valley, leading up the Bousset Valley, with its lakes of Rovine and Brocan, to Entraque, offers a beautiful approach, by way of the Italian Alpine Club châlet four hours above, to the Punta del Argentera, the highest summit in the Maritime Alps (10,794 feet). The views from this peak and from many of its neighbours have the advantage over all other Alpine views that they extend over the Mediterranean to the south. This rocky peak is not difficult from the Italian side and can also be approached from the Bagni di Valdieri, charmingly situated at the mouth of the Vallasco Valley, rich in beech-woods and running up to S. Giacomo, above which a path runs up to a glaciated valley-head and Mont Clapier. This approach to the Argentera, however, demands the laying-back of a much greater height differential.

From Borgo, too, attractive passes lead from the lush and fertile valley (the Vallis Aurea of the Romans) across to Vinadio, the Customs post at the foot of the Col de Larche (see chapter 15) and over the Col de Fenestre to St Martin Vésubie, The Bagni di Vinadio, set in a paradise of beech woods and pine forests, with several beautiful waterfalls, give access to the Becco d'Ischiator (9,860 feet) and Mont Tinibras (9,950 feet), both commanding glorious views.

Tende itself, on the French side of the pass, is the starting point for numerous attractive tours. Especially worthwhile is that to the northeast up the valley of the Rio Freddo to the Refuge on the Colle dei Signori and the ascent of either Monte Ciagore (7,535 feet) or the Cima di Marguareis, at 8,690 feet the highest summit in the Ligurian Alps. The views here over mountains and sea are hardly to be rivalled.

Another very rewarding journey is from S. Dalmazzo di Tenda, up the Levenza Valley to Sta Maria Madellena (5,110 feet) and the Val Casterino's larch forests; then up the wild Valle del Inferno, with its 14 small lakes, and on to the Monte Bego (9,425 feet), from which there is yet another magnificent view over the Riviera and the Alps. Beyond, in the valley, lie the three large terraced lakes of Valmasca, at 7,700 feet, beneath the snow-clad Monte Ciaminejas (9,556 feet).

From Cuneo, in the Piedmont Plain, the romantic Val Pejo dives into the hills, cradling the Certosa di Pejo, founded in 1173, a lovely shrine set in avenues of great trees overshadowing its half mile of cloisters, but in summertime a flourishing hydropathic health-resort. From here, or from Limone on the main Tenda road on its other flank, the ascent of the extraordinary rock ridge of the Bessimauda (Bisalta, 7,850 feet) can be undertaken. Its view over the Ligurian Alps and the Valley of the Po is the finest to be had from any summit of such modest altitude.

Of all the summits mentioned R. L. G. Irving preferred the Mont Clapier (9,990 feet), easily ascended from the Rifugio Nizza, 7,000 feet up in the Val Gordolasca, above Lantosque on the road from Nice due north to St Martin Vésuoie. This is what he wrote of it:

Of all summit views this is the one that has impressed me most. On one side the sea and the Riviera coast, beyond it the

Carrara mountains and the peaks of Corsica. On the other side, running north, then in the far distance turning east, the Alps. Monte Viso catches the eye at once, standing head and shoulders above anything near it; the Matterhorn is not hard to pick out in the Pennine Alps; further east they fade away into dim blue outlines which you may or may not be right in calling Disgrazia and Adamello. Between you and them is an immense plain covered by a faint mist through which are seen suggestions of rivers, spires of churches and smoke from busy towns.

From this valley, too, which houses the beautiful Lac Long, 8,000 feet up at its foot, Mont Gelas (10,285 feet) best attained from the Refuge on the Col de Fenestre above St Martin-Vésubie, can be climbed to offer a view only second to that just described.

Sheer lack of space forbids the description of innumerable other expeditions in this area of lovely mountain and coastal scenery.

The valley road connecting Nice with Sisteron and the road to Dauphiné has already been mentioned. From it three high and important internal passes strike northwards to Barcelonnette and Briançon: the Col de Restefond, claiming (dubiously) to be the highest motorable pass in Europe, the Col de la Cayolle and the Col d'Allos. From Barcelonnette the Col de Vars links the Cayolle with Guillestre and Briançon; and from just north of Barcelonnette the second truly trans-Alpine pass, the Col de Larche, branches off eastwards to Cuneo (see chapter 15).

All these roads pass through much higher and grander mountain scenery than those further west, consisting mostly of rather bare rock-peaks running up to over 10,000 feet, the most important being the Punta d'Argentera (10,794 feet) the highest peak in the Provençal Alps, and Mont Pelat (10,017 feet). These ranges are much frequented by rock-climbing enthusiasts.

Most of the places mentioned in this chapter are popular summer and winter resorts, and a number of others are scattered up and down the valleys and slopes, where hiking, mountaineering and fishing in high mountain tarns can be enjoyed. To mention only a few: Annot, Auron, Beauvezer, Colmars, Guillaumes, Isola, Lantosque, Manosque, Puget-Théniers, St Martin Vésubie and Valberg. Those in the Grenoble area, and that lovely city itself, are dealt with in the following chapter.

6. Dauphiné

Grenoble, the gateway to the western French Alps, lies in a wide plain astride the Isère, with the Belledonne range fronting it and a hint of the great Dauphiné massif beyond. A short ride in a cable-car to a restaurant terrace crowning a rocky spur reveals the full extent of the lovely prospect, with a bonus of Mont Blanc lifting 80 miles away to the northeast – floating, at the hour of the evening meal, like a rose petal on the lilac mists. Since the city housed the 1968 Winter Olympics, this fine university centre of 170,000 inhabitants has sprouted a rash of modern concrete architecture, but the character of the old town and its bridges across the dark-green swirling waters of the rivers has remained unspoiled.

If you are concerned with the Alps rather than cities humming with traffic and commerce, as readers of this book are supposed to be, you will need to know that the N90 runs northwards up the Isère valley to Chambéry. Beyond that busy road-junction (actually just off the highway, to its west) it continues, straight as a die to Albertville and then on by a choice of minor passes into the heart of the Savoy Alps at Chamonix under the shadow of Mont Blanc (chapter 8). Halfway between Chambéry and Albertville, the Mont Cenis road swings off to the right southwards on its way over the 'backbone' to Suza and Turin; while at Albertville itself the N90 bears south along the Isère valley to Bourg St Maurice at the foot of another 'backbone' pass, the Petit St Bernard, leading to Italian Courmayeur and Aosta. Here too the entirely internal French Col d'Iseran starts on its high journey

13 *Tenda, in the Maritime Alps*

14 *The last cornfield and the Écrins, near La Bérarde*

among the Cottian peaks. (All these major passes are dealt with in chapter 15.)

South of Grenoble lies a district of sub-alpine ridges, plateaux and folds enclosing the Montagnes de Lans, the Royans, the Vercors and the Forêt de Lente, ideal walking country liberally sprinkled with holiday resorts such as Villard de Lans, Chamrousse, Uriage and Pont en Royans. Royans is famous for the gorges of the Bourne and for picturesque Pont en Royans itself, clinging precariously to their cliffs. The Vercors is a pleasant plateau falling away into limestone cliffs at its western rim, reminiscent of scenery in the Jura, and its extensive woodlands are criss-crossed with a profusion of hiking paths. The Forêt de Lente to its west is an area of parallel cliff-sided ravines, again with wide views from their crests, westwards towards the Rhône Valley and eastwards across the Devolouy to the distant Dauphiné peaks.

The glory of Grenoble is, however, the mass of high and savage peaks lying 25 miles to its east, the massif of the Dauphiné Alps. This is traversed by the major line of the Col du Lautaret, leading to Briançon, and its spur the Col du Galibier doubling back to St Michel in the deep Maurienne valley through which runs the approach road to the Mont Cenis.

Leaving Grenoble the N91 runs past Vizille, then up through huge wooded gorges to Bourg d'Oisans, where the Col du Lautaret proper starts its attack on the huge mountain-barrier ahead. Here, leaving the main road, a magnificent staircase of a dozen hairpins swings to the left up the ochre cliffs to the popular summer and winter resort of Alpe d'Huez, perched on a sunny shelf at the foot of the 11,400-foot Grandes Rousses, which owes much of its rapid development to having staged several of the 1968 Olympic events. Standing above the treeline, it commands wide views over the high intervening snow-ranges to the spire of the 13,081-foot Meije lifting an inch or two over them.

Shortly before Bourg d'Oisans, at Rochetaillée, two very attractive minor mountain-passes diverge northwards from the main highway. Starting as a single road through the little resort of Allemont it penetrates between the Grandes Rousses and the slightly

15   La Meije from Le Chazelet

lower Belledonne by the 6,260-foot Col de Glandon to St Avre Lachambre in the Maurienne valley. At the col, an easterly arm breaks away over a second interesting pass, the Col de la Croix de Fer (6,947 feet) to St Jean de Maurienne. Both routes abound in fine mountain scenery, with wild ravines and fine waterfalls; but the most impressive view is that of the three huge Aiguilles d'Arves, which rise between La Grave and the Galibier, towering up apparently vertically to 11,500 feet southeast of St Sorlin d'Arves, early in the descent from the Croix de Fer to St Jean.

Another fine mountain road in this area, if somewhat constricted by the neighbouring mountain walls, leads from Bourg d'Oisans over the Col d'Ornon (4,460 feet) to La Mure in the broad Drac Valley, on the route from Grenoble to Corps, already mentioned in chapter 5.

For the climber and the mountain walker there are two minor roads hereabouts which both penetrate to the southern foot of the Dauphiné massif. The first runs up from La Mure, splitting into two arms at (La Chapelle en) Valjouffrey, the left-hand one leading to Valsenestra at the foot of the Muzelle, climbed from a refuge higher up, the right-hand to Le Désert de Valjouffrey, from which tracks lead to a number of walkers' cols and, at least four climbers' huts for ascents in the Olan group or the crossing of the Col d'Olan to Vallouise (see p. 97).

The second side road leaves the highway a mile or two south of Corps and passing through St Firmin winds its way up to La Chapelle en Valgaudemar, directly to the south of the Pic and Aiguille d'Olan. From here there is a wealth of high walking, pass-crossing and mountaineering on a dozen minor peaks as well as on the greater peaks to the north, the two Olans, the Cime du Vallon and Les Bans, attacked from a multiplicity of huts and refuges in the area.

A third by-road further south, halfway between St Bonnet and Gap leads to Champoléon and Orciéres. From the former a high walking col. the Col de l'Aup Martin, is an attractive route to Vallouise, while from the latter a fine mountain track, the Col des Tourettes, climbs over the eastern bastion of the group to Châteauroux, near Embrun in the Durance Valley.

Leaving the main southward route at Corps is a useful cross-country link with the Grenoble–Sisteron highway (chapter 5), climbing modestly over the Col du Festre (or de la Cluse, 4,820 feet) to Veynes on the valley road from Gap to Serres, and penetrating the wild and barren Devolouy country by way of some magnificent ravines, particularly the savage gorge of the Souloise.

Four miles east of Bourg on the N91's approach to the Lautaret, at Pont Guillerme, a very exciting minor road is well worth a diversion. Swinging off to the right, it enters the valley of the Vénéon, the Romanche's chief tributary, in a quiet unsensational way. Then at Bourg d'Arud it crosses the torrent and for 12 miles, to its end – for it is a cul de sac – at the tiny hamlet of La Bérarde, it piles sensation on sensation as it climbs through a series of wild and precipitous gorges from valley-level to valley-level, through St Christophe (4,820 feet) to Les Etages (5,230 feet), traversing some of the most awesomely rugged scenery in the whole Alpine chain, then on to La Bérarde (5,000 feet). For the non-mountaineer motorist La Bérarde has nothing to offer but the overwhelming grandeur of the Ecrins (13,462 feet) and its satellite giants from the valley-level or, if an energetic scramble of some two hours up a rough, steep and at places exposed path is acceptable, from the glorious belvedère of the Tête de la Maye (8,500 feet) one of the classic middle-altitude viewpoints in the Alps.

At La Bérarde, a climber's paradise since Whymper's day, and still only a cluster of simple buildings surrounding a chapel, you have penetrated the heart of the Dauphiné massif in all its stark grandeur. Here, seen from the Tête de la Maye, a circle of great peaks mostly showing their rockier aspects rings you, from the 13,081-foot Meije herself through her half-dozen satellites, the Pic Gaspard, Grande Ruine, Pic de Neige Cordier and Roche Faurio to the monarch of the Dauphiné, the Barre des Ecrins then on, through the Pic Coolidge, behind which the triple-peaked mass of the Pelvoux (12,973 feet, see p. 97) is obscured, to the broad Ailefroide and round to the snowy twin-summits of Les Bans, beyond which the long line of high summits from the Pic and Aiguille d'Olan to the Rocher de la Muzelle swing back towards Grenoble.

Even if you do not make the steep ascent to the magnificent watchtower, the head of the high-sided valley with its brave little sprinkling of silver-birches lining the banks of the foaming Vénéon and the ochre-and-beige mass of the Ecrins soaring above is ample reward. This is Alpine scenery at its sternest and grandest.

The little centre is a climber's and mountain-walker's paradise. Tracks lead to a number of famous club-huts high among the peaks. That past the Refuge du Châtelleret, to the Refuge du Promontoire, hard up against the Meije's southern precipices, continues as a mountaineer's expedition over the Col of the same name and down to La Grave, the climbing-centre on the Lautaret road. From St Christophe, on the La Bérarde road, another hikers' track running parallel to the Promontoire route crosses the Col de la Lauze to descend on La Grave. Other paths, penetrating the superb scenery of the massif, climb to the Refuge Adèle Planchard and across to La Grave by way of the climber's hut at the Châlets de l'Alpe, on the east side of the massif; to the Refuge E. Caron at the foot of Les Agneaux and on down, by the Refuge Cézanne to the villages of Ailefroide and Vallouise at the eastern foot of the Pelvoux (see p. 97). A scrutiny of the local guidebook will extend the list considerably.

The Lautaret (6,751 feet) is a lovely pass. Climbing through impressive gorges to La Grave, a tiny climbing-centre at 5,000 feet, it there commands one of the classic close-up road views of a great peak, the beautiful Meije (13,081 feet) whose summit is only 4½ miles distant and lifts overhead at an angle of 30°, as compared with the Matterhorn's 16° above Zermatt's main street. A much more comprehensive view of the whole group and its creaming glaciers is obtained by turning aside after the first tunnel beyond La Grave for the 20 minutes' drive up the excellent hairpins of the minor road to Les Terrasses and Le Chazelet (5,700 feet), with a picturesque chapel forming a foreground to one of the most magnificent views in the Alps. Above La Grave the main pass swings gently up to its saddle through meadows of (protected) flowers, with views of all the neighbouring peaks and glaciers, the snowy and shapely Agneaux (12,008 feet) at the far head of the green Romanche re-entrant being especially beautiful.

At the Lautaret saddle, the Col du Galibier climbs away into the rocky range on the left to its summit tunnel (8,399 feet), where a quarter of an hour's walk will take you to the enormous view from the actual col – the ice-plastered north face of Les Ecrins (13,462 feet and highest of the Dauphiné peaks) is seen at its best from here and the wide circular panorama extends from Mont Blanc, 80 miles away northwards, to the Viso in the distant Cottians to the east. The pass then winds down endlessly through the small resort of Valloire (4,690 feet) and finally by some very tight hairpins into the deep trench of the Maurienne, to join the Mont Cenis route at St Michel, a rather tedious descent of more than 6,000 feet in all (see chap. 7).

The Lautaret road continues pleasantly down the long, straight valley of the Guisane, through Monêtier les Bains (4,890 feet), behind which a ropeway runs to another splendid viewpoint, Serre Chevalier (8,760 feet), to reach the historic old fortified town of Briançon (4,396 feet) in 17 unexciting miles. It would be a pity not to spend an hour up in the ancient city and see its wonderful rampart defences and a superb bridge, built by Vauban in the eighteenth century.

From Briançon, the Durance carves its way southwards in a deep trench between the true frontier ridge of the Alps, just to its east, and the eastern bastions of the Dauphiné massif. Here, somewhat withdrawn, and hidden entirely from the north and the west, rises the third giant of the group, the triple-headed Mont Pelvoux, at 12,973 feet only a few feet lower than the Ecrins. Ten miles south of Briançon a deep valley carves its way back westwards into the range, and for the best approach to and views of the Pelvoux it is advisable to take the narrow road to the right, which runs up the valley of the Gyr to the little resort of Vallouise and the hamlet of Ailefroide beyond. Higher up stand the Refuge Cézanne, from which the mountain is generally climbed, and the Refuge Tuckett, a starting point for many of the surrounding peaks. The continuing track climbs over, by way of the Châlets de l'Alpe to descend on Villar d'Arène, on the Lautaret road, a magnificent mountain walk.

From La Bérarde climbers approach the Ecrins by way of the Carrelet Refuge and the Refuge Temple-Ecrins, at the foot of the Pic Coolidge, over which the route from that side passes; the Col de la Temple near by affords a high passage to the mountain's eastern flank above Vallouise by way of the Glacier Noir at whose foot stands the Refuge Cézanne, the eastern springboard for the ascent of the peak. While higher up, the Refuge Tuckett, perched above the tongue of the whitest glacier of all, whence its name, the Glacier Blanc, affords a choice of rock or ice routes (both have been mentioned just above).

R. L. G. Irving had a point when he wrote that the eye some-times craves for a touch of the greenery of trees and grass in the stony desert at the heart of the Dauphiné massif; but for the rock-climber and the lover of truly wild and savage mountain land-scapes there is nothing among the really high peaks of the Alps to rival the upthrust of the Dauphiné precipices. For the high-mountain walker this is a paradise, seamed by tracks in the shadow of their massive assault on the sky.

7. The Tarentaise, the Graians and the Cottians

North of Grenoble, the N90 runs straight and flat along the plain to Albertville; but if you have time to spare you will take the parallel hill-road to its west, which takes in a picturesque minor pass, the Col du Granier among the limestone, and also gives you the opportunity at St Pierre, to visit the monastery of the Grande Chartreuse and sample its wares. (Continue with due care and you will find yourself in Chambéry.)

Beyond that teeming road junction-cum-summer resort, to the north, lies Aix les Bains, sunning itself on the east shore of the pretty Lac du Bourget; and behind it, accessible by cable-car or by a winding road seven miles long, rises the splendid viewpoint of the Mont Revard, overlooking the lake from its 5,000 feet, with Chambéry in its plainlet, backed by oddly-shaped hills, and the whole chain of the snowy Dauphiné Alps in the distance. Another charming viewpoint is the 2,100-foot Col du Chat above the western shore of the lake. The whole lake-basin offers every holiday amenity from water-skiing to attractive walks up on the Jura-like plateau of the Revard.

From Aix it is only another 20 miles to Annecy and a cluster of smaller resorts ringing the narrow lake of the same name – Veyrier, Talloires, Menthon St Bernard – set in a steep-sided bowl which can be very hot and airless at times. Annecy has become a modern city, with the inevitable high-rise flats, but its old town, intersected by canals, is preserved intact and is extremely picturesque, enabling it at least to share the title of 'The Venice of the North' with Bruges. (My casting vote to Annecy every time because of its less odorous comparison.)

Behind Talloires a big ropeway runs to another famous viewpoint at the top of the blue-grey precipices of the 7,730-foot Tournette. It is a wonderful prospect, extending from the Tarentaise summits, in the Graians to the south, to the giants of the Mont Blanc group 30 miles away to the east. The road along the lake's south shore runs through the small resorts of Sévrier, St Jorioz and Duingt to rejoin our N90 from Grenoble at Albertville.

Here the N90, still following the Isère valley bends sharply south to Moutiers, then northeastwards again to Bourg St Maurice, at the foot of the Petit St Bernard and Iseran passes (see p. 102).

South of Moutiers, and bordered at its eastern fringe by the headwaters of the Isère falling from the Iseran heights lies the Tarentaise, the western group of the Graian Alps, enclosing a roughly oblong mountain complex, roughly 30 miles by 20, the Massif de la Vanoise. This is beautiful mountain country with deep pine-forested valleys running up into it, strangely-shaped limestone towers and, rising behind them, a wealth of high snow summits, crowned by the much loftier Grande Casse (12,668 feet) the Grande Motte (12,018 feet) and, in its northeastern corner, close above Bourg, the 12,468-foot Mont Pourri, with its two cones of purest snow.

The chief mountain resorts of the district are Pralognan la Vanoise (4,670 feet) and, since the coming of the winter sports era, the new ski-centres of Courcheve, Meribel and Les Menuires. Pralognan, in summer, is enchanting, even though it lies deep in the Doron Valley, close under the fierce rock wall of the Marchet, and you have to stroll for half an hour through the pine-woods to Chollière before the classically beautiful view of the snowy Grande Casse and its amphitheatre of rocky neighbours opens up. This is a wonderful centre for mountain walkers. All the best views have to be earned by a good uphill slog, though there is a cable-car now to the Mont Bochor plateau, but the most rewarding way is the mule track to the Refuge Felix Faure on the

Col de la Vanoise (8,129 feet), where the glaciers of the Casse cataract down on you, close at hand, the circle of lesser rock peaks embraces you and, beyond the little mirror of the Lac Noir, the shapely Grand Roc Noir closes the prospect to the east. The track continues down on the southern side to Val d'Isère at the foot of the Iseran (see later) and also by way of the Col de la Leisse (9,121 feet) to Modane, at the foot of the Mont Cenis.

From the refuge, glacier-lovers and climbers ascend by the smooth, wide Glacier de Chasseforêt to the foot of a number of attractive peaks, including the Dome de Chasseforêt, the Dent Parrachée and the Pointe de l'Échelle, all over 11,000 feet.

Southwards from Pralognan, a long and wearisome mule-track climbs the upper valley of the Doron to the Col de Chavière (9,206 feet) from which a steep descent leads down to the Maurienne and the Mont Cenis approach-road between Modane and Lanslebourg (see p. 103). Before the col and above it to the right, by a little lake, stands the Refuge Peclet-Polset, from which a delightful snow promenade – after the usual horrors of a steep moraine path – leads up the Polset glacier to the easy rock-belfry of the Aiguille de Polset (11,608 feet) and its neighbours the Dome de Polset and the Aiguille de Peclet. The Aiguille de Polset is one of the finest medium altitude viewpoints in the Alps, the vast circular prospect extending from the Mont Blanc range, towering 50 miles to the north, around the distant Pennines to the east and back, through the Graian peaks, to the cluster of local summits; while 20 miles to the south the giants of the Dauphiné rise in a long coronet of rock and snow from the Pelvoux to the Meije.

For lovers of gentle scenes and yet within reach of the higher regions by bus, car or on foot, close behind Moutiers in the main Isère Valley, on the road to Pralognan, the charming Spa of Brides les Bains lies scattered among the woods, a splendid centre for coach excursions throughout the district and farther afield in Savoy and Dauphiné.

The Tarentaise does not boast any giants, but by contrast with the sheer savagery of the Dauphiné and the overpowering might of the great Savoy summits, it provides mountain scenery at its loveliest and most peaceful.

At Bourg St Maurice the N90 goes straight on to attack the main Alpine barrier ahead and climbs to the saddle of the Petit St Bernard on its way to Italy (chapter 15). The road swinging southwards to the right follows the beautiful valley of the upper Isère – it was even more beautiful before they drowned the village of Tignes in the waters of a man-made hydro-electric lake – to the mountaineering and winter sports centre of Val d'Isère, buried deep between the Graian ranges. Here the road begins its climb, in great swinging curves, to the Col d'Iseran, at 9,088 feet the third highest in the Alps, leading over to Bonneval at the head of the Arc Valley and then along it back to Lanslebourg, at the foot of the Mont Cenis windings. This 'pass' was constructed for mainly military reasons and lies entirely in French territory, running parallel with the Franco–Italian frontier.

The high peaks of the French Graians run in a long comb from the 11,438-foot Ruitor, close behind La Thuile, a little resort on the eastern slope of the Petit St Bernard, through the Grande Sassière to the Tsanteleina (11,831 feet) above Val d'Isère, roughly north to south, constituting at once the main watershed and the frontier. Then follows the complex of the Iseran peaks and the long southwestward curve of the range from Bonneval towards Lanslebourg and southwards again to Briançon, where the Graians give way to the Cottians.

Descending the almost level valley from Bonneval to Lanslebourg, we come to Bessans, above which the high but not difficult Pointe de Charbonnel (12,500 feet) offers a magnificent panorama of the Tarentaise, Dauphiné and Savoy Alps as well as the eastern Graians. From Bessans, too, the very lofty and adjoining saddles of the Cols du Collerin, d'Arnès and de l'Autaret pass through a world of glaciers, some of which they traverse, and descend into the Val Malciaussia under the shadow of the 11,605-foot Roche Melon, to Viu and so down to Lanzo (see p. 105).

Lower down, at Bramans, close to the 11,500-foot Aiguille de Scolette, another splendid viewpoint, two other high passes strike

southwards up the fine ravine of St Pierre : the Col du Petit Mont
Cenis (7,220 feet) and the more famous Col du Clapier (8,175
feet) – an unlikely favourite, in my humble opinion, for the
Hannibal Stakes; for, supposing him to be in this valley at all, he
could hardly have missed the far easier, lower and more open
saddle of the Mont Cenis itself, as he passed below it, only a mile
or two away. Both these high tracks cross the 'backbone' to
descend on Susa, at the foot of the Mont Cenis proper.

That great trans-Alpine highway (6,834 feet), in use since
Charlemagne's days, is still the most direct and easiest of the high
passages from the plains of central France to those of northern
Italy. The superb lower approach through the Maurienne Valley,
from Aiguebelle, 20 miles east of Chambéry, to Modane, is so
finely engineered as to be almost a speedway. Beyond Modane
(3,465 feet), through Lanslebourg (4,500 feet) and then by six
gentle wide dog-legs up the 2,000 feet to the saddle in the main
watershed, the scenery of the Tarentaise peaks and glaciers to the
north unfolds with progressive splendour. The road then dips a
little into a remarkable hanging valley five miles long where once
stood Napoleon's barracks, now submerged in the waters of two
hydro-electric 'lakes' in successive steps of the valley-floor. Here
the Cenisio river is born, to flow down the ravine beyond and join
the Dora Riparia at Susa in the valley below. This descent of more
than 5,000 feet into the chestnut and walnut groves of sunny Italy
is achieved by a superb staircase of wonderfully-engineered hairpin windings, with the huge bulk of the 11,605-foot Roche
Melon's rockwall dominating everything on the opposite side.
There are ten highly impressive miles of motoring, till, passing
the remains of the Arch of Cottius, where the Mont Genèvre
road comes down a deep re-entrant from the right (see chap. 15)
you emerge in the white-walled, red-tiled streets of Susa (1,624
feet).

Separated from the Graians by the Mont Genèvre road-crossing
into the valley of the Dora Riparia in Italy, the main chain of the
Cottians runs south from Briançon to the Maritime Alps (chapter
5), forming the frontier between France and Italy, which runs

along their highest crests to the east of Barcelonnette, Guillestre, Château Queyras, Aiguilles and Abriès, the main resorts in the region. By far the highest peak in the group is the sharply pointed Monte Viso (12,609 feet), rising isolated on the Italian side of the frontier and visible, on a clear day, from the Pennine heights, 100 miles away. At its eastern foot the Po starts its long journey to the Adriatic. It is best approached from Crissolo, with two club huts affording access not only to the mountain and its neighbour the Visolotto – the rock-climbing on the south face of the Viso is graded as low as 'moderate' – but also to walking country well worth a couple of days' stay. The approach from the French side starts at Abriès beyond Aiguilles and is altogether bleaker and more barren and the ascent much more difficult.

Guillestre lies 20 miles south of Briançon in the main Durance Valley, here joined by that of the Guil, falling in from the east. From that interesting valley in which nestle Château Queyras, Aiguilles and Abriès, there are many peaks providing uncrowded and attractive climbing, such as the 11,000-foot Font Sancte with a superb panorama; these are also the approaches to half a dozen high tracks over the watershed into Italy. From Château Queyras the 8,755-foot Col Agnel, with a hospice at its saddle, crosses into the Val Varaita at Casteldelfino. From Abriès, eight miles farther up the valley, set in fine scenery and among splendid viewpoints like the easy Tête de Pelvat (9,633 feet) the Col de Vallante (9,170 feet) leaves the extreme head of the Guil Valley to reach the same destination. Here also starts the long track to the Col de la Traversette (9,827 feet) leading down to Crissolo; while, striking eastwards from the valley head, the 7,576-foot Col de la Croix provides the main link between French Queyras and the Val Pellice at Torre Pellice. (For the southern approaches to all these Cottian crossings see below, next page.)

Crissolo is the southern exit of the Traversette route, which descends from the Col by way of the Piano del Re (6,625 feet), close to the source of the Po, an open alp, with its impressive view of the Viso's towering south face. From all the easily access-ible summits along the passes just mentioned there are magnificent views of the great mountain and down the valleys to the Italian plain.

Twenty miles north of Turin, at the mouth of the three valleys of the upper Stura lies Lanzo, near which an arched bridge built in 1378 still spans the river. The three picturesque valleys lead respectively to Viu, the southern foot of the Col de l'Autaret (see p. 102); to Ala di Stura and Balme; and the northernmost, the Val Grande, to Forno Alpi Graie at the southern foot of the Levanna, the Graian peak above Bonneval in the Arc Valley (see below).

At Pinerolo on the edge of the Piedmont plain, 25 miles west of Turin, the main road leads up to Sestrières and the 6,600-foot col beyond it which joins the Mont Genèvre just on its Italian side at Cézanne (Cesana). A minor road dives into the foothills up the Val Pellice to Torre Pellice, just short of the frontier, at the foot of the Col de la Croix. This is one of the three parallel valleys to which the much-persecuted Waldenses of Vaud in Switzerland transmigrated in *c.* 1500 and they have maintained their distinct French-speaking identity ever since. Torre Pellice is the capital of this 'home from home'. The other two valleys are the Val Chisone, leading up through Perosa to Fenestrelle, and the neighbouring Val Germanasca.

Other roads running up into the frontier-range from Italy are that up the valley of the Maesa, a little to the west, to S. Damiano and Prazzo, at the southwest foot of the 11,155-foot Aiguille de Chambeyron, usually climbed from St Paul on the Col de Vars road (p. 88) from the French side. The other peaks of over 11,000 feet in the Cottians are the Aiguille de Scolete, Grand Rubren, Brec de Chambeyron, Rognosa d'Étache, the Dents and Roche d'Ambin, the Font Sancte and the Visolotto.

The Cottians on the whole are a rugged and somewhat inhospitable sector of the Alps, offering only the few summer resorts mentioned and a few more winter ones in recent years – Mont Genèvre itself above Briançon, Sauze d'Oulx on the south flank of the Dora valley a few miles on the Italian side, Bardonnechia in its side-valley and the now famous and sophisticated Colle de

Sestrières, 6,000 feet up on the Italian frontal slope of the Alpine chain, the crests above which overlook the distant plain of Piedmont where lies Turin, whose happy weekend hunting-ground it has long since become.

In summer the Cottians are climbers' territory, unspoiled and off the beaten track, while walkers will delight in the many wild and high trails across the 'divide', already mentioned.

Returning to the Graians, the main range runs northwest from the frontier at Mont Genèvre above Briançon through the two lofty Ambin peaks to Roche Melon (Roccamelone, 11,605 feet, the first snowpeak ever to be climbed when in 1358 a knight, Bonifacio Rotario of Asti, ascended it, to place a votive offering on its summit). The chain then runs due north, flanking the upper Arc Valley, gaining in height all the time, till with the Levanna and Albaron above Bonneval it reaches the 12,000-foot level. The continuation through the Iseran nodule and the north-western spur stretching to the Petit St Bernard has already been described.

The real pride of the Graians is its loftier eastern group, bounded on the north by the great trench of the Aosta Valley, separating it from the southern wall of the Mont Blanc group and the Central Pennines. It forms an enclave of its own, a little larger than the Tarentaise to its west, entirely in Italy. This is a lovely mountain-tract, deeply bitten into by valleys climbing steeply southwards from the Val d'Aosta and westwards from north of Turin, and rich in simple resorts like Cogne, Valgrisanche and Ceresole Reale, set in green and wooded folds at the foot of some of the most beautiful snow-peaks in the Alps – among which the sheer symmetry of the Grivola (13,022 feet) must surely take pride of place. The only higher summit is that of the broad-fronted Gran Paradiso (13,384 feet) but there are at least ten of over 12,000; yet the climbing in this area is not, on the whole, of the most difficult kind, and there is no more beautiful mountain rambling to be had anywhere than on some of the shelf-walks at the foot of these delectable mountains.

At Aosta the road coming down from Courmayeur, at the southern mouth of the Mont Blanc road tunnel (see p. 22) is joined by the Great St Bernard coming over from Martigny in Switzerland and the broad highway follows the deep, wide valley of the Dora Baltea due eastwards to Châtillon-St Vincent, then southwards, still skirting the eastern foothills of the Graians, to Ivrea and Montalto Dora, where Autostrada 5 makes light of the further 20 miles to Turin.

8. The Mont Blanc Group

If we had gone straight on at Albertville instead of following the N90 southwards to explore the Graians and the Cottians, a choice of attractive minor passes would have brought us to the Mont Blanc group, the greatest complex of elevated peaks in the Alpine chain.

The N212 running northwest for 15 miles up the Vale of Arly to Flumet proceeds over the low Col de Megève beyond that highly popular and populated summer and winter resort (3,690 feet) – with its 80 hotels and innumerable lifts now France's most frequented and fashionable skiing centre – to Le Fayet-St Gervais les Bains in the valley of the Arve. All along this road there are grand glimpses of Mont Blanc's western faces and the great Brouillard ridge crowning them. The view from Combloux, just off the main road to its west, is particularly beautiful, especially in evening light.

From Annecy (p. 99) the road to Thônes by way of the Nom Valley and La Clusaz climbs over the very picturesque Col des Aravis (4,915 feet) to descend the valley of the Arondine and join the N212 at Flumet, a beautiful drive of about 30 miles. This pass, somewhat cluttered by coaches in summer, has a wonderful view of the Mont Blanc range towering over the nearer and lower Aravis peaks and provides the most attractive drive of all the routes into the heart of Savoy.

For those who have come across France to enter the Alps by way of Geneva, the valley approach runs for 40 miles through the beautiful basin of the Arve, by way of Annemasse, Bonneville and

16 *The Noire and the Blanche (Peuteret Ridge, Mt Blanc): with the Dauphiné Alps 80 miles away*

17 *Mont Blanc from above Courmayeur*

Cluses to Sallanches, still less than 2,000 feet up. Just before Sallanches there are continuous views of the whole great snowy chain. Four miles farther up lies Le Fayet-St Gervais, already mentioned, at the eastern foot of the Col de Megève. This is a charming valley resort, in an open bowl catching the sun till late in the afternoon. Directly after St Gervais the road climbs steeply to enter the almost level upper valley of the Arve at Les Houches and runs on to Chamonix, ten miles above St Gervais, the heart and centre of the Mont Blanc region. The last four miles, with the stupendous cascade of glacier and rock sweeping to the roadside from 10,000 feet above on the right, are almost daunting in their impressiveness.

Chamonix-Plage (3,400 feet), as its modern appellation suggests, has everything – lido, casino, cinemas, 'le dancing', 'le bar', and milling crowds of worshippers of Mont Blanc (which is, incidentally, not seen well from the sprawling township, once a climbing-village, because it is far too foreshortened from so deep and so close beneath).

Indeed, it always seems to me that in the famous statue decorating the main square, Horace Benedict de Saussure and his companion are cricking their necks and straining their eyes in an effort to recognise the place where their incredible temerity landed them one day in 1786. If on your mountain holiday you are in search of peace and quiet, you will not like the most famous, perhaps, of all Alpine centres – with apologies to Zermatt, of course. If so, the road runs gently uphill along that marvellous valley with ever-improving views of the great peaks for ten miles, through Les Tines, Les Praz and Argentière, to Le Tour in the valley-bed and Montroc le Planet on the windings of the Col des Montets road over into Switzerland – all pleasant and quiet places. Moreover, if you occasionally crave the bright lights and, when it rains – as, alas, it so often does among mountains – hunger for a cinema and a chromium café, you can be in Chamonix by car or electric train in twenty minutes from any of those delightful smaller resorts higher up the vale, or from Les Houches below.

Belittle the new Chamonix as one may, this is a situation which

18   The Jorasses–Rochefort–Géant complex from the Midi

defies description. Even Baedeker, commenting that it is 'inferior to (his beloved) Bernese Oberland in picturesqueness of scenery' has to admit that it is 'superior in the grandeur of its glaciers, in which it has no rival but Zermatt'. And with due respect to the indefatigable revealer of places visited, I would argue stoutly that the famous Valaisian centre, which has elevated the Matterhorn as a monument to itself, has nothing comparable to offer in glacier scenery till you have taken a train or ropeway to high above it.

Here in the depths of a green plainlet, between massive pine and larch-forests clothing the huge slopes, the Glacier des Bossons plunges 10,000 feet almost to the main valley road, while along its pleasantly-wooded upward course, the Glacier de Bois (the tongue of the Mer de Glace), the steep icefall of the Glacier d'Argentière and the broad, shattered cataract of the Glacier du Tour come cascading down successively to the fringe of the flower-starred meadows.

While from a high shelf above the forests the russet towers of three gaunt clusters of shattered granite – the Chamonix Aiguilles go winging skyward, from the Midi to the Charmoz, to a point a savage contrast with the great surging amphitheatre of ice and snow to their right and the sharp ice-clad spires of the Verte, the Chardonnet, the Argentière and the gentler comb of the Tour to their left.

Surely there is nothing even remotely comparable to this cataclysm in the whole of the Alps?

For the visitor who does not intend to climb or glacier-walk high in the recesses behind this stupendous façade, the best views of it, across the rift of the narrow valley, are to be had from a number of famous vantage-points on the chain of the Aiguilles Rouges, which bounds the Chamonix valley on the north. All are accessible nowadays by aerial-ropeways.

The nearest to Chamonix itself and consequently to the semi-circle of summits and glaciers crowning it, is Planpraz (6,770 feet), whose terrace commands one of the most glorious views in the Alps. It is at its best in the late afternoon, when the light strikes almost horizontally through the gap to the west from Sallanches;

the reward of waiting for the last car down – yes, even of missing it and walking the steep two hours through the darkening woods – is a rich one.

From Planpraz a single loop of cable leaps the 2,500-foot cliff-face of the Brevent (8,285 feet), from which the view of Mont Blanc is even more magnificent and the prospect is extended to include the whole valley, the Aiguilles and peaks to the east as far as the Col de Balme at its head, over whose saddle the summits of the Bernese Oberland appear; while to the southwest the remote Dauphiné Alps are added to the scene.

La Flégère (6,158 feet), farther to the east on the slopes below the Aiguilles Rouges, is reached by the ropeway starting from Les Praz, on the main valley-road to Argentière. The view of the Mont Blanc amphitheatre is less grand from here, but the terrace directly faces the Aiguilles and the tongue of the Mer de Glace falling to their left, with a glimpse of the Grandes Jorasses soaring behind it, and the Dru and the massive Verte forming the centre-piece of the view. Beyond, to the east, the Chardonnet and the Argentière, with its icefall, dominate the head of the valley, closed in by the long ridge falling from the Aiguille du Tour and its glacier to the Col de Balme. Here again evening light adds much to the beauty of the magnificent prospect.

There is, of course, nothing against following an old-established practice of former 'foot-slogging' days, before the advent of the ubiquitous 'bucket' (on which be much praise now that I am 'older grown and fat') by spending the night at any of these three mountain inns to add the majesty of the sun's uprising to the splendours of its going-down.

There are wonderful 'shelf-walks' all along this side of the valley, along the bridle-path which links Planpraz with the Flégère and continues to descend eventually on Les Joux and Argentière. In high summer all the slopes through which it passes are ablaze with a carpet of the '*rose des Alpes*', the alpine mini-rhododendron, forming a gorgeous foreground to the snows opposite.

For the more energetically inclined there are fine mountain

walks in this range from the Brevent, Planpraz and the Flégère.
One of the most attractive is by the path rising from behind the
last-named to the little Lac Blanc, two hours higher up, at the
foot of the Aiguille de Floriaz (9,475 feet) and the Belvedère
(9,730 feet), the highest point in the Aiguilles Rouges, neither of
which is difficult for experienced climbers, about two more hours
being required from the lake for the ascent. Both summits open
up the view to the north over the basin of the Lake of Geneva,
while that from the Lac Blanc, with the Chamonix Aiguilles
mirrored in its still waters, is a 'photographer's dream'.

There are plenty of excursions on the Mont Blanc side of the
valley, too. You can take your choice very easily now that the
ropeway hoists you up to Plan de l'Aiguille (7,223 feet) in a few
minutes at the foot of the Aiguille du Plan. All the favoured viewpoints which used to require a day's outing on foot from the valley
are now at your command from here by paths and tracks contouring the slopes with little height differentials involved – westwards past the Glacier des Pélerins to Pierre Pointue (6,720 feet)
overlooking the tremendous icefall of the Bossons, from where a
steep and less easy climbers' path leads up to the Pierre à l'Échelle
(7,910 feet) which has a magnificent near view of the whole Mont
Blanc amphitheatre rising above the rock-comb of the Grands
Mulets (this is all part of the route to Mont Blanc: the night is
spent at the hut high on those rocks). Eastwards from the Plan you
can ramble for hours along the shelf at the foot of the Plan–
Blaitière–Charmoz chain of Aiguilles, very close to the masses of
débris thrown down by them and their three hanging glaciers, the
Pélerins, the Blaitière and the Nantillons, till you finally come to
Chamonix' world-famous belvedère, the 6,266-feet Montanvert,
overlooking the wide sweep of the Mer de Glace and the peaks
which enclose it.

The normal approach from Chamonix to this grand viewpoint
is either on foot by the path through the pine-forests, a matter of
under three hours, or by its own little electric railway. The famous
hotel caters for hundreds of thousands of day-trippers in a season
besides providing a base for all the climbs in this sector of the

massif. On a knoll close by stands the charming little 'Temple of Nature'. High overhead, beyond the broad, sinuous sweep of the Mer de Glace, soars the spearhead of the 12,320-foot Dru, with the snowy summit of the Verte, to which it is attached, rising another 1,200 feet behind it to the left, and the Aiguille du Moine (11,197 feet), remembered by many a climber as his first big rock-peak, for it is of no great difficulty from the Couvercle (see below), to its right. Set back behind a wide gap rises the tremendous north face of the Grandes Jorasses (13,795 feet), then further forward again the snowy cap of Mont Mallet (13,084 feet) and, at the extreme right-hand end of the ensuing Rochefort comb, the huge monolith of the Aiguille du Géant (13,070 feet). To the right of it, close at hand, the eastern ridge of the Grands Charmoz, from which sprouts the amazing splinter of the République, closes the horseshoe view.

Those anxious to make their first acquaintance with glacier-ice and who have not already tried their feet out at the bottom of the Bossons, nearer the town-centre, will find guides here willing if not positively eager to see them safely through the crossing to the far bank and on by the 'Mauvais Pas', hewn in the rock and protected by iron stakes, to the little inn on the Chapeau (5,278 feet), an hour and a half from the Montanvert, which commands a good view of the icefall and the valley, the descent to which by bridle-path takes less than an hour.

A longer glacier-tour in this glorious mountain-scenery leads to the Couvercle refuge at the foot of the Moine, fronting the Jorasses in all their precipitous magnificence above the curve of the Leschaux glacier. Near the present palatial two-storey Club Hut of stone there is a huge flat-topped rock on which for generations dozens of people have delighted to assemble to watch sunset or sunrise. The old Couvercle refuge, a one-storey wooden hutment designed to house a maximum of 40, stood underneath that pro-jecting slab, entirely sheltered by it. I once spent the night there in the company of 79 others and was very glad to escape into the cracking cold of the hours before dawn, to surface and draw the necessary breath. Beyond the Couvercle and approached direct by the Glacier de Talèfre stands the Jardin, an isolated rock in the centre of that glacier, at the foot of the towering Verte, Droites and Courtes. It is so called because around a spring in the rock alpine flowers are to be found flowering in midsummer.

For more experienced mountaineers, the classic route from the Montanvert leads up the Mer de Glace to the icefall of the Géant glacier, in the shadow of the granite pinnacles of all the Aiguilles and then up that glacier's less steep and snowy basin to the Col du Géant (11,060 feet), on the Italian frontier, a glacier-slog of some six hours. The ropeway descent from the Refuge to Entrèves in Italy now takes 17 minutes instead of several hours by zig-zag path as it once did. A bus will deliver you at Courmayeur (see p. 118) in another 20, thus halving the old time of 16 hours once allowed for the traverse from Chamonix.

There is of recent years a classic route for non-mountaineers, of all shapes and sizes and ages and, happily, for mountaineers who are beyond mountaineering any more, through the heart of the Mont Blanc massif. This starts a mile south of Chamonix's main square with the first section of the world's most wonderful ropeway, the section to Plan de l'Aiguille, already mentioned, where cars are changed for the fabulous single-festoon of the 5,000-foot leap to the 12,608-foot Aiguille du Midi. Here there is an inn with a restaurant, and the summit rocks are honeycombed with lifts, bridges, ice-tunnels, galleries and rock-paths, giving access to every aspect of the stupendous circular view.

From this belfry of yellowish grey granite, high above the valleys on one side and the glacier-world on the other, all the splendour available to a climber who has scaled a high alpine peak is offered to the townsman who has never seen a mountain before. Without going into details, it sweeps round from the lower Savoy ranges to the west, past a hint of the Geneva basin, through the Aiguilles Rouges (now well below the eye-level opposite), past a glimpse of the Oberland, the Valais giants, Monte Rosa and Matterhorn, to the front wall of the Mont Blanc massif plunging from the Chardonnet, Argentière and Verte and all the Aiguilles 10,000 feet to the trough of the Chamonix Valley. Across the glaciers southwards towers the Jorasses–Rochefort–Géant cluster. Then beyond the lower gap of the Col du Géant, the Graian giants, Gran Paradiso, Grivola and a dozen others rise above the unseen rift of the Aosta Valley to lean against the Italian sky; further to the right of the Col rises, in the foreground, the helmet-like head of the 'Little' Tour Ronde and – the rest of the world and the sky to the west is blotted out to the zenith by the creaming, streaming snows and blue-crevassed, plunging ice-falls and glacier-tongues of Mont Blanc, near enough to touch and still bulking 3,000 feet overhead.

But this is by no means the end of ropeway marvels. From the Midi a subsidiary line of cables, served by small four-seater cars, swings high above the Vallée Blanche and the head of the Géant glacier, in full view of Mont Blanc's magnificent southern precipices and all the other peaks ringing the basin, to the 11,300-foot Pointe Hellbronner, 300 feet above the Col du Géant and connected with it by a short cablecar section, affording easy access to Courmayeur. So the modern lowlander can now enjoy in comfort all the marvels of the high-mountain scene, not long ago only to be captured by long and arduous uphill struggle of body, hand and foot.

Or can he? A high proportion of those who are unceremoniously yanked in 20 minutes to the top of the Midi are coach-passengers straight from the heat of the plains and valleys, unsuitably clad and shod, who have apparently not even been properly warned that the air is thin and it is likely to be cuttingly cold up there, in the icy breath of the snows and glaciers. This seems to me an inexcusable omission on the part of the authorities. Many too are elderly people whose heart conditions may be quite unequal to the ordeal. I have seen women in thin summer frocks and low shoes, men in open-necked shirts and shorts, chilled to the marrow and suffering acute discomfort; not to mention numbers in the throes of severe mountain sickness, resulting from the all too swift change of atmospheric pressure. This, to anyone who has ever been mountain-sick, might seem a peculiar form of 'enjoyment'.

Yet, for those who know enough to take the necessary warm

clothing, who are strong and fit, and who have eyes to see, the 'ascent' of the Midi may in some cases prove the ultimate revelation, opening their eyes to the undreamed glory of the high places, beckoning them to return to this dazzling world-out-of-the-world by their own efforts and to their lifelong profit, which they might otherwise never have reaped. I should not like to hazard a percentage-guess, lest I be written-off as a pessimist.

Courmayeur (4,360 feet) the Italian counterpart of Chamonix, is quite different in character, lying spread out on a broad, sunny southward-facing slope hard up against the immense rocky precipices of the southern wall of the Mont Blanc group. The old village with its narrow, cobbled streets and the ancient church (the clock in whose crooked tower obligingly strikes the hour twice at a minute's interval, just in case you did not hear it the first time) are still there; but modernity, voracious as elsewhere, is rapidly nibbling into it with tall ultra-modern hotels, tinselly shops and, erupting all over the surrounding knolls and slopes, a rash of trim whitewashed villa-estates of wealthy *Torinese* industrialists. Between the town and the ancient village of Dolonne to the west of the Dora Baltea, bursting its way to freedom and the plains through a nearby gateway in the hills, the amenities of once-quiet flowery meadows have not been improved by the lorry-traffic thundering down the stilt-borne motorway descending from the southern exit of the Mont Blanc road-tunnel, four miles and a few hundred feet above at Entrèves, beyond a narrow neck in the foothills.

Entrèves, too, straddling the junction of two high valleys facing one another, the Val Veni to the west, the much longer Val Ferret to the east, is the start of the Col du Géant–Hellbronner leg of the Mont Blanc ropeway network. Every visitor to Courmayeur will wisely wish to be whisked up to the magnificent viewpoints 6,000 feet overhead on the rim of that titanic wall, from which the Peuteret ridge of Mont Blanc, incorporating the savage black sail of the Aiguille Noire and the exquisite white ice-sculptures of the Blanche, sweeping up to the monarch's huge southern pillars and precipices, is a truly magnificent sight. Close at hand beyond the

Col soars the 400-foot monolith of the Dent du Géant's summit-block, dominating an immense panorama of the Graians and the Pennines, stretching away to Monte Rosa's gleaming five-towered castle-keep and the dark spike of the Matterhorn, 80 miles away to the east, and to the long line of the Dauphiné summits a similar distance to the west. (The Col, 11,300 feet, like the Midi, is well above the snow-line, so the same considerations of clothing and basic physical fitness apply.)

The two valleys at the foot of the great wall are both interesting and quite different in character. The Val Veni, starting below the shattered cataract of the huge Brenva Glacier, rises gently past the bare slopes at the base of the soaring Aiguille Noire, to the tongue of the even larger glacier curve of Trélatête falling from the beautiful *Aiguille* of that name and, just beyond it, reaches the green glacier-lake of Combal, the home of little icebergs even in summer. Beyond this point the valley is called l'Allée Blanche, along which the track rises steeply to the Col de la Seigne (8,240 feet), the last leg of the favourite three-days' pass-walk of the 'Tour du Mont Blanc', usually undertaken from the Chamonix end (see below). The broader and more luxuriant Val Ferret, into which a narrow motor-road climbs from Entrèves, then runs straight and almost level past the towering mass of the Grandes Jorasses for some miles till, beyond the Aiguille du Triolet and Mont Dolent, the Franco-Swiss cornerstone of the range, it is barred by the low frontier-ridge with Switzerland, over which the Col Ferret bridle-track gives somewhat tedious access onwards to Orsières and down to Martigny in the Rhône Valley. This lovely, open valley, rich in flowers along the banks of the infant Dora, babbling and foaming down between great boulders, is an ideal spot for a day's rambling and picnicking in the shadow of the great peaks.

A steep side-road leaving the Courmayeur-Entrèves road to the left, leads in a few minutes to the tiny chapel of Notre Dame de Guérison, decorated with frescoes and beautifully perched against the background of the Brenva Icefall. This is another photographer's plum, and the short detour is well worth while.

Of the other expeditions round Courmayeur, one of the finest viewpoints in the surrounding green and wooded-ridges is the Mont de la Saxe (7,755 feet), a lovely day's path-walking, with an ascent of some three hours and a superb prospect over the whole southern wall, close opposite. Almost as fine, and more accessible by a series of linked cable-cars from Dolonne, is the charming flower-starred Alpe Chécrouit (5,650 feet) set among the meadows, pines and bilberries of a saddle in the Mont Chétif–Crammont ridge, with a breathtaking view of the Peuteret ridge surging up to Mont Blanc's much-foreshortened summit, incredibly high above. The view is improved by a short stroll up to the little Lac Chécrouit, where the great peaks are seen reflected in the dark, still, photogenic waters of the small tarn.

Further afield, and more mountainous, but well within the compass of any strong uphill walker, is the ascent of 8,955-foot Crammont, considered by many to be the best of all the points from which to view the southern aspects of the group. This is made from Pré St Didier, the charming little resort about four miles down the valley-road to Aosta, from which the summit is reached by a steep track in about four hours.

The 'grand tour' of Mont Blanc, already mentioned as usually being undertaken from Chamonix, entails three days of splendid if strenuous mountain-walking. The first leads in about six hours, by way of the Pavilion de Bellevue (rightly named) and the Montjoie Valley, to Les Contamines (3,843 feet); the second, passing the châlets of Nant Borrant, leaves that valley by the Col du Bonhomme (8,140 feet), from which there is a splendid view of the Tarentaise, and descends to Les Mottets (6,225 feet); on the third, the path ascends again to the 8,240-foot Col de la Seigne, overlooking the whole length of the Allée Blanche, at the foot of the enormous southern precipices of the chain, and affording near views of the Aiguilles du Glacier and Trélatête and their respective glaciers. It then descends past the Châlets de l'Allée Blanche with glorious views of that valley and the Aiguille de Trélatête overhead to the Combal lake, from which issues the Veni arm of the

Doire or Dora and below which the valley is called the Val Veni (see above).

There is no space to go into the innumerable mountaineering possibilities available to climbers from Chamonix, Courmayeur and the huts and refuges lavishly scattered about the area. The normal route from Chamonix up Mont Blanc (15,874 feet) is a long, exhausting snow-and-ice trudge, the night being spent at the Grands Mulets. All its neighbours afford classic climbs as well as new routes of extreme difficulty; these will all be found in a multiplicity of excellent climbing guide-books available.

There are, however, two relatively minor high peaks in the group, one on the Chamonix side, the other above Courmayeur, which are worth a special mention; for they should afford much pleasure to the (guided) novice and the elderly climber who still loves to move about above the snowline but prefers to moderate his raptures. They are the Aiguille du Tour (11,640 feet) at the extreme eastern end of the range, ascended from Le Tour (a convenient halt halfway up the Col de Balme chair-lift eases the long slog to the hut) with a night at the Refuge Albert Premier, then up the Chardonnet glacier to the Col du Tour and thence by an easy rock-climb to the summit with its wonderful panorama, three to three and a half hours from the hut; and, at the other end of the range, the charming Tour Ronde (12,250 feet) nestling in the vast shadow of Mont Blanc's south face. This is a snow trudge over the Géant glacier, then steeply up a *couloir* to a little belfry of granite boulders on the very rim of the Brenva wall, looking out southwards over Courmayeur, the Aosta Valley, all the Graians beyond it and, eastwards away to the distant Valais giants. The kindly ropeway will take you from Entrèves to the Col du Géant in 20 minutes, your legs from there to the top of your mountain in three to three and a half hours, according to their age and condition. The return to the Col will require three hours or a good deal less, depending on how lively they are after their uphill exertions.

If you plan to leave Chamonix bound for Switzerland, both road and rail climb up to the Col des Montets (4,740 feet) beyond

Argentière and down to the frontier at Le Chatelard; here the routes divide, one road and the railway climbing away to the left by way of the holiday resorts of Finhaut and Salvan and dropping into the Rhône Valley at Vernayaz. The direct road route, keeping to the right, climbs through Trient to the Col de la Forclaz (4,985 feet) and so to Martigny (see following chapter).

Since 1965 when de Gaulle, by a remarkable coincidence of timing, opened it during the very week when the Swiss were celebrating the Matterhorn centenary at Zermatt, there has been another exit from the valley – the great seven-mile-long road tunnel under Mont Blanc, approached by a couple of windings above Les Houches and emerging in Italy at Entrèves, from where a fine modern motorway, carried high above the valley bed on stilts, runs down to Pré St Didier on the way to Aosta. Its opening shortened the journey from Geneva to Northern Italy by 130 miles, but much of the benefit is lost owing to the bottleneck caused by the narrow approaches at its northern end between Sallanches and Chamonix.

9. The Bernese Oberland

Martigny (1,550 feet), a typically tidy Swiss industrial town and busy road-junction lies spread across the Rhône Valley highway at a point where it makes an almost right-handed bend before running eastwards almost as straight as a ruler for 35 miles to Brigue.

The deep sub-alpine rift carved by the river here separates the modest ridges of the Vaudois range to the north from the loftier spurs of the main Pennine range, some 20 miles to the south. Close behind the screen of those snowless mountains of Vaud, their sunny slopes close-terraced with vineyards, rise the southernmost snows of the Bernese Oberland, running roughly parallel to the Pennines at a distance of about 30 miles. The wedge of the Bietschhorn (12,970 feet) dominating the Loetschental (Valais) is a prominent object from the Rhône Valley road or railway long before Brigue is reached.

For the traveller coming across France, the direct approach to the Oberland is by way of the road and rail links through the Jura, down by Delle, Delémont and Solothurn through Bienne, the lakeside industrial centre, and so to Bern itself, the capital of the Swiss Confederation, straddling the Aar with the graceful arches of its airy bridges.

Bern is a lovely old city, rich in ancient Swiss architecture, clock-towers, churches, colonnades and arched gateways, but truly modern as well in its amenities, hotels, luxury shops and transport. The old town stands on a bluff to the south of a great loop in the river, deep down in its gorge. Its chief glory is the

Bollwerk (Bastion), a fine promenade in front of the parliament building and government offices, looking out over the new town and its sprawling suburbs across the river-moat. Here, if you are lucky with the weather, you can make your first acquaintance with the great Oberland snow-peaks, gleaming white in a seemingly endless chain, from the Wetterhorn to the Blümlisalp, 40 miles away beyond the plain and the basin of the unseen Lake of Thun. To sit on one of the benches on that high terrace at the heart of the capital at sunset and watch the miracle of rose and flame floating, apparently unattached to the darkened world, on a grey mist, is an unforgettable introduction to the Alps. I wish I could enthuse as warmly about a possibly more generally-known attraction of the Swiss capital – the celebrated bears (Bären = Bern) typifying the national emblem. It is quite a long journey out to the pits which house these famous beasts, and I, who am allergic to zoos, thought they looked small, scruffy, undignified and pathetic the only time I made it. No notice should, of course, be taken of this purely personal reaction by those who like looking down at bears in pits : I happen to prefer lifting up my eyes to the hills, that's all.

Interlaken, the earliest of the great lowland tourist-centres, is the true gateway to the Oberland. The 40 miles of the journey across the intensely and tidily cultivated plain (everything is tidy in Switzerland) through Münsingen and Thun beyond is an exciting one on a clear day : the snowy chain ahead gains in stature at every kilometre, the centrepiece consisting always of the beautifully balanced triptych of the Eiger, Mönch and Jungfrau.

Thun, at the Bern end of the lake to which it gives its name, is a charming town with an old castle, much beloved by painters, Turner among them. The railway provides an enchanting journey to Interlaken, hugging the west shore of the lake, curving in and out of green baylets with the main-road never far from it, for there is not much room between the wide blue lake and the foot of the green, wooded hills. Halfway along the lake stands sunny Spiez, overlooking it on two levels, an elevated terrace housing the main town and important railway junction – for here the

Loetschberg line bears away eastward to Kandersteg and through its tunnel to the Rhône Valley and Brigue – the lower cradling a charming land-locked harbour fringed with poplar trees, with an old castle at the tip of one of the enclosing arms. Dominating the town from a little to the west rises the perfect 7,763-foot pyramid of the Niesen, a historic viewpoint complete with funicular railway from Mülenen, though its tip must be somewhat out of joint since the construction of the Schilthorn ropeway above Mürren (see below, p. 132).

Just after Spiez road and rail skirt one of the prettiest little bays in the world – Faulensee, with its three waterside inns and white boats bobbing in the tiny harbour below the church; beyond which the rest of the journey to Interlaken skirts bay after bay, headland after headland, now well above the lake, now at its very edge.

The other road (of more recent conversion to a motor highway) from Thun to Interlaken along the east shore is a little longer, but provides finer views of the snowpeaks, particularly of the Blümlisalp, seen to great advantage from a mile or two beyond Thun, at Hilterfingen. It need hardly be mentioned that the lake shores are studded with hotels, restaurants, cafés and tea gardens, from which to feast the eye on the lovely contrast between blue-green waters and dazzling snows.

Interlaken, the largest of all the Swiss alpine (sub-alpine, really) resorts sprawls its hotels, shops, bandstands, Kurhaus, ornamental gardens and swimming-pools all over an open plainlet about five miles by two, between its two lakes : that of Thun and its smaller, more enclosed neighbour of Brienz, to link which the Aar flows dark-green through the town. Its chief scenic glory and the reason why it stands where it does is a world-famous portrait (head and shoulders) of the Jungfrau (13,670 feet) framed as a miracle of white symmetry between the tall dark hills which form the jaws of the Lauterbrunnen Valley to the south: the sole and matchless snowpeak to be seen, across open park-land, from the resort's main thoroughfare and promenade, the Höheweg, beautifully trimmed with formal cushions of flowers. (Always supposing that as you sip your elevenses in one of the open-air cafés along its golden mile you can see anything for the bonnet-to-boot procession of crawling cars and coaches between you and the view.)

If you want to add the Jungfrau's mighty neighbours, the Mönch and the Eiger, to the prospect – and I should recommend it – you will stroll up a small completely wooded hillock 20 minutes behind the noise and bustle of the town, the Heimwehfluh (funicular and café available). This is one of the classic middle-distance views in the Alps. The Harder (4,350 feet), overlooking the plain and the same three peaks from the other (northern) side of Interlaken entails a pleasant walk of about two and a half hours uphill through the woods, or a journey by funicular. Here is a terrace restaurant and lovely walking on the paths which contour the slopes facing that glorious trio of peaks.

Apart from its beautiful situation, Interlaken has grown up where it is because it is the perfect hub of the local universe. To the south, easily accessible by road and rail, lie Lauterbrunnen and the higher and more famous resorts to which it leads – Grindelwald, Wengen and Mürren. To the east, along the all too narrow and crowded lake-side road through Brienz's wonderful old main-street and the extension of the main railway from Interlaken Ost, lies Meiringen, where the low and pretty Brünig Pass swings northwards over to the Sarnen Valley and Lucerne, while a mile or two ahead, beyond the famous gorge of the Aar (an incredibly narrow rift, well worth a visit) Innertkirchen provides the junction to two major passes : the Susten climbing over to the Gotthard, and the Grimsel leaping over the watershed to near the source of the Rhône at Gletsch (see chapter 11).

Until the second war the shortest road-link between the Oberland, the upper Rhine Valley and the Engadine was the Grimsel–Furka–Oberalp trio of passes; a long and arduous journey, seeing that the first two are major undertakings 7,000 and 8,000 feet high. For centuries there had been a mule-track from the Gadmental, near Innertkirchen, leading over the lofty Susten saddle to the lower sector of the Gotthard pass in the Reuss Valley. An imaginative decision was taken between the wars to convert this

*19/20 From the
Schilthorn:*

19 The Gspaltenhorn

*20 Jungfrau and
Ebnefluh*

21　*The North Face of the Eiger*

to a motor-road, thus bypassing the Grimsel and the Furka and halving the time needed to reach the foot of the Oberalp at Andermatt.

The Susten Pass (7,300 feet), which took eight years to build, was opened in 1947 and is a superbly engineered modern motorway, its perfect grading and 30-foot width catering for the huge coaches of today, its western side defeating a 3,000-foot precipice by a daring and spectacular staircase of built-out corners, tunnels and half-tunnels. On this prodigious ascent there are lovely views back to the three clean-cut snowy Wetterhörner (12,250 feet), rising magnificently beyond the Innertkirchen bowl. Having surmounted this main obstacle, the road clings its almost straight way past the Steingletscher hotel (6,120 feet) to the summit, facing at close range, all the way, across a rubble-filled chasm, the shattered icefall of the Stein glacier, which pours from between the gracefully curved snowy saddles and sharp peaks of the lovely Sustenhorn (11,520 feet) and Gwächtenhorn (11,245 feet) into a grey-green lakelet at their feet. This is another high-mountain close-up comparable with the great ones provided by the Stelvio, Grossglockner, Bernina and Lautaret roads. At the summit the road tunnels for 400 yards under the saddle proper (7,420 feet) – well worth the ten minutes' stroll up a path for its fine view down the eastern (Uri) side – and then, after four banked hairpins, slashes its way along the great rock wall containing the broad, green Maiental for ten miles without another turn till, just short of its exit into the Reuss Valley, it is forced to bore a way through a towering barrier of cliffs in a spiral tunnel, leap the thundering torrent by a slender 50-foot arch of concrete and resort to a couple of steeply banked hairpins to join the Gotthard road at Wassen (see p. 186).

The Grimsel (7,100 feet), though completely different in character, is just as wonderful. From the depths of the Innertkirchen bowl it climbs by successive steps up a green and wooded valley, the uppermost rocky treads of which are occupied by two turquoise hydro-electric lakes, for once not too unsightly. At Handegg (4,510 feet) where the valley contracts to a narrow chasm between the cliffs, the Aar, boiling down from the glaciers high above, used to take a stupendous leap of 250 feet sheer into an inferno of spray rising from a gloomy pit below. I am told that it is still allowed to do so by courtesy of the electrical engineers, when the sluices of the Räterichsboden dam are opened at certain times of the year; sad experience dictates that the summer touring season is not one of them. The sector from Handegg to the Hospice is one of the most fantastic on any of the great passes; since there was no room in these fearsome ravines for a road, the builders just strung it from ledge to ledge, often only a few feet above the seething glacier-grey torrent, now blasting it out of the living rock, which is still left overhanging, now forced to tunnel through the vast flying-buttresses rising vertical to the narrow strip of sky above – a Gustave Doré scene.

The Hospice, reached by a short spur-road, stands on the crest of the huge Grimsel Dam, more than 100 feet high, containing a regular-sided man-made storage tank of yellowish water, a mile and a half long, capable of holding 20 billion gallons and supplying half the power for the railways of northern Switzerland. Contemptuously ignoring this desecration, the lower Finsteraarhorn peaks and glaciers soar above its farther end. As so often when man meddles with the mountains, the Grimsel scene is on so colossal a scale that his puny scratchings are in the end only visible as minor changes in detail, effortlessly absorbed by the overpowering and changeless majesty of the surroundings.

The pass road curves upwards through the titanic crater-like wilderness of multi-coloured rock, much of it mauvish and all polished smooth, at the bottom of which all this is set, to reach the watershed and the summit-car-park, from which there is a lovely vista back over all the long road you have come. In the other direction the great view opens up over the deep Gletsch cauldron, with the Rhône Glacier streaming down into it below the Galenstock's white dome, the Furka slashing its way up the wall opposite, and the six great windings of your own road twisting their way down the Maienwang to Gletsch 2,000 feet below. And until you level out among the hotel buildings there (see p. 176) some aspect or other of that view will be with you as you drive on down. The choice of wonderful day-tours by coach or car from Interlaken is thus unlimited. However, here again, as at Chamonix, if you are in search of comparative peace and quiet among high mountains, you will be content to treat this overcrowded, noisy almost-city as a curtain raiser.

The Vale of Lauterbrunnen must surely rank high in the 'Miss Beautiful Valley' competition. From the moment you enter it at Wilderswil on the edge of the plain, its flower-starred meadows, its woods, its steep slopes and cliffs winging high overhead, the foaming grey glacier-torrent of the babbling Lütschine, its dappled light and shade as it rises at first very gently, are an enchanting approach to the great barrier of peaks ahead.

At Zweilütschinen, where the two arms of the torrent meet, the valley opens up for a moment and throws out an arm up towards Grindelwald (see p. 139) with the three summits of the Wetterhorn rising superbly at its far end, ten miles away. The main valley then contracts again and ascends steeply to Lauterbrunnen, and suddenly the whole sky ahead is usurped by the glorious white shoulders and draperies of the Jungfrau. Five minutes later, less than half an hour by road from Interlaken, you are in Lauterbrunnen (2,615 feet), where the valley railway ends and gives way to the triangular Wengen–Scheidegg–Grindelwald mountain network; while on the other side the old funicular runs straight up the slope to Grütschalp and the short electric-tramway to Mürren.

Beyond Lauterbrunnen's narrow main street the road runs on through level green meadows between ochre cliffs rising vertical on either side, to Stechelberg, the last village in the valley below the Schmadribach fall's amphitheatre, crowned by a wall of snowy peaks and glaciers. Almost immediately after leaving Lauterbrunnen, to the right of the road, the remarkable waterfall of the Staubbach leaps down over the rim of the cliffs 980 feet above, in a free fall sheer to the valley level; but its slender skein of water never gets there, for it dissolves into fine 'dust' before it even arrives, drenching the bright green cushion at the foot of the precipice. Half way to Stechelberg, on the other side, are the Trümmelbach Falls, by which the melting glacier-water of the Jungfrau's snow and ice thunder their way spectacularly and dauntingly through the rock-caverns they have gouged for themselves inside the cliff; a stupendous spectacle from the stairways and galleries provided.

Just before Stechelberg, in a meadow to the right, stands the valley terminal of the Schilthorn ropeway, Switzerland's answer to Chamonix's Midi lift, opened in 1967 and almost as wonderful. If its summit panorama does not quite bear comparison with that of its sister-marvel, it is because the top of the Schilthorn (9,754 feet) is 2,500 feet lower, stands facing the snowy range opposite and does not itself rise from a vast glacier-world on which it can look down. And while the scimitar-view from distant Titlis above Engelberg and Lucerne through the perfectly-proportioned Eiger–Mönch–Jungfrau sculpture to the near-by Gspaltenhorn and Blümlisalp glaciers is wide and glorious, there is nothing in it which can begin to compare with the magnificence of Mont Blanc's neighbourly cataclysm upon the Midi.

Here, in 1969, capitalising to the full on the lovely mountain background, the terraces flanking the rotating restaurant 'Piz Gloria', and the snow-shields below, which make the ski-runs from the Schilthorn down to the valley an expert's delight, the James Bond film *On Her Majesty's Secret Service* was shot, superbly, I am told. (I must be the only person in the world who has never seen a James Bond film; and, in any case, I am – if I can still find it – all for peace and quiet among my snow-peaks; two qualities I understand are not usually pursued to full advantage in that gentleman's adventures.)

From the engineering point of view there is little to choose between these two daring assaults upon the high places. The difficulties of the Schilthorn terrain have dictated three stages, involving two changes of car en route. The bottom sector, lifting the passenger from the valley level to the Mürren shelf, 1,500 feet above a vertical precipice, is a miracle of ingenuity, the 'dog-leg' sector from Mürren itself meeting the leap from the valley at

Gimmelwald, where the first exchange is made, by synchronised cars. The cost of this enormous engineering feat was £2,000,000. The fare is as steep as the cable itself and worth every centime of it on a clear day. One small caveat: be sure it *is* a clear day for the Schilthorn's summit has a nasty little habit of veiling itself, even in fine weather, with its own private cloud-system by midday; and a revolving restaurant can be seen, if desired, at the top of the Post Office tower in London. If the fog is down, you will see little else.

Mürren (5,500 feet), that historic resort, thanks to Arnold Lunn the cradle and nursery of British skiing, stands on a narrow shelf, somewhat precariously perched between the foot of the Schilthorn and the 1,500-foot sheer drop to the Stechelberg meadows. Players on its cliff-side tennis courts must always go in fear that a high bounce will have to be retrieved from the valley. It has a splendid échelon view of the Mönch and Eiger, across the gulf and above the Wengernalp and Scheidegg slopes; but the Jungfrau from here is a total loss, since the limestone cliffs which are its pedestal (the 'Schwartz Mönch') loom up far too close opposite, and the loveliest of snow-mountains is reduced to a foreshortened jumble peering over them, prodigiously high overhead. Mürren's own snow-range is the continuation from the Jungfrau, right round to the Büttlassen at the head of the valley, seen to great advantage only from here. The pleasant village has of course all the amenities; and walks and excursions abound, from the gentle Almendhubel, a little way behind it, to the lovely length of the shelf running back towards Lauterbrunnen, always through pine-woods and among flowers, and on, high above the valley through Grütschalp, crossing at least one splendid waterfall, to charming little Isenfluh, below the crooked fingers of the much-climbed Lobhörner. The views of the Eiger, Mönch and Jungfrau from this three-hour stroll are incomparable.

Longer and more mountainous expeditions will lure the mountain walker up to the inn at the Obersteinberg châlets, close to Mürren's own particular snow chain, which swings gently round overhead from the Ebnefluh through the beautiful helmet-shaped Breithorn to the Tschingelhorn, with their splendidly glaciated

faces. The little tarn, a few minutes above, on the way to the
Tschingel glacier and finely situated Mutthorn hut, from which
the 10,000-foot snow-ridge of the Petersgrat, with its surprise view
of the towering Bietschhorn, is crossed to Fafleralp in the Loetschental, is worth the small extra exertion. Or again there is the
crossing, up in the shadow of the shattered Gspaltenhorn (which
signifies just that) and the Büttlassen, of the Sefinen Furgge (8,583
feet), either down to the Kiental (one day) or up again over the
Hohtürli (9,100 feet), famous for its views of the Blümlisalp and
the beautiful Oeschinensee in which the several peaks of that
broad mountain are mirrored to perfection (two days, the night
being spent at the Blümlisalp Hut), to Kandersteg (see p. 141).

So much for the Mürren side of the valley, so rich in wonders.
Back at Lauterbrunnen, where you leave your car parked or
garaged, for you are going up into a region where the worst
enemies to be met in street or on bridle-track are a hotel's electric
luggage-trolley or two guides wobbling slowly on bicycles deep in
conversation, you take the little cream-and-green train at the other
platform, for Wengen and Kleine Scheidegg on the opposite slope.
Twenty minutes of steep climbing, twisting and tunnelling up the
less daunting and lower cliffs on this side brings you out on
Wengen's wide green shelf, a sun-trap below pinewoods at the
foot of the rocky Männlichen–Tschuggen–Lauberhorn comb,
sheltering it from the winds.

Wengen (4,450 feet), like Mürren, uncontaminated by
fumes because impracticability and local opposition combined
have prevented the building of a road up to it, has not changed
much in character since I first knew it in 1913, in spite of the
building of a modern state school, a swimming-pool, a recently
completed artificial ice-stadium (coals to Newcastle?) and the
Männlichen ropeway. Its short main street has hardly altered;
flanked by its hotels, shops and *konditoreien*, it still curves gently
into the incomparable background of the Jungfrau's glaciers
creaming down from those shapely shoulders. There is now a
pretty little modern church overlooking the valley. At the top of
the sheltered hollow, close under the dark pine-forests, there is the

ropeway station and surely the most beautiful swimming-pool in the world, whose deep-end mirror's Wengen's own mountain in its azure water. The local paths and walks are as they have always been, and if there are many modern châlets and a few new hotels, they are not obtrusive and their gardens and balconies are a blaze of colour.

Even if there was nothing else to do at Wengen, it would be enough to pick your spot and feast your eyes on mountain and valley, but there is plenty. Nearest and shortest is the gentle Steinwaldweg round through the woods above the village roofs; here, in the early morning, the peaks at the far end of the valley gleam sharp and golden, and the Silberhorn, that pure cone of unsullied white on the Jungfrau's broad breast, catches the first low beam of the sun and glows in lonely greeting against the shadowed wall behind it.

An hour away to the north up through the meadows and the flowers a little copse of pine, where red squirrels frolic, crowns the ridge known as the Leiterhorn, a modest 500 feet and a mile above the red roofs nestling among the green below. From here the Jungfrau, mightily risen in stature above the Wengernalp slopes, and at her most symmetrical perfection, fills all the left-hand sector of the sky, while to her right, beyond the green and lovely depths of Lauterbrunnen, the dome of the Breithorn and the attendant peaks at the far head of the valley ring the horizon on a lower level. I wonder if there is any more beautiful place, at so modest an altitude, in which to undo a packed lunch and dream away the long lotus afternoon?

There are many other delightful short walks in all directions, such as Staubbachbänkli, with its view directly opposite of the famous waterfall across the valley. But for those bent on things more strenuous and farther afield, the classic day's expedition is the three hours of the bridle-path up over the open slopes and through the woods, criss-crossing the railway, to Wengernalp and the Kleine Scheidegg, at the foot of the glaciers streaming down from the Mönch and the Eiger. Wengernalp (6,160 feet) is reached in two hours, and here you are suddenly close under the huge rocky precipices of the Jungfrau's base, beautifully crowned by the Silberhorn and Schneehorn, above which the summit soars, a little set back. Here on a hot summer's day the snow-avalanches roar down the rocks all day. There is a little knoll ten minutes to the right of the station with a bench on its crest, where it is pleasant to rest in the sun and watch for the next one to come down. ('Surely the Wengern Alp must be precisely the loveliest place in this world . . .', Leslie Stephen rhapsodised.)

The path, much less steep now, leads on in another 40 minutes past the foot of the Mönch and its glaciers to Scheidegg, for a century famous as a high summer-resort, for half a century as a skiing-centre – is not the Lauberhorn, world-famous for its down-hill racing course, one of the knobs overlooking it? Of recent years it has become notorious as a grandstand for successes and tragedies alike (telescope 50c. a goggle) on the north face of the Eiger, which looms, all 6,000 feet of it, black and repellent – also apparently alluring – above the roofs of its hotels.

The Kleine Scheidegg (6,770 feet) – giving it its proper name to distinguish it from its big brother, the Grosse Scheidegg, five miles to the east, which closes in the far end of the broad green bowl cradling Grindelwald, seen from here as a huddle of roads and houses – is a busy mountain-railway junction. Here the line from Lauterbrunnen meets the 'leg' ascending from Grindelwald, which again is joined down in its own valley, the Lütschental, by the line to Zweilütschinen in the Lauterbrunnen valley (see above, p. 131), thus completing the triangle. But the real pride of this Clapham Junction of the Hills is the Jungfrau railway, onto whose little trains half a million people a year change, in order to see one of the modern wonders of the world.

The amazing dream of a Zürich visionary and engineer, Dr Guyer-Zeller, took 12 years to build and cost 28 lives and 12,000,000 gold francs; Zeller himself died long before it was completed in 1912. After climbing a green slope to Eigergletscher, at the rim of that glacier, the line dives into a tunnel below the Eiger and for its six-mile and 3,700-foot ascent to Jungfraujoch (11,340 feet) never emerges again, the route having been blasted and bored out of the living granite of the two great mountains through and under which it passes. At Eigerwand station, the train stops long enough for you to look out through the wide vaulted windows, which are a landmark on the North Face, over the green map of foothills the climbers see during the lower part of their climb. Then the tunnel swings back on itself inside the Eiger and, at Eismeer, the only other station, you are looking out of similar windows over the shattered ice-world on its reverse side to the grim precipices of the Schreckhorn and Lauteraarhorn. Then an almost level run takes the train right through the core of the Mönch to the Jungfraujoch terminus beneath the broad saddle between the two mountains.

Lifts take you up to the luxury hotel, restaurants, terraces and observatories high above the great sweep of the Aletsch Glacier's 17-mile southward curve – the longest ice-river in the Alps. There is an ice-rink in the bowels of the rock, and a network of tunnels and galleries giving access to the broad snow-plateau of the Joch itself on the upper level and to the glacier on the lower.

The view is world-famous and comparable to that from the Midi rather than any other mechanically approached vantage-point above the snowline. On either side of the saddle rise the summit-masses of the Jungfrau and the Mönch, easily climbed here; below you to the south the Aletsch sweeps in a broad white curve, cradled between high peaks, including the imposing Aletschhorn, down to Concordia, Eggishorn and Belalp, hidden by the final bend.

Beyond the gulf of the unseen upper Rhône Valley, rise the Lepontine Alps, Helsenhorn, Cherbadung and Monte Leone, to close the southern view. To the north, the prospect is at first bewildering, apparently limitless – all the valleys, foothills and lakes of northern Switzerland, to the plains beyond Thun and Bern, to the Jura beyond and, on the far rim of the world, the dark line of the Black Forest, far beyond Bâle, in Germany. All of it, 7,000 feet or more below you as you stand on the edge of the Oberland's northern wall. And all of this for the equivalent of a good restaurant meal. Go to it, I counsel you, but again with the proviso that the weather is settled, and even then as early in the day as possible before the peaks put on their cloud-necklaces.

Back on our chosen day's round – not our Jungfraujoch day – from Scheidegg an almost level track contours below the Lauberhorn and Tschuggen, high above the lovely vale of Grindelwald and always in full sight of the Wetterhorn and Eiger, and leads in less than an hour to the inn on the Männlichen summit itself (7,700 feet). This again is a superb viewpoint. On the left you look down on Grindelwald, with the distant Lucerne peaks just lifting over the saddle of the Grosse Scheidegg, dominated by the Wetterhorn cliffs, nearer at hand, and the dark blunt head of the Schreckhorn again to its right. Then, close in front, the Eiger, Mönch and Jungfrau, the central trinity, to whose right your gaze plunges down to the roofs of Wengen on its shelf and Lauterbrunnen on the valley-carpet another 1,500 feet below them, with the ring of peaks at the far head of the valley biting into the horizon sky. The centre piece to all this is the dark cone of the Tschuggen (8,278 feet) rising in front of the snows, a wonderful foreground contrast. Its steep north ridge, facing you, is an ideal introduction for a novice to an easy but extremely airy Alpine ridge; it can be climbed guided in less than two hours from the inn on the saddle, and in fact provided me with my first experience of finding myself using my hands on a narrow crest with a drop of some thousands of feet to the valleys on either side.

Back on your day's round after visiting the Männlichen view and consuming your favourite tipple in the afternoon sun outside the inn, you can be wafted back to Wengen by bucket in seven minutes, or walk down the hour's slightly crazy zig-zag path in the face of the cliff. In 1926 I came *up* it – at the end of a track-season and trained to a hair – in 67 minutes, as against Baedeker's two and a half to three hours' allowed time. Only one of the guides in the region was prepared to believe me, my own Hans Burgener: and then only after I had sprinted 60 yards flat out in heavily-nailed climbing-boots down Grindelwald's main street, which odd performance seemed to convince him that *anything* was possible (mountain guides *never* run and this was obviously an entirely new idea to him). Anyway, it happens to be true, and I repeated the offence at the age of 50, just to check whether I had been dreaming things; that time it took me 20 minutes longer which, allowing for age deterioration, seems to prove my case. You could, of course, have been wafted up to the Männlichen saddle – 7 minutes by cable car – in the first instance, but you would have missed a glorious day's round.

The other famous member of the trio of resorts at the foot of the Oberland chain is Grindelwald (3,450 feet), the lowest and most townified-touristy of them, which has grown and is growing prodigiously since I first knew it and my wife and I did most of our climbing with Hans for seven seasons from what was then a village, sophisticated perhaps, but still a village.

Its chief visual glory is the Wetterhorn (12,149 feet), whose further 9,000 feet of sheer cliff surmounted by a snowy bell-tower appear to rise out of the end of the busy main-street and go straight up to hit the sky. It is a glorious peak, and there it is whenever you want to look at it, right in front of you: powdered with new snow it can be beautiful beyond description. Its proximity is, however, an illusion. From the village to the Gleckstein Hut on one of its low shoulders above the splendid Lauteraar ice-cascades, was once a five-hours' slog (now shortened somewhat by the new chair-lift to Pfingstegg); from there to the marvellous summit by an interesting 'mixed' climb of snow, rock and ice, another five or more; the beige and brown pillars of cliff propping up that summit have their foundations in the Grosse Scheidegg, the journey to which up a road of many windings takes an hour by the postal-motor service from the village.

The broad saddle of the Grosse or Hasli-Scheidegg (6,436 feet) closes the Grindelwald bowl in at its eastern end, separating it from Meiringen's Haslital beyond. A bridle-path descends from it to Schwarzwaldalp and the narrow postal-motor road through Rosenlaui (4,364 feet) to Meiringen itself (see p. 126 above). There is hardly anything of Rosenlaui except a historic hotel and a school of mountaineering; but a mile on the Meiringen side lies one of the most beautiful meadows in the world, the Gschwandtenmaad. Thick with flowers, dotted with trees, it is quite flat and looks up at the sky-raking precipices of the nearer Wellhorn and the Wetterhorn behind it, displaying from this side the pyramidal aspect of its icy summit, and the huge cascade of the Rosenlaui Glacier's ice-fall pouring down in the middle-ground almost at your feet. A place for picnics, photography and procrastination, if ever there was one. The descent to the valley then takes you past the beautiful Reichenbach Falls – where Sherlock Holmes came off (temporarily) worst in an encounter with Moriarty – to Meiringen.

From the Grosse Scheidegg there is a long and splendid day's round, high above the Grindelwald bowl's northern side, by way of the Oberläger huts to First, then on up to the charming Bachalpsee, another Narcissus-pool for the great peaks, and, for the young and very fit, up the steep windings to the Faulhorn inn (8,805 feet) which commands another classic view of the Oberland giants. All day long you are face to face with the magnificence of the Wetterhorn, Schreckhorn, Finsteraahorn – that shy 14,026-foot monarch of the range, a lance-head shooting up in the background – the snowy wall of the Fiescherhörner, then the Eiger, Mönch and Jungfrau; and, away to the west, above the velvety green comb of the Lauberhorn, Tschuggen and Männlichen, the more distant Blümlisalp.

This used to be a mountain walk of from ten to 12 hours, but now there is the Grindelwald – First chair-lift to take you airily down in half an hour and save you 3,500 feet of knee-jarring descent at the end of the long day. The advent of this cable-lift is a godsend to those who only wish to sun themselves and stroll gently for an hour or two on a glorious high shelf facing an incomparable view. A day spent up there is a Grindelwald 'must'.

Lower down, there are walks in profusion on woodland paths, or steeply up the meadows where the wild flowers riot. On a pre-breakfast photography prowl I once came back, never having left the path, just stretching out my hands to left and right, with a posy for my wife containing 30 different varieties. Everyone visits the two Grindelwald glacier tongues, at last moving forward again after many years of recession, the lower falling from the Schreckhorn and Fiescherhörner deep into the bottom of the valley; the upper from the Lauteraarsattel, between Schreckhorn and Wetterhorn, farther up with an inn for refreshment and close inspection conveniently at its foot.

And, as you take your leave by road or rail down the luxuriating valley to Zweilütschinen on your way out to Interlaken, there, behind you all the way, is the triple-headed surge of the Wetterhorn to remind you that you will be coming back.

The other centres in the southern sector of the Oberland – I always think of it as the 'lesser Oberland' – are visited by returning to Spiez (p. 124), where the Loetschberg Railway branches off to the left, first to Mülenen at the foot of the Niesen and of the Kiental on the other side, and then up the pretty Kandertal till a series of amazing spirals lifts it up to Blausee, a lakelet of a really startling blue, and so to Kandersteg (3,900 feet) at the entrance to the Loetschberg tunnel. All the way up this wonderful section of railway-engineering there are fine views ahead of the beautiful Balmhorn (12,175 feet) and Altels (11,930 feet), much the highest peaks in the southern Oberland chain.

Kandersteg is a pleasant, sunny resort, lying in an open plainlet entirely surrounded by high hills. Its own particular snow-mountain the 12,000-foot Blümlisalp, stands somewhat withdrawn beyond the lovely Oeschinensee (5,200 feet) already mentioned, an hour and a half's easy uphill walk or still more easily accessible by the Oeschinen chair-lift, from whose upper end a path descends in quarter of an hour to the near shore of the lake. This is an Alpine jewel, with the glaciated rocks of the Blümlisalp's four main summits rising sheer from its opposite rim, and often mirrored in its placid surface.

To the south, where the railway tunnel burrows into the base of the hills on its seven-mile journey to Goppenstein in the Loetschental, a wild and beautiful valley, the Gasterntal, opens up and provides attractive walking all the way up to Selden's little hotel, above which a somewhat vertiginous path leads to the

Wildseligen Hut, from which the Balmhorn is climbed; and in the other direction, beneath the ramparts of the Doldenhorn, the long glacier trail by the Kanderfirn starts on its way to the Mutthorn Hut (see p. 134) and so back to the Lauterbrunnen Valley.

Kandersteg's 'special' is, however, the fine excursion to or over the Gemmi Pass (7,640 feet) in a breach between the Balmhorn–Altels complex and the Wildstrubel, leading over to Leukerbad and the Valais. The first trying slog can now be curtailed by taking the Stock chair-lift beyond which a stony wilderness leads to the Schwarenbach Inn (6,780 feet), the starting point for numerous climbs in the neighbouring range – Rinderhorn, Balmhorn, Altels and Wildstrubel among them. Soon afterwards the track runs for half an hour along the shore of the gloomy Daubensee, frozen over for the greater part of the year; soon after that it reaches the Gemmi saddle, on which stands the Hotel Wildstrubel (providing a night's shelter for those sensible enough to want to see the sunrise).

The surprise view which suddenly opens here – improved by a diversion to the Vordere Plattenhorn (8,595 feet) less than an hour to the east – is one of the great Alpine panoramas, from the nearby Wildstrubel's Lämmern Glacier, out across the great rift of the Rhône Valley to all the Valaisian giants surging up beyond. Three thousand feet below you, at the foot of the vertical precipices of the Gemmi's southern wall, lies Leukerbad, a huddle of small dice.

The descent of that sheer precipice into the Valais is achieved by a narrow zig-zag path carved out of the rock, at places almost like a spiral staircase, protected by rails at the giddiest spots. Those who complain that they have no head for heights once preferred to remain in the Oberland; now they bypass it in a cable-car.

Westwards from Kandersteg, the Bonder Krinden pass (7,832 feet) offers a high crossing to Adelboden (4,450 feet) in the parallel Engstligental, another popular summer and winter resort, the favourite climb from which is the Wildstrubel, by way of the club hut on the Engstligen Alp.

Lenk (not to be confused with Leuk), at the head of the Simmental, still farther west, another good centre for walking, climbing and skiing, is reached from Adelboden in six hours by way of the low Hahnenmoos and is a starting point for both Wildstrubel and its own Wildhorn (10,708 feet), a westerly neighbour in the long, less lofty continuation of the watershed between the Oberland and Valais, which finally terminates in the Diablerets (10,650 feet) above its own well known resort Les Diablerets, Villars-Chesières nearby and Aigle in the Rhône Valley, many miles to the west.

The main valley roads to Adelboden and Lenk both start at Spiez (see p. 124), the former running up the fertile Engstligental with fine views of the Doldenhorn, Balmhorn and Altels, in ten miles. The road to Lenk follows the broader Simmental as far as Zweisimmen, where it branches off to the left from the main road link between the Oberland and Vaud which continues over the low Saanen-Möser pass to Gstaad – lately become the haunt of the famous and the wealthy – and Gsteig, then over the picturesque Col de Pillon (5,070 feet), to Les Diablerets, Le Sepey and down into the Rhône Valley at Aigle. Another pleasant minor pass motor road goes off to the right at Zweisimmen over the Jaun Pass (5,000 feet) to Vevey 60 miles away on the north shore of Lake Geneva; while at Saanen the road divides, the modern but slightly lower Col des Mosses (4,740 feet) loops away through Chateau d'Oex to rejoin the descent from the Pillon at Le Sepey.

The only other valley of importance here is the lovely Loetschental, opening to the east and almost parallel with the Rhône Valley a few miles to the south, at Goppenstein, the southern exit of the Loetschberg tunnel. (The Loetschental is of course geographically in the Valais, but for the sake of convenience is here included with the Oberland.) Unfortunately it is some years since I was last there, but I am told that the opening-up of the road all the way to Fafleralp, almost at its head, has in no way spoiled the remote charm and peace of that beautiful corridor, cradled between the Petersgrat (p. 134) and the southernmost of the

Oberland's high ridges, which run westwards and parallel with it from the Aletschhorn, above Concordia on the Aletsch Glacier, with its southern flanks falling towards the Rhône Valley.

The road runs up through the picturesque old villages of Kippel (where till comparatively recently the road ended, giving way to a bridle-path) and Ried, then to the ancient weather-blackened châlets of Blatten and past a tiny, much sketched, painted and photographed chapel, to the Fafleralp Hotel (5,825 feet), situated on an open, green and wooded alp with a little tarn of its own, a little short of the well-named Langgletscher's snout. Four hours' toil up the glacier brings one to the magnificently placed Hollandia Hut above the Loetschenlücke (10,500 feet), a nick in the wall of the main Oberland massif, looking down on the great cruciform basin where the curve of the Aletsch meets the Jungfraufirn and the Grünhorngletscher at Concordia. This hut is the starting point for climbs in the range facing Mürren, to the west of the Jungfrau, so well seen from the Schilthorn (see above, p. 132) – Ebnefluh, Mittaghorn and Grosshorn, as well as of the 13,720-foot Aletschhorn, towering to the south beyond the Loetschenlücke's saddle.

The valley, which is bounded on the south by a chain of fine peaks, the Distelhorn, Schienhorn and Loetschentaler Breithorn, culminating in the immense wedge of the Bietschhorn (12,570 feet), climbed from the Bietschhorn Hut above Ried, is a stroller's and walker's paradise. A number of local excrescences, like the Tellispitze and the Burstspitze, can be climbed without much difficulty by those experienced in rough mountain-scrambling. Above Fafleralp there are two lateral hanging valleys, the Inner and Ausser Faflertal, leading to the foot of the Petersgrat and its traverse to the Mutthorn Hut (see p. 134). From Ferden, lower down the valley, the Loetschenpass (8,840 feet) provides an interesting eight-hour link with Kandersteg; and there are several high tracks southwards to the Rhône Valley.

This southernmost and least modernised of the high valleys deserves a visit before, in its turn, it is submerged in the general tide of sophistication or even of proliferating hydro-electric

22   *The Märjelensee, with the distant Weisshorn*

schemes. As such, it seems a suitable place with which to close this survey of the region.

If there should be a sneaking suspicion that I have a slight bias in favour of the Oberland, it is possible that it is well-founded. I saw the Jungfrau for the first time at the age of six, spent my honeymoon at Wengen, returning again and again, and at Grindelwald, also revisited a dozen times, my wife and I formed a life-long mountain-partnership and friendship with Hans, that prince charming among guides, his splendid wife and their delightful family, all daughters. Now, whenever I go back there, I walk five minutes up the hill, to sit in the sun with Frau Burgener outside one of the most beautifully-situated châlets in the world, talking over old times. And whatever else may have proved transient, the Wetterhorn – as it happens, the first big climb a young couple did with Hans – still goes winging its matchless way to heaven above our heads.

23   *The Aletsch Glacier from Jungfraujoch*

10. The Valais

The Lake of Geneva, crescent-shaped and 70 miles long, is by far the largest of all the Alpine lakes. Along its north shore runs the gently rounded, wooded range of the Jura, reaching a height of over 5,000 feet at its highest points; along the southern the much more abrupt ridges of Savoy attain an altitude of more than 7,000 feet, screening the Mont Blanc group 40 miles to the south, with their rocky, sharply indented summits.

If you have come across France by road, heading for Geneva through Dijon, Dole, Poligny and Champagnole you drop down out of the Jura into the great lake-basin either by the Col de la Faucille (4,341 feet) direct to Geneva itself or by the Col de St Cergue (4,000 feet) to Nyon, 14 miles along the lake's northern shore. On a clear day the summits of both these little passes offer wonderful wide views over the lake to the distant ring of the Alps, from the Oberland right round to the Valais and, nearest of all, but still impressive at 50 miles, the splendid surge of the Mont Blanc group. It would be a pity not to park the car and take in this comprehensive introduction to the Alpine scene.

Geneva is a lovely city – or rather two cities, the north shore of the lake being occupied by the modern town with its string of hotels along the Quai du Mont Blanc facing the mountains beyond the lake and the 300-foot jet of a world-famous fountain; farther along the shore stands the Palais des Nations and a complex of United Nations office buildings gathered about it. On the south shore, linked with the modern city by the fine Pont du Mont Blanc bridging the neck of the lake where the Rhône issues from it, lies the Old Town, with its lakeside promenades and gardens, fashionable shops, cathedral, museums and university. A most gracious, historic and cultured place in which one could profitably spend many days. The trouble about Geneva, in my experience, is that, thanks to its hospitality to commissions, conferences and conventions, it is almost always impossible to find a room to sleep in even for one night.

Both shores of the 70-mile lake are studded with resorts – Thonon and Evian on the southern (French) side, while the Swiss side boasts one charming town after another, Nyon, Rolle, Morges – where in the right conditions Mont Blanc, for all the 40 miles between, can be seen reflected in the lake through a gap in the hills – then the great city of Lausanne, cathedral-crowned on its hill terrace, with the pretty harbour of Ouchy at its feet (you can bypass the city's traffic jams by keeping on the lake shore level through Ouchy); and on, below the terraced vineyards of Lutry and Cully, to Vevey. The 10 miles from Vevey onwards, almost to the head of the lake, have become a cluttered, endless built-up area consisting of Clarens, Montreux and Territet, beyond which stands Chillon's castle, after which a more open road leads to Villeneuve and the lake's end. Unless you particularly wish to visit this string of famous resorts, you can avoid the tedious urban crawl, bypassing it along the *autoroute* (Geneva–Lausanne–Villeneuve) which runs behind them 'inland'. Along all the latter part of the drive, the Savoy Hills, culminating in the 7,300-foot Dent d'Oche opposite Montreux, form a striking background to the wide steely-blue waters; and as you approach Villeneuve, the broad mass of the Dents du Midi (10,695 feet), crowned by five turrets, rises snow-streaked to an impressive height to the right of the V-shaped gateway to the Rhône Valley.

The main valley road now runs almost due south, deep between the walls of the Vaudois ridges, masking the Diablerets on the left, and the high Savoy foothills to the right, through Aigle, at the foot of the Col de Pillon link with the Oberland (p. 143), to Bex (where the road up to the pleasant and popular resort of Villars-Chesières (4,120 feet) winds away up the left-hand slope),

St Maurice and Martigny (p. 123). There is much fine walking and climbing to be had among the Vaudois Alps; the classic viewpoint being the Grand Muveran (10,043 feet), which can be reached by a path from near Bex, but it is a matter of some eight hours from the valley to the top, so that the presence of a club hut at the Frête de Sailles (8,530 feet), about three hours below the summit, is not unwelcome.

At Martigny the valley takes an acute-angled bend to the east and the highway sets out on its 35-mile almost straight course along the hot, smiling sub-alpine trench at the heart of the Valais, to Brigue. From that long trunk, five parallel valleys branch out southwards into the great 40-mile long chain of peaks and glaciers constituting the backbone of the Pennine Alps, Swiss on this side, Italian on the other, of the frontier which runs along their crest. All five are lovely and lead through and up to grand mountain-scenery, increasing in stature and magnificence the farther east you go.

The first of them runs up directly behind Martigny's old town and fortress-tower through the deep and narrow gorge of the Drance, beyond which a plainlet opens out, housing the little town of Orsières, where the branch railway line from Martigny ends.

Beyond Orsières the valley sub-divides, the left-hand branch, the Val de Bagnes, running up deep into the heart of the range, past the foot of the great glaciers falling from the east face of the mighty Grand Combin (14,164 feet), one of the most splendidly glaciated mountains in the Alps, through Lourtier to Fionnay (4,900 feet), a small centre noted for its woods and flowers, and the lovely walks to the Alps of Louvie and Corbassière (7,300 feet) with magnificent views of the Corbassière glacier and the whole Combin group. From Fionnay there is a splendid two-day walkers' route up the valley, through Mauvoisin where there is now a man-made lake, to the Chanrion Hut (8,071 feet) at the head of the valley, and on between peaks and glaciers, offering one grand view after another, over the 9,140-foot Col de Fenêtre de Balme, the Italian frontier, and down through the Val d'Ollomont into the Valpelline and so to the bus route to Aosta.

The right-hand branch beyond Orsières is the long and not very interesting Swiss Val Ferret, running up to the low watershed at the Col Ferret, below the corner-stone of the Mont Blanc group's southern wall (see above, p. 119).

In between them the Great St Bernard Pass road strikes up the combe of the Val d'Entremont on its way to Aosta and Italy.

Orsières, however, throws out two other roads, one on either side, that to the east climbing up in a bank of splendid hairpins to the popular summer and winter resort of Verbier (5,000 feet), overlooking the Orsières basin, high on a sunny shelf at the foot of the rocky comb the highest point of which is the 8,123-foot Pierre à Voir, from which there is a classic panorama of the Rhône Valley, 6,000 feet below, the far-off Oberland, the nearer peaks of the Valais, the Combin magnificently at hand, and the Mont Blanc group. Verbier itself has a beautiful view of the latter; and the Combin, partly hidden from the village, is seen to great advantage from the many walks on the plateau, especially that along the almost level shelf-path from the top of the chair-lift to the Cabane du Mont Fort an hour and a half away, at the foot of the 10,925-foot peak of that name. The Pierre à Voir is reached from another lift up an easy path in the opposite direction; the last 200 feet are, however, very steep, the path being cut into the almost vertical rock of the summit-tower. For those who find this too much of an undertaking, the Croix de Coeur saddle, half an hour short of the Pierre, is a good consolation prize.

The other road, to the west of Orsières, winds steeply up to the charming little resort of Lac Champex (4,823 feet), set in a deep bowl on the shores of a narrow boating-lake whose dark, transparent waters mirror the Grand Combin, rising at its eastern end beyond the unseen Val de Bagnes. Chair lifts open up a number of pleasant walks, attractive glacier-tours and climbs among the eastern peaks and glaciers of the Mont Blanc group by way of the Saleinaz and Julien Dupuis huts (8,830 and 10,300 feet respectively). The glacier-crossing from the former to the fine viewpoint of the Fenêtre de Saleinaz (10,710 feet) is well worth while, and the Julien Dupuis is a good starting point for the easy two and a half hour ascent of the Aiguille du Tour from this side (see p. 121).

The second lateral valley to branch off southwards from the Rhône Valley does so at Sion, where two ancient castles dominate the main road and the great slopes above to the north are clothed for miles in vineyards producing some of Switzerland's best wines. Mounting in wide sweeps to Euseigne, noted for its remarkable 'earth pyramids' close to the road, where the valley divides into two, the more important road climbs up through woods into the almost flat meadows of the Val d'Hérens to its main resort, Evolène (4,520 feet). The other runs up the Val d'Hérémence past Pralong, where the valley becomes the Val des Dix, and to the Cabane du Val des Dix (8,694 feet) at its distant head, close to the foot of the fine snowy pyramid of the 12,700-foot Mont Blanc de Cheilon. The upper part of the valley, once much more attractive, is now completely occupied by a man-made lake with the usual unnatural looking shores which are a feature of these necessary providers of hydro-electric power. From the hut Arolla can be reached in four hours by crossing the Durand glacier, one of several similarly-named glaciers in the Valais, and the short rock-passage of the Pas des Chèvres (see p. 153).

The road to Evolène, a pleasant resort (4,520 feet), with great attractions for walkers, runs straight on up the Val d'Hérens to Les Haudères, opening up splendid views of the Dent Blanche, a pyramid from this aspect, ahead to the left in the background. Here the road splits again, the right-hand branch climbing steeply in curves to the higher level of the Arolla Valley and continuing along its fine scenery to the famous climbing centre of Arolla at its head. The other branch runs up briefly to Ferpècle (5,910 feet), where the Val d'Hérens ends, at the foot of the great twin glaciers of Mont Miné and Ferpècle. A path above Ferpècle brings you in two hours to the Alpe Bricolla (7,960 feet) with a magnificent view over the huge glacier, above which the Grand Cornier and the enormous Dent Blanche tower to the left, the right-hand rim being contained by the rocky comb of the Arolla peaks. The Alp is the starting-point for the long but highly rewarding route up the glaciers to the 11,418-foot Col d'Hérens and thence down to the

Schönbuhl Hut at the foot of the Matterhorn's north face and so to Zermatt, an unforgettable 12 hours of glacier work.

Arolla (6,400 feet) provides everything a walker or a climber could wish for. It stands beautifully placed only a short walk from the tongue of the glacier falling from Mont Collon (11,955 feet) which, with the mitre-tip of the slightly higher Evêque peering over its right shoulder, fills the head of the valley, a symmetrical flat-topped castle of rock and ice. Not seen till some way out of the village, to its right rises the beautiful and gentle crown of the snowy Pigne d'Arolla (12,470 feet) and, still further westwards, the icy precipices and sharp tower of the Mont Blanc de Cheilon (12,700 feet).

Pleasant walks among the famous stone-pines ('Aroles') take one to the slopes below the frontal glaciers plunging from the Pigne and the Cheilon. An attractive but steep walk of two and a half hours leads past them to the 9,353-foot col of the Pas des Chèvres (see above) overlooking the Durand glacier and the great peak above it; a difficult descent of a small rock-face, where the rope is a sensible precaution, leads down to the glacier, which can be crossed to the Cabane du Val des Dix in another two hours. A gentle and attractive walk leads down the Arolla valley to Satarma, where stands an isolated 'needle' of interest to climbers on an off-day, and up from there to the exceptionally clear Lac Bleu de Lucel (6,791 feet), with a fine close-up of the precipices of the Aiguilles Rouges d'Arolla (11,975 feet), a rock-climber's paradise and offering a long day's end-to-end traverse of their many crests.

The opposite (eastern) side of the valley is bounded by the long rocky chain rising steeply above Les Haudères and running due south through the Bouquetins (12,625 feet) to the Mont Brulé (11,880 feet), dividing the Arolla Valley from the high basin of the Glacier du Mont Miné. The climbers' peaks in this range include the Grande and Petite Dents de Veisivi, the Dent de Perroc, and the Aiguille de la Zà, a popular rock-climbing 'first' high peak for novices, presenting no great difficulties except the single celebrated slab below the summit, and that is not too difficult even for a novice. All these summits are from 11 to 12 thousand feet high, and can be approached direct from the valley by the Alpe de Zarmine (7,750 feet) or from the reverse side by spending a night at the Bertol Hut.

Arolla, moreover, harbours a 'must' for mountaineers disinclined to wrestle with stiff rock or climb one of the very high peaks – a glacier-and-snow walk to 12,300 feet at one of the most glorious viewpoints in the Alps – the Tête Blanche. An afternoon of path-walking, high above the Arolla glacier, brings you in two and a half hours to the Plan de Bertol and thence, in about the same length of time, up the fairly steep Bertol glacier to the luxurious two-storey Bertol, or Neuchâtel, Hut – a benefaction of the Suchard family – beautifully perched at 11,155 feet on a platform below the tip of the Clocher de Bertol, a sharp pinnacle in the col between the Aiguille de la Zà and the Bouquetins just opposite. From the platform the magnificent tooth of the Dent Blanche (14,318 feet) is seen at its best across the trough of the Mont Miné glacier and, in the opposite direction there are splendid views of Mont Collon and the wide, almost level trench of the Otemma Glacier; while, over the snow-edge to the south, a sliver of the Matterhorn's black summit and of its neighbour the Dent d'Hérens lift tantalisingly, but in promise of good things to come.

Next morning – early enough, let us hope to ensure a summit sunrise – a gentle snow-trudge will land you in two to three hours, according to age and inclination, on the domed crest of the Tête Blanche, from which there is a superb circular view of all the great giants still thrusting overhead – Grand Cornier and Dent Blanche close at hand, Weisshorn, Rothorn and Gabelhorn appearing over the dividing ridge, Dom and Täschhorn beyond them and, above the cornice at your feet, overhanging the escarpment on the Zermatt side, the towering northwest faces of the Matterhorn, a dark and forbidding monolith, rising to a sharp spear-head from this aspect. Armour-plated with gleaming ice, the Dent d'Hérens seems close enough to touch. The views back over the heads of the Zà and Veisivi summits and the Evolène valley sweep away to the Oberland peaks in the distance beyond the Rhône gulf, while through a gap near the Bouquetins there is a far-off glimpse of Mont Blanc. On one exceptionally clear morning, through another window in the continuing comb, we identified the tiny teeth of the Maritime Alps, biting sharply into the horizon sky, 130 miles away to the south.

For those who do not wish to return to Arolla, this delectable glacier-crawl can be extended by dropping down a few hundred feet to the Col d'Hérens – to join the route from Ferpècle already described (p. 153) – then descending steeply, always facing the Matterhorn precipices, to the Schönbuhl Hut and Zermatt.

Returning to the Rhône valley highway, the next town is the thriving industrial centre of Sierre, from which a fine side-road on the left climbs to the sunny plateau of Montana–Vermala–Crans – pullulating holiday centres a little blemished by the too prominent presence of many large sanitaria – commanding a glorious panorama southwards across the Rhône Valley trench to the whole chain of the Valais giants.

A mile or two along the highway, beyond Sierre, a road swings steeply up the southern wall of the valley in splendidly exposed but protected hairpins and, higher up, tunnelling and contouring its way through narrow gorges into the third of the parallel valleys – the Val d'Anniviers.

Above the entry gorges, in an open hanging basin stands Vissoie, the valley's main 'town' and road-junction, picturesquely screened by poplars. Here three roads separate, the main valley road running straight ahead to Ayer and Zinal at its head. The right-hand one penetrates the narrow Val de Moiry and soon reaches Grimentz, famous for its main street fringed by wonderful ancient châlets; you had better reach it soon too, for I am told that a development scheme for turning it into a modern resort with – you will never guess – blocks of high-rise flats lies on the planning table. Above Grimentz the bridle-track continues up the deep and bleak Val de Moiry along the lake resulting from recent hydro-electric expansion to the Cabane de Moiry (7,100 feet) at the lower rim of the fine Moiry glacier cascading from between the Pigne de la Lex and the 12,000-foot Pointe de Bricolla. Here climbing and scenery alike, if not on the grandest scale, are a positive delight.

The road to the left out of Vissoie swings up the slope in a series of splendid hairpins to St Luc, that charming little village, high on a green slope at 5,400 feet, ringed with pine-woods and looking out southwards over the whole length of the valley and the semi-circle of great peaks sweeping round its head from the Weisshorn to the Dent Blanche and Grand Cornier. For me the peak which is the valley's particular delight, from wherever you see it, is Lo Besso (12,058 feet), whose graceful mitre-headed pyramid rises a little stand-offishly in front of the great snowy amphitheatre dominating Zinal and the Durand Glacier behind it.

Walks and scrambles, high above the valley, steep and less steep, shorter and longer, abound; the least exacting being the almost level stroll through the pine forest to Chandolin (6,550 feet), one of the highest permanently inhabited villages in Switzerland, beautifully perched between a backward view of the Val d'Anniviers and a forward one out over a famous landslide-scar plunging into the blue depths of the Rhône Valley, to the Oberland ridges beyond.

From St Luc a high-level track runs the whole length of the valley's eastern slopes past the Hotel Weisshorn across the lovely Alps of Barneuza and Cottier, above Zinal, and on to the Alpe d'Arpitetta commanding the finest view of all, of the great peaks ringing the Durand Glacier (the most important of this name : see p. 152). Earlier escape routes to the valley and Zinal are available all along it. The views to the great peaks ahead, the whole length of this shelf-walk are indescribably lovely.

The finest medium-altitude viewpoint in the district is undoubtedly Bella Tola (9,845 feet), reached in four hours from St Luc by a comfortable bridle-path. The summit of this stony mountain cradles a small deep-set glacier in a crater, and the last part of the path may be under snow even in mid-summer, but there is no real difficulty about the ascent. The view is one of the finest of its kind in Switzerland. All the Alps of the Valais as far as Mont

Blanc stand up magnificently to the south and west, the Weisshorn being especially prominent; to the north across the rift of the Rhône, 8,000 feet below, the Oberland peaks lift in range after range, with the huge and forbidding wedge of the Bietschhorn dominating the nearer scene.

Branching off eastwards some way below Bella Tola, the track to the 9,100-foot Meiden Pass, above the Alpe Tounot, is the prelude to a marvellous two-days' walk over into the Tourtmanntal (see below) in six hours and then in another ten over the Augstbord Pass (9,500 feet) – the ascent of the nearby Schwarzhorn in an hour yields a considerable bonus, for the view from its summit (10,500 feet) is even finer than that from Bella Tola – past its little lake at the foot of the Weisshorn's northern icefalls, with superb views opening up over all the Zermatt peaks from the Mischabel to the Matterhorn, and at the last endlessly and steeply down into the Nikolaital (the Zermatt Valley) at St Niklaus. If there is any path-walking in more magnificent mountain scenery anywhere in the Alps, I have yet to discover it.

Zinal (5,500 feet), not quite at the head of the valley, is a small climbing-centre deep-set in a flat bowl somewhat short of the Durand Glacier's dirty snout and too shut-in to give a view of the high peaks surrounding it. The long moraine-track beyond it leads first to the Cabane du Petit Mountet (7,100 feet), then onto the grubby and crevassed glacier's surface and in another three hours to the Hotel du Mountet (9,450 feet), magnificently situated at the reverse foot of Lo Besso – a four-hour climb – in the amphitheatre overlooked by the Rothorn, Obergabelhorn, the Dent Blanche towering opposite above its icefall, and its lower neighbour, the Grand Cornier. Two difficult glacier passes, the Triftjoch (11,615 feet) and the Col Durand (11,400 feet) provide experienced climbers with routes to Zermatt on the other side of the range. Sunset and sunrise from the Mountet are well worth the rather tedious approach by moraine and a somewhat uninspiring glacier.

On the west side of the valley, approached by path from either St Luc or Ayer, is the wide Alpe de la Lex (7,200 feet), from which there is a delightful day's not too difficult rock-climbing to be had above a short *nevé-couloir* leading to the foot of the four small pinnacles of the Aiguilles de la Lex (10,800 feet), delicately poised between the Val de Moiry – where the Cabane de Moiry is another starting-point for the same climb – and the Val d'Anniviers. All the way up to and along this airy day's round there are glorious views of the Weisshorn and the near-by Besso to the east; and at the foot of the steep snow-slope filling the couloir by which the descent is made from the last of the four towers – perhaps turrets would be more accurate – the gentian-starred Alp is an ideal resting-place facing the snows before jarring down the path back to the valley. Other ascents here include the Pigne de la Lex (11,100 feet), and the col between it and the Aiguilles affords an easy passage from Zinal to the Moiry Hut in the neighbouring valley. (Once again, no attempt has been made to deal with the innumerable climbing possibilities among the great peaks at the head of the valley, which are amply covered by the climber's guide-books.)

The Tourtmanntal, the fourth lateral valley rising southwards from the Rhône Valley is the shortest and least-frequented, but by no means the least attractive. It runs due south, and, in its beautifully-wooded four hours of footpath-walking alongside the foaming torrent and its waterfalls, rises from 2,000 feet at Tourtmann to almost 6,000 at Gruben (or Meiden), deep in pine-forest an hour below the splendid Tourtmann Glacier; this great icefall creams down from between the Diablons, Weisshorn, Brunnegghorn and Barrhorn and is best seen from the Alp Senntum, just above Gruben, at its foot. For non-walkers there is now a cable-lift to Oberems in a quarter of an hour and a non-postal bus service of seven-seater minibuses up the very narrow road beyond the lift (in summer only).

From Gruben there are two high passes, the Col de Tracuit (10,675 feet), involving a crossing of the Tourtmann Glacier, and the non-glaciated Pas de Forcletta (9,475 feet), to Zinal, while the seven- or eight-hour crossing by footpaths to St Niklaus and the Zermatt Valley is made by the Augstbord Pass already described; though serious mountaineers may prefer one of three difficult passes, all over 11,000 feet, the Barrjoch, Brunneggjoch and Biesjoch.

Continuing the Rhône Valley route, at Gampel, soon after leaving Tourtmann, the steep lower ravine of the Loetschental, below Goppenstein, falls into the main valley on the left; and from this point, all the way to Visp, the wonderfully engineered Loetschberg railway can be seen gradually descending the northern slope by a succession of tunnels through spurs and airy viaducts over deep ravines on its way to Brigue, six miles beyond Visp.

Visp, with its beautiful view to the towering Balfrin (Mischabel group) through the high cleft of the valley-jaws to the south, is the point of entry to the last and by far the best known of the five lateral valleys. This is the starting-point of the famous rack-and-pinion railway and, more recently, of a fine motor road, leading to the most universally known of all Alpine summer and winter resorts, Zermatt; though, mercifully, a majority decision just taken has again barred the resort itself to the invasion of external motor-traffic, tourists having to leave their cars at Täsch, three miles short of the straggling township, famous for its historic and narrow main street.

The first four miles are more or less flat and somewhat hideous with commercial enterprises including the local electricity works. At Stalden the valley divides, the right-hand branch being the long and spectacular Nikolaital, leading to Zermatt in 22 miles of scenically wonderful rail or road travel; the left-hand arm, entered by a beautifully arched road-viaduct, gives access by an excitingly engineered road through the gorges above which stands the area's other great resort, Saas Fee, in the wild parallel valley to the east.

The journey up the Nikolaital has been over-described. Suffice it to say that the valley is so deeply scored between two enormous mountain-ranges that parts of it never see the light of the sun in winter. Tremendous glacier-tongues snake down from its rim, incredibly high above, descending from the Weisshorn to the right and the Mischabel–Dom–Täschhorn chain to the left as you gradually ascend successive steps in the valley through St Niklaus,

Randa and Täsch, past the evidences in the valley-bed of at least two annihilating landslides, one of which eliminated Täsch in fairly recent memory. As the valley opens out beyond Randa, first the massive bulk of the Breithorn, then the sweep of the Gorner and Theodule glaciers and finally, with devastating effect, just before reaching Zermatt, the Matterhorn itself, unbelievably high in the firmament, loom into sight at the head of the valley.

Zermatt (5,300 feet), once visited only in summer by thousands of tourists for its scenic values alone, is now the winter Mecca of tens of thousands of skiers who come from the far ends of the earth to sun and disport themselves on the open slopes above the valley, in the shadow of the most publicised mountain in the world. Besides the Gornergrat railway they have two major ropeways and a dozen ski-lifts at their disposal, which is fortunate, as there is little skiing to be had in the deep, steep-sided and consequently somewhat sunless valley.

In spite of the millions of words already written about Zermatt's show-piece and, indeed, its original *raison d'être*, the Matterhorn, any author of a book about the Alps might be arraigned for negligence if he did not add his paragraph. It is unique among mountains. Completely isolated from its neighbours, a gigantic monolith, it soars to nearly 15,000 feet, the perfect wedge, its four faces supported by four ridges : if one was asked to draw 'a mountain' one would draw it like that, just as Nature has. From most aspects, especially the most spectacular one which is the pride of Zermatt, it looks almost vertical and entirely inaccessible, neither of which it is. In fact, from the mountaineering angle it is a big fraud, which has paved Zermatt's streets with gold. For, since the only difficult place on the ordinary route up the Hörnli ridge has been liberally decked out with fixed cables, any really fit person unaffected by vertigo or advancing years can climb it in fine weather, guided and under his own steam, or propelled up and down it by that of the accompanying professional (they have never refused a client yet, and once they have hooked their fish they rarely fail to earn the tariff for landing him, or her, there and back).

I stress the suitability of the weather, because the Matterhorn can be *very* dangerous and has claimed a high tally of victims owing to two main causes; the onset of sudden murderous storms and the continual bombardment by falling stones from its crumbling edifice – assisted by clumsy climbers, ahead and over-head, dislodging their own private landslides. Apart from these hazards, the long staircase of the Hörnli ridge is so free from difficulty and danger that in summer it is festooned with parties head to tail, as on a motor-way, and as many as 200 bodies in various stages of euphoria or exhaustion have been known to reach the summit on a single fine Sunday. The record for the course is three hours, up and down (in 1953 by the guide Alfons Lerjen and a client called Biener). Those unaccustomed to such hard labours can take as much as a whole day before being re-delivered like sacks at the point where they began. I know of two Austrian school-boys who strolled up it with a young sister in tow; and have met an Englishman who had just climbed it, guided, as his first essay in mountaineering, an experience he had greatly enjoyed, but having tucked that scalp under his belt, felt no desire ever again to climb a mountain. Such is the Matterhorn, in every way the most remarkable, challenging, stupendous, but not, I think, the most beautiful, mountain in the Alps. Lucky Zermatt!

In summer Zermatt is still a walkers' and, of course, a climbers' paradise, and here again the ropeways have opened up immense possibilities for the less energetic uphill walker, who can now stroll gently for hours on the high alps and slopes at the foot of the peaks without having to use up his energy in getting there. The scenery, wherever your footsteps may lead you, is stupendous, literally surrounded as you are by the highest and most magnificent peaks and glaciers in Switzerland.

For the tourist in search of viewpoints, whether he enjoys the long and beautiful slog uphill by way of Riffelalp, Riffelberg and Roten Boden or prefers the comforts of an overcrowded train, the Gornergrat (10,300 feet) will provide everything he requires. There is no comparable belvedère in the Alps; for here, high above the great frozen river of the Gorner Glacier, you are at the centre of a complete circle of great and glorious mountains, whose lynch-pin for most will be the astonishing isolated obelisk of the Matter-horn, dark and arrow-headed on its glacier plinth. (For me, oddly enough, the cynosure is the dazzling white blade of the Weisshorn, biting keen-edged into the blue in the opposite direction : but then, these things, like the beloved's face, are a very personal matter.) The whole thing is so marvellous – from Monte Rosa's cataract of snow, past the domes and castles of the Lyskamm, Castor and Pollux and the Breithorn, to the Matterhorn's corner-stone; then round, through the Dent Blanche, Gabelhorn, Rothorn and Weisshorn, to where, beyond the Nikolaital's exit and Visp, the Bietschhorn soars, 35 miles away, and back along the rocky Mischabel–Dom–Täschhorn comb to the nearer Rimp-fischhorn and Strahlhorn closing the circle – that preferences are invidious. A hundred years ago Mark Twain, standing at that spot, which he had presumably reached on foot, described it in his inimitable way :

> I had a magnificent view of Monte Rosa, and apparently all the rest of the Alpine world, from that high place. All the circling horizon was piled high with a mighty tumult of snowy crests. One might have imagined he saw before him the tented camps of a host of Brobdignagians. But lonely, conspicuous and superb rose that wonderful upright wedge the Matterhorn, its precipitous sides powdered over with snow and the upper half hidden in thick clouds which now and then dissolved to cobweb films and gave brief glimpses of the imposing tower as through a veil.

Since he visited the place, a cable-car ropeway has been added to the attractions, wafting you another 500 feet up to 'Stockhorn', widening the view and bringing you much nearer to the Nordend face of Monte Rosa. If you really want to go to the Stockhorn (11,600 feet), again improving the prospect by so doing, I recom-mend the easy and attractive hour's walk along and up the shaly ridge, close above the glacier, from 'Stockhorn', the ropeway

24   *The Oberland from the Simplon Pass*

terminal, to the actual rocky little summit of that name, in which the long spine of the Gornergrat abruptly ends. Though you cannot see over the broad saddle between you and the Cima di Jazzi beyond it, you are left in no doubt that sunny Italy and – if you have ever visited it – Macugnaga are there, far below, just over the rim (see p. 233).

Every able-bodied visitor to Gornergrat should walk down at least as far as the Riffelberg Hotel, with the Matterhorn growing in stature at every step and its impertinent little imitator, the Riffelhorn, rising rapidly out of the basin below. For at Roten Boden half-way down, there are two lovely lakelets in the Riffelhorn's shadow, the first mirroring Monte Rosa and the Lyskamm at one end and the Matterhorn at the other to perfection, the second, a little lower down and smaller, performing the same service for the beautiful Dent Blanche. This is another of the places I should unhesitatingly choose for the unwrapping of a packed lunch followed by a postprandial photography session.

There are literally dozens of excursions to be made from Zermatt, and this book, as already mentioned, is limited in space. There is a ropeway now to Schwarzsee's dark little lake and the chapel by its shore. Here there is a splendid view right up the Gorner Glacier from its tongue to Monte Rosa, and another down the length of the Nikolaital, with the rocky masses of the Dom (14,942 feet, the highest peak entirely on Swiss soil) and the Täschhorn (14,738 feet) streaming above it to the sky. Another chair-lift some way down the valley from Zermatt runs to Sunnegga, just below the much-photographed Grünsee, from where the Matterhorn is at its most shapely. This ropeway gives access to miles of lovely path-walking all over the eastern flank of the valley (the ski-paradise in winter). Findelen, that 'must', whose châlets and tiny whitewashed chapel have served as foreground to thousands of Matterhorn photographs, commercial and amateur, is not far off, tucked away in its deep fold below the tongue of the Findelen glacier, the path up whose moraine leads, with fine views of the Rimpfischhorn and Strahlhorn, to minor climbs on the easy Unter- and Ober-Rothorn (11,190 feet) and to

25 *Aerial view: Matterhorn–Weisshorn–Dent Blanche*

the start of the great glacier crossing over the Adler Pass to the Saas Valley (see below, p. 169). Contouring the slopes southwards, a beautiful shelf-path takes you all the way to Riffelalp, while the Dent Blanche, Gabelhorn, Wellenkuppe and Rothorn range opposite shows to great advantage all the way through windows among the stone-pines. From Sunnegga, too, you can walk up quite comfortably to the Gornergrat by a path crossing the debris-covered slopes; or you can take the long and pleasant path through the pine-forest back to the valley. And there, magnificent and amazing, overhead, wherever you go, is that pillar of the sky, the Matterhorn.

On the other side of the valley a discouragingly steep path up the Trift Ravine leads to the Trift Hotel (7,870 feet), the pushing-off place for the Wellenkuppe (12,830 feet), a high but not too difficult snow climb, and its higher neighbour, the 13,365-foot Obergabelhorn, a much tougher proposition altogether. It is also the starting-point for the ascent by path and finally over a small glacier, in three hours, for the Mettelhorn (11,188 feet). (The direct ascent from Zermatt, avoiding the Trift path, takes five hours.) This is one of the finest vantage points in the neighbour-hood, especially noted for its splendid close-up view of the Matter-horn.

Then there are long and more gentle walks up the valley, past Winkelmatten through Blatten to Zmutt and the Staffel Alp above it, two hours from Zermatt, at the Matterhorn's northern base; and on by the path on the north side of the Zmutt glacier, with magnificent views of the peak and its splendidly icy neigh-bour, the Dent d'Hérens, all the way to the Schönbuhl Hut (8,860 feet) in four to five hours. From the hut the Tête Blanche (see p. 154) can be climbed by the Schönbuhl glacier in three hours.

At a much higher level both of altitude and difficulty, there are a dozen classic glacier-passes, beloved by mountaineers. The two most favoured 'internal' ones, both leading in a 12-hour day across to Mattmark in the neighbouring Saas Valley, are the Adler Pass (12,460 feet) and the Schwarzberg-Weisstor (11,850 feet).

Of those leading across the frontier ridge into Italy, the easy Theodule Pass (10,900 feet) known to have been used as early as the fifth century, once the most frequented on foot, is now crossed by a linked network of ropeways on either side or even by 'snow-cat'. Those farther east are made of sterner stuff. The Schwarztor (12,274 feet), between the Breithorn and Pollux, and the Verra or Zwillings Pass (12,668 feet) between the 'Twins', Castor and Pollux, both descending on Fiery in the Val d'Ayas, are long, difficult ventures. The Lys Pass (14,030 feet) crosses a nick between the Lyskamm and the Ludwigshöhe summit of Monte Rosa to the Gnifetti Refuge and so down into the Gressoney Valley. Higher still is the Sesiajoch (14,370 feet) between Monte Rosa's Signalkuppe and Parrotspitze, leading down eventually to the Val Sesia at Alagna. The two main ones to Macugnaga in the Val Anzasca are the Alt and Neu Weisstor, the former (11,811 feet) between the Jägerhorn and Fillarhorn to the north of Monte Rosa, the latter (11,745 feet) just beyond the Cima di Jazzi in the frontier ridge, so well seen from the Stockhorn, with a descent on the Rifugio Eugenio Sella, and so down to the high Anzasca valley.

If my preoccupation with these great and pleasurable days for a mountaineer seems out of keeping with the general policy of this book, there is a very special reason for the deviation. For it was precisely over these passes that during the Second World War, a number of prisoners of war attempting to escape from Italy to Switzerland – naturally, a small proportion of some thousands of prisoners and refugees who made their way by less hazardous routes around the Lake of Lugano, Lago Maggiore, in the Simplon area and elsewhere – fought their incredible way to neutral territory.

The following quotation from Claire Engel's admirable *History of Mountaineering in the Alps* gives a vivid picture of the difficulties and hardships these indomitable men faced in their desperate bids for freedom; it explains why so few succeeded and so many perished miserably from exhaustion, exposure, frostbite and an icy death in the yawning glacier-crevasses:

The Alps were in very bad condition in 1943. Huge crevasses were gaping beneath a thin layer of snow. Trained mountaineers could have avoided the worst dangers, but the men who went that way had no mountain experience whatever. They were exhausted by months in prison camps and weeks in hiding, ill-fed, badly clothed (some of them wearing shorts in January) with dilapidated shoes. Many of them were Australians and South Africans who had never seen snow, and it goes without saying that they had never crossed a glacier. They had no ice-axes; sometimes they were given ropes, but they did not know how to use them. Italian 'guides' were not guides at all, but smugglers, who charged exorbitant prices and never went farther than the frontier. And since, in many cases, the way down was much worse than the way up, and while the guides retreated safely towards Italy, the fugitives had to force a way down some of the worst glaciers in the Alps.

Mr Baedeker's descriptions of these passes point the moral with almost greater force. Of the Schwarztor he merely says 'rather difficult'; the Zwillings Pass is 'not free from danger'. Of the Neu Weisstor he warns : 'a giddy descent, along perpendicular cliffs and over precipitous snow-slopes'. The Alt Weisstor is 'more difficult'. All the Italian slopes are categorised as 'exceedingly steep, and dangerous because of falling stones'. The Lys Pass is 'difficult (beware of ice avalanches)'; the passage of the Felikjoch is 'not recommended on account of the constant danger of ice-falls'. And these warnings are aimed at experienced climbers and practised mountaineers, who in peacetime pit their skill, knowledge and trained endurance against the challenge of the peaks and passes, bent on a day's pleasure.

Yet parties of from two to 30, some of whose members had their feet wrapped in rags and suffered hideously from frostbite, kept on forcing a way, even in winter conditions, up the grim Italian precipices, through the notches barely lower than the great peaks on either side, and down the ice-mazes of frighteningly crevassed glaciers on the Swiss side, where Swiss soldiers were always on the look-out to bring the frozen, exhausted half-dead survivors down to shelter, hot tea and food.

It is not known how many perished in these suicidal bids for freedom; but, over the years, the crevasses have surrendered the perfectly ice-encased and preserved evidence of some of those who struggled over Europe's highest roof-tree to a grim death on the 'safety' of neutral ground. This is a macabre chapter in the history of the 'Playground of Europe' which, for lack of adequate documentation, has never been given the prominence it deserves.

While Zermatt and its mighty obelisk stand floodlit at the head of the Nikolaital, far up the parallel valley of the Saaser-Visp (an hour by the road which branches off at Stalden) lies secluded Saas Fee, some 800 feet above the valley floor and Saas im Grund, the largest village in the valley. The motor road hairpins its way up to a car park just short of the first hotels, beyond which no mechanical transport is allowed. In the days when legs were more popular (as a means of progress), the walk up, in under an hour, by the 'Kappellenweg', a charming path passing a number of small woodland shrines, was considered one of the minor show-pieces of the locality. It can, of course, still be enjoyed by the motor-borne visitor who comes to stay but the short-term coach tourist of these days is deprived of such gentle delights.

Saas, not long ago a quiet, picturesque châlet village, occupies – and during the last two decades the occupation by a veritable army of buildings has become seam-bursting – a grassy bowl sheltered on all sides, at the feet of the mighty Nadelhorn–Dom–Täschhorn comb, whose eastern rock faces soar almost too close and high for comfort of sufferers from mountain claustrophobia, a disease more common than one might expect. Into the southern end of this small basin the huge Feegletscher's icefall cascades from the wide snowfields supporting the cushion-like Alphubel and the more rampant Allalinhorn, split almost centrally by the rocky spur of the Längfluh – the resort's counterpart to the Gornergrat.

Since 1965, the aerial ropeway to the top of the spur and since 1969 the Felskinn reaching even higher, has not only made this magnificent viewpoint accessible to non-walkers, but opened up splendid ski-domains on the broad snow-slopes above it, as well as converting such easy and attractive summer-ascents as the Alphubel (13,235 feet) and Allalinhorn (13,803 feet) to relatively short expeditions, relieved of the long grind up to the hut, and shortening the transit of the high glacier passes to Zermatt already mentioned. The new ropeway to the Hannig (7,736 feet) has similarly offered fresh possibilities on the slopes to the north.

The view from the Längfluh (9,347 feet), which provides a glorious survey of all the surrounding giants to the west and east, as well as down the valley northwards to the Oberland far beyond the Rhône trench, is as essential an experience for non-mountaineers as is the Gornergrat from Zermatt.

Eastwards, Saas looks out across the rift of the Visp's narrow valley on the splendid chain of peaks running north to south from the 13,127-foot Fletschhorn to the Laquinhorn (13,140 feet), Weissmies (13,226 feet), Portjengrat (12,005 feet) and the rather lower Sonnighorn, on whose farther side the glaciers and high valleys, dropping down to the lower reaches of the Simplon road, lead to Domodossola and the Italian Lakes. Mountaineers of no great experience can leave the valley at Grund or Almagell and cross the range by the 10,735-foot Zwischenberg Pass, just below the south arête of the Weissmies, descending the Val Vaira to Gondo on the main Simplon highway; or by the slightly more difficult Rossboden Pass (10,499 feet) to the châlets of Eggen, near the Simplon summit, descending a valley devastated in 1901 by a vast landslide following the bursting of the Rossboden Glacier. There are several other fairly low and easy ways across; but the magnificent traverses of the Laquinjoch (11,475 feet) between the Laquinhorn and Weissmies, and of the Fletschjoch (12,050 feet) between Fletschhorn and Laquinhorn are major mountaineering undertakings.

Besides the delightful strolls on local paths, this eastern rim of the Saas bowl, overlooking the valley, offers fine walking farther afield. The Plattjen (8,469 feet), a small peak with a fine view and a small hotel half an hour below the top, is a path walk of about two and a half hours. The Egginer (11,080 feet) and Mittaghorn

(10,350 feet) close by, are climbs, but of only moderate difficulty. From the Plattjen a somewhat airy path, provided with wire-ropes at the more exposed places, leads in another two and a half hours to the Britannia Hut (9,905 feet), a British gift in 1912 to the Swiss Alpine Club, splendidly situated opposite the Allalinhorn. (An extension of the walk by ten minutes eastwards and 200 feet upwards, to the 'summit' of the Klein Allalinhorn, will add considerably to the splendour.)

The Hut is an alternative starting-place for the Allalinhorn and Alphubel climbs and also for the long high glacier crossings to various points in the Zermatt Valley by the Alphubeljoch (12,475 feet), the Mischabeljoch (12,560 feet) and the rather more difficult Feejoch (12,505 feet).

Leaving Saas up on its sunny shelf, and following the main valley of the Fee Visp southwards beyond Saas im Grund, the valley road runs alongside the torrent, rising gradually through the village of Almagell (like Grund, a starting-point for the Weissmies, Portjengrat and neighbouring climbs) to Mattmark, where in 1955 an ice avalanche, breaking away from the tongue of the Allalin Glacier hard by, overwhelmed the imprudently-sited camp of the engineering gangs engaged on the hydro-electric works and reservoir, whose dam now straddles the upper reaches of the valley. Mattmark is the eastern terminal of those great glacier passes, the Adler and Schwarzberg-Weisstor, already mentioned. From it, the bridle path leads up in four hours, by way of the Distel Alp and finally over rocks and snow beside the Tälliboden glacier to the Monte Moro Pass (9,390 feet), the frontier saddle with Italy between Monte Moro and the Joderhorn, both only a few hundred feet higher than the pass itself.

This historic passage, for centuries affording the classic highway from Valais to the Val Anzasca and Macugnaga, is famous for its incomparable summit view of Monte Rosa's towering southeastern precipices close opposite, which continue to confront you magnificently all the way down to the Alp Bill – in itself a lovely viewpoint and wonderful loitering territory for an idle day – the cable-car will, of course, save you what was once the whole knee-jarring descent by wafting your weary limbs down to Macugnaga (see p. 233) and your first night in Italy.

How many, I wonder, during the splendid day's crossing of that lofty saddle will spare one thought to the hundreds of refugees and prisoners of war who attempted it as an escape route from Nazi-occupied Italy to the longed for refuge of Switzerland's freedom, only to die of exposure and exhaustion amid its wintry snows?

11. Upper Valais and the Road to the Rhine

Six miles beyond Visp, at the point where the Rhône Valley loses its plain-like character in a last little broadening-out at the foot of surrounding mountain barriers, lies Brigue. The busy town straddles two major routes – the Simplon to the south; and, to the east, the direct link with eastern Switzerland, the Rhine Valley and the Engadine, the Arlberg and Austria, by way of the narrow upper valley of the Rhône to Gletsch and over the passes beyond, the Furka and the Oberalp.

Brigue's prosperity rests on the age-old command of the trade route to Italy over the Simplon saddle 5,000 feet above it, as witness the splendid palace of the Stockalper family, which founded its fortunes by levying the tolls on it for centuries. When in 1805, Napoleon, for purely military reasons, ordered the construction of a *'route pour fair passer les canons'* in aid of his Italian campaigns – his early passage of the snowy Great St Bernard had cost him 30,000 men – the great carriage road now, after years of prodigious engineering work transformed to a first-class motor highway, came into being.

In 1906, after unforeseen difficulties claiming several years, 39 lives and 87,000,000 francs, the railway tunnel – at 12 miles the longest in the world – was opened and has since carried a volume of Swiss–Italian express and goods traffic second only to that of the St Gotthard, opened more than 20 years earlier. The entrance of the twin tunnels can be seen a mile or two beyond the busy station and the extensive marshalling yards occupying much of the little plain. Needless to say there is now a shuttle-service for cars through 20 minutes of darkness for those motorists prepared to miss the glories of one of the loveliest roads in the Alps; if there were nothing else, the near view of the massive Fletschhorn (13,127 feet) dominating its upper reaches would be more than enough.

The road assaults the mountain barrier to the south uncompromisingly from the very edge of the town and in two hours of the most varied atmospheric, scenic and floral beauties, deposits you in sunny Italy, looking down, for the last brief, steep descent on the pink and red tiles of Domodossola's roofs, sprawling across its wide plain.

The road and rail links with eastern Switzerland and the Grisons immediately twist and climb together out of Brigue through the narrow gorges carved by the Rhône (here a tumultuous torrent) and gradually ascend in company from one step to another of the upper Rhône Valley (the Goms) for 30 miles to Gletsch, a mile above which the river issues from its birth-place in the Rhône Glacier.

The northern wall of this long, narrow trench is formed by the not very high range containing the lower sweep of the Aletsch Glacier, descending in a great 17-mile curve from Concordia and the Jungfraujoch (see p. 137). Along its grassy ridge lie a number of exceedingly pleasant alps, small resorts offering endless walking possibilities, with glorious views over the glacier basin on one side and the main chain of the Lepontine–Valaisian peaks across the valley to the south. The most westerly of these, Belalp (7,011 feet) situated on a separate shelf at the foot of the easy Sparrhorn (9,928 feet), is reached by a ropeway from Blatten, five miles from Brigue. From the pretty little chapel close to the hotel there is a fine view of the tongue of the Aletsch plunging to the gorges below, as there is from the almost level miles of shelf-walking to the west, with added prospects across the Brigue bowl to the great Valaiian peaks, the Fletschhorn rising dominant in the centre above the Simplon saddle.

On the grassy crests to the east are Riederalp and Bettmeralp, and hours of easy path walking through the stunted firs of the

Aletschwald bordering the glacier, or high above the Rhône Valley, past several small lakes to the Eggishorn hotel, with glorious views southwards all the way. The once famous Hotel Jungfrau (Eggishorn) above Ried, at the foot of that superb viewpoint, the 9,626-foot Eggishorn itself, ascended by bridle-path in two hours from the hotel, is now bypassed by the cable ropeway from the valley to the summit, the immense view from which, embracing the whole sweep of the Aletsch Glacier, extends from the Gotthard peaks to Mont Blanc, 60 miles away to the west. It would be a pity if the lavish provision of mechanical modernity deprived you of the two-hour stroll from the Hotel Jungfrau, high above the Fieschertal and its icefall, to the little Märjelensee, bordering the Aletsch at the eastern foot of the Eggishorn, on whose almost black surface the little icebergs disport themselves, white, blue and green, even at midsummer.

All these charming places which had to be earned a few years ago by four or five hours of uphill plodding, are now accessible by ropeway from Mörel, Betten and Fiesch along the valley road; and all are amply supplied with ski-lifts for winter purposes.

The main valley continues pleasantly upwards past Mörel, Lax and Fiesch, just before which the attractive Binntal opens up to the south. Binn itself (4,783 feet) is a charming little place high up this lovely valley, at whose head rise the 10,637-foot Ofenhorn and the Helsenhorn (10,742 feet), neither of them difficult climbs for a mountaineer. This is a strollers' and walkers' paradise, with the local Eggerhorn and Breithorn providing much easier scrambles for the inexpert. There are several walkers' passes, too, across the frontier into Italy, a favourite being the 7,910-foot Albrun.

At Reckingeso the Blindental leads southwards to the Blindenhorn (11,102 feet), while at Münster the valley of that name falls in from the north, descending from the Löffelhorn; two miles farther on lies Ulrichen, recently promoted to the role of an important road junction by the opening in 1970 of the new motor road over the 8,130-foot Nufenen Pass (the highest entirely in Swiss territory) to Airolo in the Ticino. This was always a favourite ten-hour pass walk; now it provides the motorist with a quick short-cut from Brigue to Airolo without taking in the Furka and Gotthard passes beyond Gletsch. From the summit there are fine views back to the Aletsch peaks and the Finsteraarhorn with its glaciers above the Grimsel, as well as of the Gotthard group to the east. Just beyond the saddle rises the Ticino, whose upper course the road follows down into the high Val Bedretto, not the most amiable of valleys, and so to Airolo, at the foot of the Gotthard.

Ulrichen is the starting point for another favourite walkers' pass to Italy, the Gries Pass (8,070 feet), which diverges from the Nufenen route at Altstaffel, an hour above which there is a brief crossing of the level Gries Glacier. The pass, with a fine view back to the Bernese Alps, forms the frontier. The path then descends the combe of the Griesbach, soon to be joined by the Tosa torrent, a series of sharply divided levels descending to an inn on the third, some seven hours from Ulrichen, facing the famous Tosa Falls, which leap 500 feet to the fourth in three broad cascades. The track then continues down the Val Formazza (the valley of the Tosa), through Andermatten to Foppiano and the bus route to Domodossola, at the foot of the Simplon.

Beyond Ulrichen the main valley contracts to an exceedingly narrow gorge, through which the road and railway cling their way above the brawling Rhône to emerge in the stony plain of Gletsch, deepset beneath high slopes on every side.

Gletsch (5,708 feet), a small cluster of hotels and a railway station, faces the Rhône Glacier across a level mile of debris. Perhaps one should say 'faced', for when I first knew it, the splendid, shattered icefall cascaded to the level floor of the valley and the infant Rhône came seething out of a beautiful arch of blue ice. (There is a print in the Belvedère Hotel, where the Furka road's top winding almost touches the upper rim of the ice, showing that in the early nineteenth century the tongue of the glacier filled the whole plain, almost to the first houses; which proves that it is not only economies which are subject to recessions.) Now there is only a beautifully-coloured wall of smooth ice-polished rock 1,500 feet high, with the scrag-end of a dilapidated shoulder of dirty ice hanging crookedly a third of a way down it, and the Rhône emerges as the combined sum of a dozen trickles uniting at its base.

From Gletsch the Grimsel road leaps up the northern slope in six magnificent hairpins, on its way to Innertkirchen and Interlaken (see chapter 9). The road to the east (the railway soon takes to a long tunnel under the Furka saddle ahead) contours the southern slopes with fine views of the Rhône Glacier basin above the icefall and the shapely snow-dome of the Galenstock (11,805 feet) with its attendant spiky rock peaks. It then slashes its way up a 1,500-foot wall in a series of sensational hairpins to Furka Belvedère close to the glacier's rim, and yielding a splendid view back over the Gletsch basin to the now distant Valais peaks, among which the dark tip of the Matterhorn and the gleaming spire of the Weisshorn usually show to advantage.

The crossing of the level glacier (a local guide will take care of those unfamiliar with such obstacles) then sharply up to the charming little lake on the Nägelisgrätli (8,747 feet), mirroring the Galenstock in its calm surface, and on down the track to the Grimsel Hospice in about four hours is as pleasant a day's excursion as any in the Alps, for, all along its lovely way, it commands all the views just described.

The Furka Saddle (7,990 feet) lies a mile farther on up the road, and here it is imperative to park by the Hospice, for here, added to the Belvedère prospect, is the classic view of the Finsteraarhorn, its glaciers and attendant peaks, rising above the Grimsel saddle opposite.

The pass then descends through the Furka Ravine to Realp in the Urserental (see chapter 3) and proceeds across its level green floor to Hospental, where the Gotthard climbs away southwards across the main watershed into the Ticino. A mile farther on lies Andermat, road junction, summer and winter resort. Here the lower sector of the Gotthard comes up through the Schöllenen Gorge from Goeschenen, Altdorf and Lucerne to the north, and the continuation of our road eastwards to the Rhine Valley immediately winds up a bare, grassy slope to the not very interesting Oberalp Pass (6,720 feet), where it enters the Grisons (Graubünden); it then skirts a narrow lake in company with the railway, to drop down beyond it by some fine modern windings, below the source of the Vorder Rhein in Lake Toma, high on the slopes of the Badus opposite, through the village of Sedrun to Disentis (3,760 feet), the first town in the Rhine Valley proper.

Disentis, overlooked by a fine Benedictine Abbey on a hill to its north, faces, across the valley to the south, the entrance of the valley bringing down the Medelser or Mittel Rhein, as well as the road coming down from the Lukmanier Pass (6,290 feet) at whose southern end lie Olivone and Biasca in the Ticino (see chapter 12).

The main valley road, not so long ago rough and narrow, now a fine motor highway, continues to follow the Rhine through Trun and Ilanz, where one of the approach roads to the popular holiday resort of Flims climbs away to the north (the other starts a little farther east at Reichenau) to Chur, the main road and rail junction in the area.

(The whole of this journey from Brigue to Chur as well as up to St Moritz in the Engadine, is traversed by the narrow-gauge 'Glacier Express' of the Furka and Albula railways daily in seven and a half hours, the rolling-stock being specially suitable for the enjoyment of the scenic beauties along this remarkable line. Through-carriages from Zermatt avoid a change at Brigue.)

Flims (3,618 feet) with its pretty warm-water lake, the Cauma See, stands on a sunny shelf overlooking the great Rhine Gorges of Conn, facing south, and is equally popular in summer and winter. The broad plateau with its larch and fir-woods is lavishly provided with strollers' paths and there are many attractive expeditions in the neighbourhood, including the 8,665-foot Flimserstein whose broad summit plateau offers a long day's easy scrambling as well as fine views northwards towards the Tödi group (chapter 12) and southwards towards the Engadine. Another fine day's excursion is the path leading in five hours to the Segnes Hut (7,152 feet), fronting the rocky teeth of the Segnes group (Piz Segnes 10,175 feet), and opening up wide distant views of the Bernina snows, gleaming beyond the lower Engadine ranges.

The continuation of the journey eastwards beyond Chur belongs properly to the chapters dealing with the Arlberg, the Inn Valley and the Alps of western Austria. The moment seems appropriate to retrace our steps and visit one or two areas we have by-passed in our direct passage through central Switzerland.

12. From the Northern Swiss Alps to the Ticino

If, in search of the Alps, you enter Switzerland by way of Belfort, Mulhouse and Bâle, there are two clear choices ahead of you. Straight on, through Zürich, Walenstadt and Sargans lies the long lowland road to Liechtenstein, the Arlberg and Austria. Half-right, the shorter runs over the plain and the foothills, through Olten, in an hour or two, to Lucerne, where you are on the threshold of high Switzerland.

Zürich is a splendid and highly civilised modern city, with fine streets, churches, museums, art galleries, hotels, shops and, it is creditably reported, banking establishments. It stands at the head of a long, narrow lake, both shores of which are literally sprinkled with towns, their names mostly ending in – *kon*, and its waters gay with white and coloured sails. The high road to Austria follows the south shores and, after leaving the end of the lake, tunnels through a projecting shoulder of the hills and drops down to the small and charming Walensee, above whose opposite shore rises the jagged chain of the Churfirsten, seven rock summits about 7,000 feet high, approached and much scrambled on and climbed from their northern side in the Toggenburg valley, pretty unspoiled ramblers' country far from the madding motorways. The main places here are Wildhaus, Alt St Johann, Stein and Wattwil. Still farther north lies the delightful hill country of Appenzell, while between them rises the 8,215-foot mass of the Säntis, accessible by path (and of course ropeway) and crowned by a meteorological station. This is the most northerly high summit in the Swiss Alps and its views over northern Switzerland, the Lake

of Constance, Swabia and Bavaria, the Tyrolese mountains, the Grisons and the Alps of Uri, Glarus and Berne are incomparable.

At Näfels at the head of the Lake of Zürich a road diverges to the south and ascends the Valley of the Linth to Glarus, at the heart of Zürich's own Alps, beloved of the city's weekend motorists, walkers and climbers. Here stands the huge Glärnisch (9,500 feet), its magnificent precipices rising sheer above the three-mile long lake of Klöntal, supported by numerous lower ridges, their paths and crests rich in wide views over lake and plain, good high-mountain air and healthy exercise. The main centres, besides Glarus, in this attractive area are Linthal, a mile or two farther up the Glarus Valley and, high above it at the head of a funicular, the very popular summer and winter resort of Braunwald (4,115 feet).

Just beyond Glarus a road leads off to the left up the Sernftal to Elm, the highest village in that valley, the scene in 1881 of one of the greatest rockfalls in the history of the Alps, overwhelming the village and valley and killing 115 of its inhabitants. Conspicuous from the village and reached without much difficulty is the curious natural phenomenon of the Martinsloch, a hole 72 feet high piercing the main range and visible on the other side from the Segnes Hut (see p. 178). At the right time on several days of the year the sun can be seen shining directly through it. Besides commanding interesting climbs from the Martinsmaad Hut, three hours above, Elm is the starting point of two fine walking passes to the Rhine Valley: the Segnes (8,615 feet) leading via the Segnes Hut to Flims, and the Panixer (7,897 feet) to Ilanz (ibid).

Above Linthal the Sandalptal leads up into the heart of the splendid but somewhat neglected main group of the Alps of Uri – a neglect probably due to their slightly remote withdrawal from the main highways. They are not really well seen even from the Klausen Pass road, too close at their feet, and not at all from the neighbouring Rhine Valley, except from the crests of the range bounding it to the north. Here, grouped along the northern edge of the considerable Clariden Glacier rise a dozen splendid peaks,

27   *Macugnaga and Mte Rosa from the Alp Bill*

most of them nearly 11,000 feet high, the two Windgällen, Grosse Ruchen, two Scheerhörner and the Claridenstock; while its southern rim is dominated by the magnificent Tödi (Piz Rusein, 11,887 feet), the giant of the group – 'The King of the Lesser Mountains' and incidentally not an easy one to climb – and still farther south are Piz Urlaun (11,060 feet) and the Bifertenstock (11,240 feet) better approached by the Val Puntaiglias rising from the Rhine Valley at Trun (p. 178). The most attractive approach to the western end of the group is by the lovely Maderanertal from Amsteg on the Gotthard road, described below.

Returning to the main route eastwards to Austria, from Walenstadt at the eastern end of its lake, it is only a few miles of motorway to Sargans, where the road divides, the left-hand branch continuing to Vaduz, and through the principality of Liechtenstein to the Austrian frontier, where at Feldkirch the long rise to the Arlberg begins; while the road to the right, remaining on Swiss territory, swings south to Chur and the upper valley of the Rhine.

The 60 miles from Bâle to Lucerne are pleasant with a hint of things to come. Enough has been written about the famous tourist resort and the lovely starfish-armed Lake of the Four Cantons on which it stands; in any case, its Alpine benefits are fringe ones. The old rack-and-pinion railways will still take you (electronically now) up to those two celebrated vantage points, the Rigi (5,905 feet) and Pilatus (6,995 feet), for a first sight of the snows of Glarus and Uri and the more distant Oberland. As an introduction to the Alps they are a 'must' for newcomers. If you have only time for one of them, make it Pilatus, rising to the north of the town, which has the advantages of being much higher, some miles nearer to the main objective and above all a real mountain, tall and precipitous, so that your head will know that it is on a height; moreover its gorgeous view takes in more of the lake and adds the fine group at its head to the prospect. To stay the night at the Kulm and see the sunrise from the Esel, close by, is a perfect introduction to the Alpine world; it will also provide one of the most enchanting sights I know, on the eve of that revelation – the tiny points of

Lucerne's myriad lights glittering up through the indigo velvet of the night from 4,500 feet sheer below your feet. (The speediest way of ascending the peak is by the ropeway from Kriens on its western side.)

The bay at the eastern foot of the mountain is occupied by the little lake-port of Stansstadt, looked down upon its own belvedère, the 6,065-foot Stanserhorn, the third of Lucerne's famous observation posts. Behind it a steep valley runs deep into the hills to the south, terminating at Engelberg (3,350 feet), crowded in summer and winter alike, at the foot of the first really high range thrown up by the northern Alps, whose highest summit is the snowy Titlis (10,627 feet) with the rocky teeth of the Spannörter in attendance. Walks, scrambles and climbs abound above this pretty valley, from which the track over the 7,265-foot Jochpass leads over, by way of the tiny resort of Engstlenalp on its little lake, to the Hasliberg shelf, Innertkirchen and Meiringen in the Haslital (p. 126).

The pass has long been accessible by ropeway and so, for the last year or two – tell it not in the presence of those who once thrilled to their first Alpine climb up its snowy dome! – is the summit of proud Titlis itself. (The project of a ropeway to the summit of the Matterhorn has, so far, repeatedly been refused planning permission.)

The other long valley, rising southwards from Stansstadt with low hills on either side, through the resorts of Sarnen and Lungern and past their modest lakes, eventually peters out in the low, heavily wooded ridge separating it from Meiringen, the Haslital and the Lake of Brienz. This slight obstacle is crossed by the gentlest of passes, with road and rail in close company, the 3,396-foot Brünig, from whose pine-clad saddle there is a superb view to the Wetterhörner and their Oberland neighbours, some ten miles away across the plain, into which the winding descent is a matter of a few minutes.

So much for Lucerne's southern purlieus. Fringing all the bays and promontories on its northern shore, through Küssnacht, Weggis, Vitznau and Gersau to Brunnen, there is an enchanting lakeside road. Unfortunately it is normally so crowded with traffic and the main streets of those delightful summer resorts are so narrow that it is quite impossible to make any headway along it. So, unless you are merely out for a sightseeing drive and if you really want to get to Brunnen and 'points beyond', you will take the highway which runs through Arth-Goldau, carefully keeping the long saddle-back of the Rigi between itself and lake-shore delights.

At charming Brunnen the lake takes a right-angled bend to the south and the road skirts and tunnels the cliffs precariously – this is the modern development of the famous Axenstrasse – past Tell's legendary chapel, to Flüelen at the head of the lake and Altdorf's lovely ancient Swiss architecture beyond it. Here the long climb up the Reuss Valley to the Gotthard begins, while to the east the 6,390-foot Klausen Pass branches off to run up along the fringe of the Clariden–Tödi group, described above, and drops down into Linthal and Glarus.

The Gotthard road goes on up the long Reuss Valley, climbing through Amsteg, Wassen (where the Susten Pass, 7,422 feet, falls in from the west) to Goeschenen (3,640 feet), where the railway tunnel dives into the great frontal wall of rock on its way to Airolo, seven miles beyond. The whole of this sector of the road is made fascinating by the marvellously engineered main railway line to Italy, surmounting successive steps in the valley and lateral gorges in a bewildering series of spiral tunnels and wonderfully airy viaducts.

At Amsteg the Maderanertal opens up to the east. This valley leading up to the snow peaks of the Clariden–Tödi group is one of the most beautiful in the Alps and unspoiled by the presence of a main road and other modern encumbrances. It is a rambling and climbing paradise of the old-fashioned type, well off the beaten track, 'the world forgetting, by the world forgot'. At its head, some four hours from Amsteg, stands the Hotel Pension zum Schweizer Alpenklub (4,442 feet), among pleasant woodland walks, in the shadow of the Düssistock and Schneehorn (10,815 feet). From here the peaks of this fine group and the splendid glacier expeditions over the Clariden Pass (9,740 feet) to Linthal, or the equally high Planura and Sandalp Passes to the Rhine Valley, are close at hand for the climber.

The Gotthard Pass, that great north–south axis, by rail and road, for traffic and trade, affords an ideal literary link between two areas bypassed in the earlier chapters, which pursued a direct west-to-east course through central Switzerland: the northern area just covered and the sub-Alpine, Italianate Ticino to the south.

Beyond Goeschenen a marvellous modern motor road forces its way through the tremendous Schoellenen Gorge, where the old carriage road and famous 'Devil's Bridge' can be seen above to the left, to emerge by a tunnel at Andermatt in the Urserental (chap. 3). Retracing our steps a mile to Hospental, we leave the valley again, to swing south over the main watershed close to the highest Gotthard peaks, the 10,000-foot Pizzo Centrale and Lucendro, at the Gotthard summit (7,926 feet); and then, in next to no time, down the superb new motorway (on stilts), which has replaced the 48 hairpins of the old Val Tremola descent – still worth a visit – to Airolo, 4,000 feet lower down at the head of the Val Leventina. (A car shuttle-service by rail through the nine-mile tunnel is available from Goeschenen to Airolo, if you want to miss all this.)

The descent of the Val Leventina, at first narrow and steep-sided, with the sky incredibly remote above, as far as Biasca, is made exciting by the wonderful companionship of writhing road, rushing river and contortionist railway, forced to even more desperate spiral acrobatics than on the northern side. Lovely waterfalls cascade from high up the cliffs and wooded slopes as you drop down through Rodi Fiesso to Faido (2,465 feet), the capital of the Leventina – charming small mountain resorts these with plenty of attractive excursions, such as that to Lake Tremorgio, high in the hills, to be enjoyed from them.

At Biasca (970 feet), in the first level plainlet, the road to the Lukmanier Pass (6,290 feet) and Disentis swings away northwards up the broad Val Blenio, whose débris-covered lower reaches soon give way to slopes covered in vines, walnuts and chestnuts. The road ascends through Malvaglia and Aquila to the small resort of Olivone, where the actual pass begins, striking up the Val Sta Maria for ten miles to reach the saddle dividing Ticino from the Grisons; from there it follows the gorges of the young Mittel Rhein to its junction with the Vorder Rhein in the broad main valley at Disentis (see p. 178). All the way up from Olivone to Casaccia, just below the pass, there are splendid views of the snowy Adula (Rheinwald) range and especially of the 12,500-foot Rheinwaldhorn, its highest peak. There are several lateral valleys rising from the Val Blenio into the heart of those fine mountains: the Val Malvaglia from Malvaglia itself, the Val Soja from Aquila and the Val Camadra, north of Olivone.

From Biasca southwards, you are suddenly driving straight down the pleasant, wide and flat Ticino Valley, between lush meadows, through village after village typically Italian in character. Everything is hot, southern, sub-Alpine; even the language is Italian in this Swiss canton to the south of the main Alpine chain.

Twelve miles farther on is Bellinzona (760 feet), the fine old capital of Ticino, with its many church towers. Here the lovely Val Mesocco (Misox), deep and steep-sided, falls in from the northeast, and up it for 20 miles to Mesocco, through one pretty village and town after another – Soazzo, Grono, Roveredo, close-built in sunny meadows around their slender white campaniles, among the surrounding vineyards and orchards – runs the road to the San Bernardino Pass (6,768 feet). At Grono the valley splits and a charming sideroad runs up the almost parallel Val Calanca for 12 miles to its chief village, Rossa.

Mesocco (2,495 feet) is a considerable resort. Just before it is reached, on a rock below the town, stands the magnificent four-towered medieval ruin of Misox, which has given its name to the whole district. Here the pass proper begins, climbing the upper valley to the pleasant summer resort of San Bernardino (5,270 feet). There are charming woodland walks here, to the Belvedère, the pretty Lago d'Osso, as well as longer excursions and climbs, including the sharp tooth of Piz Uccello (8,911 feet). Since 1967, a four-mile-long road tunnel, intended to ease the congestion on the St Gotthard by attracting traffic over (or rather under) the San Bernardino, has rendered the passage of the actual saddle unnecessary. Visitors to it, unattracted by the darkness, will still find there by the little lake of Moësola the small hospice where, in the fifteenth century, St Bernard of Siena preached the gospel and so bequeathed his name to a pass (and a tunnel). This runs from San Bernardino to Hinterrhein (5,350 feet) on the Grisons side of the watershed, near which there are fine views of the Rheinwald peaks. The old road then descends alongside the nascent Hinter Rhein to Splügen (4,790 feet), where the Splügen Pass (see p. 194) climbs away southwards on its way to Chiavenna, near the head of Lake Como in Italy; and thence, by a series of truly remarkable gorges, bored by the furious torrent, to Thusis (2,369 feet) and on down to the Rhine Valley at Reichenau (see chapter 11).

Shortly after leaving Bellinzona, in its wide open plain, the main Ticino highway divides, the direct road straight ahead swinging easily up over a small, wooded spur, the Monte Ceneri, surmounted in a few easy curves by the low 1,850 feet 'pass' of that name; and then for 15 miles down the wide, wooded Vedeggio Valley, crowded with villages and villas, to Lugano.

Lugano (905 feet) is the most over-populated, over-visited – and in high summer the most impossibly congested – of all Switzerland's famous lake resorts, where too many cooks have spoiled the broth and not only Lunn has been vile. Which is a pity, because its lake is perhaps the loveliest of all, with enchanting villages straggling along its shores – Gandria, most sketched of all lakeside haunts, Porlezza, Morcote with its superbly perched abbey-church – it own splendid crow's-nests of Monte Salvatore and Bré (3,600 feet), and overlooking its southern end one of the finest middle-height viewpoints in the Alps, Monte Generoso (5,590 feet), famous for its sunrises on Monte Rosa, all the great Pennine peaks and Milan and other towns in the plain to the south.

As for Lugano's own inimitable hill-roads, twisting their precipitous way high to bird's-eye views of the green unruffled lake, with ancient villages and churches huddled on every shoulder and terrace of those lovely hills – stay a day or two, if you can find room anywhere around Lugano, and sample them all, especially out of season at blossom time. Among short drives I do not know of a more repaying half-hour than the ascent to Monte Bré, either by day or when the shimmering lights of the town, 2,000 feet below, twinkle up on the dark velvet of a warm spring night like a diamond coronet.

Southwards of Lugano, the new *autoroute*, in company with the main railway to Italy, crosses the lake by a causeway and swings through the narrow neck at its southern end through Capolago and Mendrisio to Chiasso, the large railway junction on the Italian frontier, just across which lies Como, on the edge of the Italian plain. Milan lies only 30 miles ahead by *autostrada*.

At the road junction south of Bellinzona, mentioned above, the right-hand road runs level to the head of Lago Maggiore, a few miles away, along the wide trough through which the Ticino now flows down to it, broad and placid.

Here, strung out along the western shore of the lake, lie the famous tourist centres of Locarno, Ascona, Ronco and Brissago, forming an almost continuous built-up area along a coastal road far too narrow and tortuous to cope with its heavy traffic. These sophisticated and over-crowded summer resorts, with their multiplicity of hotels, lake-bathing, swimming pools, speed-boating and water-skiing, need no description except the rather obvious one that they are beautifully situated in a sub-Alpine paradise.

Many of the visitors to them, however, seem totally unaware of a number of lovely valleys opening into the tall green hills at their backs, to the west, such as the beautiful Val Maggia, with its offshoots, the Valle da Campo and the Val di Bosco, rich in rock-scenery, lush vegetation, waterfalls, picturesque villages and small hill-resorts, which runs up for 17 miles through Cevio to charmingly situated Bignasco (1,448 feet). Or again, the Val Melezza, perhaps better known as the Centovali, into which it merges, through which a somewhat narrow and at times airy but wonderfully exciting road twists its way, high above immense gorges to the Italian frontier at Camdo and on to Domodossola, at the foot of the Simplon, 20 miles of unusually varied scenic beauty.

At Brissago the lakeside road crosses from Swiss Ticino into Italy, the broad northern arm of Lago Maggiore being neatly halved between the two neighbours. This is a convenient point at which to end our traverse from northern to southern Switzerland, the Italian Lakes being dealt with in chapter 15.

13. The Engadine

Beyond Chur (chapter 11), the level Rhine Valley road runs northwards to meet the west–east Zürich–Arlberg artery at Sargans. From Chur itself there is a short cul de sac road leading steeply up into the southern hills to the delightful summer and winter resort of Arosa (6,000 feet) – one of the highest in Switzerland with its two little lakes and a famous chapel on a knoll. Thirty miles to the south lies one of the most beautiful areas in the Alps, the Engadine, a high open trench falling gradually from 6,000 feet at its western end to 3,500 at its eastern exit, in a distance of 50 miles. There is nothing comparable in the whole Alpine system.

The most direct and easiest motor road runs from Chur through a pretty but unexciting valley past Lenzerheide (4,845 feet), a genial summer and winter resort among meadows, to Tiefencastel, the main junction of the valley roads leading up to the high trench above. For scenic beauty I would however prefer to retrace my steps along the Rhine Valley to Reichenau, and drive into the mountains there up the valley of the Hinter Rhein, broad and open at first, to Thusis, with its long, straight, gently tilted main street, flanked by hotels.

Thusis (2,369 feet) is the northern starting point for two major passes (neither of which concerns the Engadine) – the San Bernardino, described in the previous chapter, and the Splügen, dealt with later in this. For the first 16 miles they share the same sensational road, a marvel of engineering, forcing a precarious way through a series of stupendous gorges bored by the Hinter

Rhein's raging waters, descending from the glaciers of the Rhein-wald group, ten miles away and 10,000 feet above.

The first is known as the *Verlorene Loch* – the 'Chasm of the Lost' – the road assaulting the craggy wall to the right most courageously. The short, rock-girt ravine is followed immediately by a small open bowl in whose meadows lies the hamlet of Ron-gellen. The valley then narrows rapidly again and the road bores into the dark and fantastic gorge of the Via Mala – sufficiently sombre and awe-inspiring to merit so sinister a name. Here, between cliffs of grey rock, the Rhine has carved a deep and gloomy passage, often not more than a yard wide, down which it thunders in a series of foaming cascades and whirlpools. Thread-ing its way high above, the road is forced to cross and recross the chasm; this it does on modern bridges which have replaced the old stone arches; but the loftiest of them has been left to lend a most picturesque effect to this tremendous manifestation of nature's irresistible forces. For all its grim and daunting character, the scene is one of great and impressive beauty, with the hamlet of St Ambriesch, occupied only in summer, perched high up on a rocky plateau above the second bridge.

A third bridge brings the road out of the enclosing jaws of the ravine into the pleasant little plain of Schams, among whose con-trasting meadows and pines is the village of Zillis, where the tiny church contains some remarkable thirteenth-century roof paint-ings.

Crossing the Rhine again, at the thermal baths of Bogn, with the hamlet of Clugin – where another picturesque old church houses fourteenth-century frescoes – on the other side of the river, the road soon reaches the remarkable little township of Andeer (3,210 feet), still bearing every mark of its importance as a staging and trading post in the days of the prime hegemony of the two passes. Here, the unusual external wall-designs on the Padrun house and the frescoes on the Conrad house are well worth inspection.

Beyond Andeer the Averser Rhein comes down the long, high Aversertal, which leads up to Cresta Avers (6,440 feet), the highest Swiss village inhabited all the year round, to meet the Hinter Rhein. Beyond Cresta a famous and beautiful walkers' track ascends a saddle above the Jufern Alp and drops down to join the Septimer on its way from Bivio to Casaccia (see below).

The main road now penetrates the far less intimidating Roffla Gorge, crosses a level widening in the valley and, passing through the *Rheinwaldthörli* tunnel ('The Little Rheinwald Gate') continues among pines and firs till at Rütenen the Rheinwald peaks, with pyramid-shaped Piz Tambo prominent, suddenly lift into view ahead. Splügen (4,790 feet) in its high, level valley-bed, rather like a minor Urserental, is soon reached. Like Andeer, it bears the mark of its importance in the great trading and coaching days: stately and patrician residences and huge old warehouses, now fallen into disuse.

Here the passes part company, the San Bernardino running straight as a ruled line to the west, the Splügen equally straight to the south till it hits the mountain wall and starts its climb over it into Italy.

If you have chosen the Reichenau–Thusis approach to the Engadine, it would be a pity to miss this diversion as far as Splügen and back, for the wider Schyn Gorges of the Albula torrent along the road to Tiefencastel, fine as they are, cannot begin to compare with those just described.

Tiefencastel (2,821 feet) is a busy and highly picturesque road junction, from which two roads climb over into the Upper Engadine – the Julier and the Albula – while a third branches eastwards to Davos and the Fluela Pass beyond it, leading into the Lower Engadine.

Davos (5,115 feet) is famous not only as a summer and winter resort (for here are the Weissfluh and the Parsenn ski-runs) but for its long history of a sanatorium for chest-complaints and the origin of much celebrated literature inspired there, from R. L. Stevenson to Thomas Mann. Beyond Davos lies another well-known resort, Klosters (4,000 feet), the nearest centre to the Silvretta Group (see below), which also commands the Parsenn and other winter delights; there is a direct road from the lowlands to Klosters, leaving the Rhine Valley highway at Landquart (p. 209).

Tiefencastel is in itself a remarkable and much photographed spot. Here, where a lofty stone arch spans the roaring torrent penned between precipitous rock walls 60 feet below, the junction of four major roads and two rivers, the Albula and the Julier, is crammed onto a narrow shelf. Two white-walled hotels face each other across the first lift of the Julier road, the gaily-painted balconies at the back of one overhanging the ravine. Crowning a hillock beyond the stream stands the slender-towered church, and that is all there is of the place. But if you look up the steep mountainside beyond the church to the rocky comb of Piz Curver (9,764 feet) against the sky, you will see a similar church-tower, white in the sunshine, doing a perfect imitation act on a jutting terrace hundreds of feet up the green slope, marking the village of Mon.

Of the two Engadine passes ahead to the south, taking almost parallel courses, the Albula (7,595 feet) is a pleasant enough road, the chief feature of interest all the way along its 25-mile course, through the charming resorts of Bad Alvaneu, Filisur, Bergün and Preda, being the remarkable sustained engineering feat by which the 3ft. 6in. gauge Albula railway twists and spirals up successive steps in the valley in a series of bewildering loops and spiral tunnels through the mountainside and across wonderfully airy bridges and viaducts – a Gotthard in miniature. The finest examples are the Schmittentobel bridge between Alvaneu and Filisur, and the marvellously beautiful curved viaduct 200 feet high by which the branch-line to Davos leaps a wild gorge near the latter village. Ahead there are fine views of Piz d'Aela (10,958 feet) and later Piz Kesch (10,738 feet) and other rocky peaks streaked with snow. At Preda the railway burrows under the dividing range by a four-mile tunnel, emerging in the Engadine at Bevers, while the road climbs to the bare saddle of the pass (7,595 feet), skirting a lakelet on the way, to descend through a narrow, stony valley on Punt (5,546 feet) in the green levels of the Engadine a mile or two east of Samedan, from which it is another four to St Moritz (6,080 feet). The upper levels of the pass are, incidentally, a favourite hunting-ground for botanists and entomologists, since some extremely rare plants and insects exist there.

The Julier (7,493 feet) is, in my opinion, in a different class altogether. I would take it among the 'greats', if only for its 'surprise' summit-view and the magical first glimpse of the Engadine lakes on the descent into that lovely valley – it should therefore be driven, at least on first acquaintance, from Tiefencastel up, and not from the Engadine down.

The road at first climbs pleasantly, looping its way upwards through the hay meadows for six miles to the first little plateau, housing the tiny but enchanting resort of Savognin (3,900 feet) with the rocky walls of Piz Michel, the Tinzenhorn and Piz d'Aela rising grandly behind it. Another six miles of climbing and twisting brings you to the terrace (4,793 feet) where once stood the hamlet of Marmore, drowned under the dirty-coloured waters of the reservoir built in 1954 to provide distant Zürich with additional electric power. The road follows the shore of this artificial lake and then winds up rock-strewn slopes for another five miles to the highest balcony in the valley, where stands the large village of Bivio (5,827 feet).

Travellers on foot can here take to the 7,600-foot mule-track over the Septimer Pass, famous since Roman times, to Casaccia in the Val Bregaglia (see below). At its summit one track breaks away down to Maloja at the head of the Engadine, another to cross the 8,000-foot Stallerberg Pass descending through Cresta Avers to the Splügen road at Andeer (see p. 193). Pass walkers will find along this fine route some magnificent views of the Bregaglia peaks across the deep rift of the valley as well as of the more distant Bernina giants to the east.

Above Bivio, the Julier road swings desperately up a bare, savage and boulder-strewn slope in a series of contracting hairpins to the bleak, narrow saddle with its swampy little tarn, slung between Piz Albana (10,184 feet) and Piz Polaschin (9,900 feet), at 7,500 feet.

To enjoy the summit view to the full, it is best to park your car and walk a little way down the forward slope to pick your vantage point. You will find yourself looking out through a V-shaped window between the grim and stony slopes of Piz Julier (11,105 feet) and Piz Polaschin sweeping down from overhead, to the Engadine's unseen trench before you. Beyond it rise the long snow-dappled ridges of Piz Rosatsch and Piz Mortel (11,300 feet), joined by the low, dark sweep of the 9,000-foot Fuorcla Surlej saddle. And, close behind that snowless, sombre-hued barrier, overtopping it by 3,000 feet of rock, ice and snow, there rise into the sky the gleaming heads of Tschierva (11,713 feet), Morteratsch (12,315 feet) and Bernina (13,295 feet) herself, the polished blade of the Biancograt slashing like a knife from the deep notch between the great peaks to her proud 13,000-foot crest.

The downward road from the pass follows the Ova de Vallun torrent with hardly a curve till the last steep slope down into the Engadine above Silvaplana's roofs causes it to take a trio of wide sweeps through the pinewoods. And here is the second 'surprise' of the Julier road.

The great white peaks have long since retired behind the intervening screen, though Piz Corvatsch (11,320 feet) and its neighbours are a fine enough skyline. Now there suddenly opens at your feet a contrasting picture of the most exquisite gentleness and colourful beauty. A few minutes ago you were among bleak and cheerless boulder-littered slopes of grey rock-rubble. Here you are looking down across the heads of dark pine-lances, perhaps 300 feet below you, on the gently curving shores of two unruffled lakes whose colour defies description, set in lush green meadow-land only less beautiful than their own deeper turquoise and backed again by the richer colour of the pine forest steeply banked at the foot of the opposing wall of the valley. Perhaps it is the violence of the contrast, but this seems to me to be one of the warmest, loveliest, most peaceful downward glances among all the mountains I have seen.

A few minutes later the Julier drops through a typically narrow space between Silvaplana's houses (5,958 feet) into the bustle and heavy traffic of the main valley road. If you are bound for St

Moritz you turn left; for Maloja, right. Either way you will be bowling along by the edge of one or other of those enchanting lakes in one of the world's loveliest valleys.

The Julier is, incidentally, one of the few really high passes which the shovel and snow-plough keep open proudly all the year round. In winter, the Engadine is of course one long, crowded, luxurious winter sports centre; so the visitor puts on his chains and sails merrily over the 7,000-foot pass to the snow and the sunshine, the ski-lift and the Samba. Let us hope that as he passes between banks of snow piled 15 feet high along his strip of magic carpet, he gives a thought to the relays of hands operating the shovels in all kinds of bitter mountain weather and to the snow-plough teams who spend the cracking winter nights up there on the wind-swept heights.

Since the Engadine begins at Maloja, a few yards from the freak watershed described in chapter 1, let us for the moment leave it, somewhat capriciously, and examine the Maloja Pass (5,959 feet), by which it is approached from the head of Lake Como and Chiavenna, 5,000 feet below to the southwest in Italy also at the foot of the Splügen Pass, tumbling down over its high gap in the range to the north (see above).

At Castasegna, seven miles up the Val Bregaglia, the valley of the Mera, lies the Swiss frontier, beyond which the road winds pleasantly up through pinewoods to Promontogno (2,685 feet) clustering in a plainlet at the junction of the wild Bondasca Valley and the Mera. Here the grand Bondasca ravine bites deep into the mountain mass to the south, crowned by the splendidly savage rock spires of the Cacciabella, Sciora and Bondasca peaks, a crescent of shattered rock and hanging glacier whose greatest glories are the Cengalo (11,070 feet) and the stupendous smooth northeast face of Piz Badile (10,853 feet), one of the last great climbing problems in the Alps to be solved, as recently as 1938. The mountain walker in search of sublime scenery will want to pause at Promontogno and walk all the lovely three hours' length of the Bondasca Valley's steep rift, to the Sciora Hut (7,057 feet) at the feet of those great precipices.

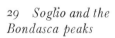

28   *The Bernina Group from Fuorcla Surlej*

29   *Soglio and the Bondasca peaks*

30 *Edelweisshöhe on the Glocknerstrasse*

31 *The Rosengarten from Carezza (Dolomites)*

The motorist with less time to spare, but who would still wish to see that splendid semi-circle of peaks, will either drive in a quarter of an hour up the narrow road which winds up the opposite slope or walk up in an hour either from Promontogno or Stampa, through the shade of the famous chestnut groves to Soglio (3,570 feet), the historic Bregaglia home of the de Salis family in the middle ages – now an excellent hotel (Pension Willy) – and perhaps the most perfectly situated village in the Alps: certainly the most photographed.

Some of the ancient rooms are still on show in their original state and the register is bright with famous names. A stroll through the little white-walled village street, at least 10 feet wide, with its wrought-iron balconies and scarlet geraniums, leads in a few minutes to gentle grassy slopes from which the huddle of grey roofs about the slenderest of white church towers, set against the marvellous background of the valley below and the Bondasca gorge with the sharp spires towering above, is seen at its lovely best.

From Promontogno the Maloja road ascends three successive terraces, all marked by villages with euphonious Italian names – Stampa, Vicosoprano, Casaccia (at the foot of the Septimer, see above) – up the Val Bregaglia, whose Italian identity the Swiss are prone to hide under the collective name of the 'Bergell'. All the way up, there are clear traces, along the mule-track used by walkers, of the old Roman road from ancient Clavenna into the territory of the Rhaetii beyond the saddle at its head.

At Casaccia the road suddenly swings up the sheer and narrow 2,000-foot escarpment barring the way, through a dense cloak of pines clinging to it, by a dozen splendidly-engineered, beautifully graded hairpins, well surfaced and of comfortable width. A moment later you cross the rim of this precipitous wall and find yourself at 6,000 feet looking eastwards along the level wide trench of the Engadine.

It is well worth while parking the car here and getting out to study this unique phenomenon in the geological conformation of

the Alps. For here, at some time or other, this southern side caved
in, and the waters draining the Bregaglia peaks, instead of flowing
northwards into the basin of the Inn, were diverted southwards to
pour into the Italian lakes.

Maloja, where the painter Segantini lies buried, is no longer the
fashionable resort it used to be, but the walks all around it are
lovely, especially the hour's gentle rise to the dark Cavloccio Lake
(6,266 feet) on the way to the Forno Group behind it – an area
beloved by climbers operating from the Forno Hut, three hours
farther up, across the Forno Glacier. To the left from the lake, the
very long but interesting Muretto Pass (8,390 feet) crosses a small
glacier between Monte del Forno (10,545 feet) and Monte
Muretto (10,197 feet) into Italy's beautiful Val Malenco to Chiesa
(four hours from the pass) and eventually down it to Sondrio in
the Valtellina. The Muretto Pass is one of the few places from
which the huge Monte della Disgrazia (12,067 feet) is seen in all
its magnificence.

From Maloja to St Moritz is 12 miles of sheer joy, skirting the
blue-green lakes of Sils and Silvaplana, with pine forests sweeping
down to them on the left and the fine range capped by Piz Corvatsch (11,310 feet) opposite. At Sils Baselgia a road crosses the
floor of the valley to the right to the favourite resort of Sils Maria,
behind which rises one of the most beautiful hanging valleys in the
Alps, the Fextal, running up to the fine horseshoe of glaciated
peaks – Piz Chapütschin, Glüschaint, Tremoggia and half a dozen
more, all 11,000 feet or more high – which form the northern rim
of the Bernina Group (see below, Pontresina). The road up this
valley is barred to motor traffic and its meadows are so thick with
(legally protected) flowers that you cannot put your foot down
without breaking them and the law.

From Sils Maria there is a lovely level walk back to Maloja
along the south bank of the lake past the promontory of Isola,
where the rugged Val Fedoz opens up at the foot of Piz la Margna
(10,353 feet), whose blunt rocky head, in spite of its modest elevation, dominates the valley from St Moritz and all view points
around it. For the innumerable beautiful valley paths and wood-

land walks in the Upper Engadine area I can only refer you to local guide books : space forbids more.

The road now runs along the lake to Silvaplana at the foot of the Julier, which small resort has for some years past staged an unusual additional attraction : a large colony of those supposedly bashful glacier-haunters, marmots, which eat happily out of the hands of children close to a garage on the busy main road at the Maloja end of the village.

From Silvaplana a narrow road crosses the valley to the hamlet of Surlej where one of the great path walks of the district starts up to the 9,055-foot Fuorcla Surlej, four hours above. This high saddle, also reached by paths from Sils and from the Hahnensee near St Moritz, separates the Engadine from the Rosegg Valley to the south, into which the track descends with wonderful views of the Rosegg Glacier and its peaks to a narrow road leading down that lovely vale to Pontresina (see below). The inn on the saddle stands just below the glacier falling from Piz Mortel (11,300 feet) and its slightly higher neighbour Piz Corvatsch, accessible in three hours and yielding a superb view, from the Disgrazia to the southwest, over the whole Upper Engadine and the Bernina giants, and extending eastwards to the Wildspitze lording it over the Ötztal Alps in Austria. Since 1968, more easily still, since the construction of the ropeway from near Surlej to 'Corvatsch' (10,843 feet), high on the rocky spur descending from the two peaks, to provide a paradise for skiers in summer as well as winter. From there the ascent is only 500 feet and a matter of an hour.

The close-up view from the Fuorcla onto the great Bernina peaks opposite which appear as a 'surprise' when you reach the saddle, reflected in the little tarn among multi-coloured boulders, is one of the 'great' middle-height Alpine views, and those who spend the night at the inn to see the sunrise will remember it for the rest of their lives.

Beyond Silvaplana the road runs through pine forests along the smaller lake and village of Campfer (just above which, for up to £20 a day, you can enjoy the amenities of the mountain-Ritz known as the Suvretta House) and soon reaches the city-resort – I use the term advisedly – of St Moritz, looking down on its own small lake, convenient as an airfield and a racecourse in winter – the Mecca of the millionaire and the purlieu of the playboy. For me its only attractions are the paintings in the Segantini museum and chocolate and whipped cream with assorted marvels of pâtisserie, at Herr Hanselmann's world-famous *konditorei*, where the crowds and the steam-heated atmosphere are so thick that you will almost inevitably absorb the local 'flu-germs with your elevenses!

After which, let it be added that nothing, not even the Grand Babylon by the mountain lake, can destroy the supreme beauty of its surroundings. Above the welter of hotels and shops, to the north are the progressively difficult ski slopes of Chantarella, Corviglia and at the top of 10,045-foot Piz Nair (railway and then ropeway), another glorious viewpoint, commanding the whole Upper Engadine and the Bernina peaks dominating the Pontresina valley to the south.

Beyond the clutter and clatter of St Moritz's traffic-jammed high street, the valley road descends in three wide curves down the slope which has been immortalised by the Cresta toboggan and bob-sleigh runs sharing them, to Celerina (5,700 feet) at their foot and Samedan, in the lower level now reached.

At Samedan (5,670 feet) across the level green floor of the plainlet which houses the Engadine Airport, the lateral valley leading to Pontresina and the Bernina Pass opens up southwards. Pontresina (5,900 feet), although its long, narrow and sloping main street is nearly as congested in the high season as that of its more fashionable neighbour, remains a charming and less sophisticated resort. Here again the walks and excursions are countless – the lovely Rosegg Valley has already been mentioned – (Muottas Muraigl, 8,058 feet, also attainable by funicular, is Pontresina's own particular belvedère, looking out over the whole necklace of the Engadine lakes). The ropeway to the Alp Languard has shortened the long drag up to another of the great Alpine viewpoints for non-climbers, Piz Languard (10,715 feet) directly overlooking the Bernina Group – the third highest in Switzerland – and ranging over an enormous sweep of the Alps from the Adamello in Italy to the Wildspitze in Austria's Ötztal.

Above Pontresina the windings of the Bernina Pass (7,644 feet) climb to its saddle in the main Black Sea–Adriatic watershed ten miles away, from which it plunges excitingly 6,200 feet into the Vale of Poschiavo and Tirano in the Italian Valtellina. Up this great southern wall of the mountains for hundreds of years the mule-trains maintained an endless traffic in the famous Valtellina wines, a cask on either side of the mule, with all the excitements of the smuggler's craft thrown in. And so since time immemorial the Bernina has had a second name – 'the Wine Pass'. On its way up, from Pontresina its supreme glory is at one of the hairpins known as the Montebello Corner (6,500 feet), where the road rises clear of the screening forest and suddenly reveals the dazzling view over the great Bernina peaks close at hand. This is to my mind the finest and most beautiful view at close quarters of the peaks and glaciers of a great group of snow-mountains to be had from any road in the Alps. For me, the perfect proportions of this semicircle of mighty peaks, all reaching the 13,000-foot level or near it, all unusually snowy-breasted because of their northerly aspect, some soft and undulating in contour, the Bernina herself sharp-ridged and knife-edged, with the great expanse of the riven icefall and tongue of the Morteratsch glacier perfectly centralised below, and all in middle-distance, where they stand up without undue foreshortening, give this glorious prospect pride of place for sheer beauty of form and texture.

There is, by the way, a side road a mile or so beyond Pontresina, branching off to the Morteratsch Inn, below in the valley, half an hour from the glacier's dirty snout. The half hour is better spent by climbing the steep zig-zag path to the wooded spur of Chünetta (6,876 feet), for its splendid view of the glacier's morained and crevassed sweep up to the great peaks ranged at its head – Piz Palü (12,825 feet), Bellavista (12,087 feet), Zupo (13,120 feet), Crast Aguzza (12,705 feet), Piz Bernina (13,295 feet), Piz Morteratsch (12,315 feet) and Piz Boval (10,150 feet). Beyond

Chünetta a splendid path leads, high up above the glaciers, to the Boval Hut (8,068 feet) an hour and a half farther on, a grand walk.

At Bernina Haüser, a couple of lonely stone buildings five miles farther on, a great many things happen nowadays. This has always been the starting point for the lovely walk up the Val dal Fain, a gorgeous protected flower reserve (noted too for its marmots) bending away to the Italian frontier at its head; and the path on the opposite side of the valley to Diavolezza and its famous glacier tour, one of the easiest in the Alps. Now, a little farther up the road, two aerial ropeways lead up the opposing mountain sides, the one on the right to Diavolezza, the other to a new skiing area on Piz Lagalb (9,833 feet).

Diavolezza (9,767 feet) has for a century been visited by countless thousands for its glorious close-up view of the Bernina peaks – Palü being particularly impressive – from high above the Pers Glacier. This is another of the places where sunrise excels even itself, but the spectacle is truly magnificent at any time of day. Glacier walkers and, more recently, skiers have used the inn at the top as a resting place on the 'Diavolezza Tour', continuing down the Pers and Morteratsch Glaciers all the way to the Morteratsch Hotel. With the provision of the ropeway, summer-skiing on the slopes near the Diavolezza Inn itself often involves queuing at the bottom for the cable-car, such are the crowds.

The road to the pass climbs on, below the glacier falling from Piz Cambrena (11,843 feet), past two dark lakes, and finally tunnels to the summit, with its superb downward glimpse into the blue-green depths of the Vale of Poschiavo and the eye of the little lake of Le Prese, 6,000 feet below. The railway, which has followed the road all the way up, crosses the saddle at Alp Grüm (6,850 feet), closer to the mountain wall and the Palü Glacier streaming down the reverse side of that peak, but the view into the depths is equally impressive. The southern side of the pass belongs properly to chapter 15 (see p. 234).

Below Samedan, the main valley of the Engadine falls gently by a series of long steps and terraces through the resorts of Bevers,

Punt (where the Albula pass falls in from the north) and Zuoz to Zernez, where the Lower Engadine begins. Here, to the south, lies the fine walking territory of the Swiss National Park, through whose beautifully wooded central valley – with a touch of the Canadian pine forests about it – the long road over the low Ofen Pass (7,070 feet), commanding a distant view of the Ortler, leads to Santa Maria and down, across the Italian frontier at Münster, into the Adige Valley, the highway to Merano, Bolzano, the Ortler Group and the Dolomites.

Beyond Zernez, the Engadine, bounded on either side by rocky ranges of no great height, is less interesting but still scenically very attractive, as the long road falls gradually past Süs and Lavin to the considerable and much favoured combined resort of Schuls-Vulpera–Tarasp (3,950 feet) crowned by a fine castle on a rock in the middle of the valley.

The short lateral valleys on either side are full of lovely things, with delightful villages and small resorts perched on high, green shelves, such as charming Fétan (4,400 feet) near the mouth of the Val Tasna, and Guarda to the north. Here, screened by the lower containing range and approached from the heads of the valleys, rises the fine Silvretta Group – Piz Linard (11,200 feet), Silvrettahorn (10,655 feet), Piz Buin (10,880 feet) and Fluchthorn (11,165 feet) – another area beloved by glacier walkers and climbers, through whose snowfields and crests runs the Swiss–Austrian (Arlberg) frontier. Several attractive glacier passes lead over to Klosters (pp. 195 and 209).

At the head of the wooded Val Sinestra, to the north of Schuls, is the health resort of that name, with its thermal springs and lovely walks, many of them on level ground.

Below Schuls the long valley road runs pleasantly down to Martinsbruck (Martina) (3,400 feet), at the foot of the 50-mile trench and then down the picturesque gorges of the Inn, crossing the Austrian frontier at a bridge, through Finstermünz, its ancient tower deep in the river bed below, to Pfunds and Landeck (2,550 feet) at the eastern foot of the Arlberg (see chapter 14).

At Martinsbruck a road to the right climbs up a low containing

spur to drop into the open plainlet of Nauders on the main road
from Landeck to the Adige Valley. Here begin the gentle ascent of
the Resia (Reschen–Scheideck Pass, 4,947 feet), from which the
road drops down into that wide and beautiful valley to continue
on its way through Spondigna at the northern foot of the Stelvio
Pass (see p 237) to Merano and Bolzano.

14. North Tyrol, Bavaria and Salzburg

In the Rhine Valley, 15 miles north of Chur, stands Sargans, where the road from Zürich and Walenstadt comes in from the west. A little farther down the Rhine along the northward road leading to Bregenz, Constance, at the far end of its long dull lake, and South Germany, is Buchs, where the road to Feldkirch, the Arlberg and Austria branches off to the right, skirting the tiny mountainous Principality of Liechtenstein, only 25 square miles in area. Coming from Chur you can take the road on the east side of the valley and approach Feldkirch through the picturesque little 'capital', Vaduz, overlooked from a hill above by its princely castle. At Feldkirch you will find the Austrian frontier and a busy railway junction straddling the lines from Switzerland and Germany to Western Austria by the Arlberg railway; beyond, railway, road and an appalling prominence of pylons (if that is the correct collective term) head straight for the barrier of the Vorarlberg mountains ahead, along 15 level miles to Bludenz, an industrial town with an interesting old quarter, where the 18-mile haul to the Arlberg Pass and rail-tunnel begins.

To the north of Bludenz lie the large and attractive area of the Allgäu Alps, a charming district of foothill peaks and valleys shared by Germany and Austria's Bregenzerwald; to the south, between it and the Engadine, the much higher Alps of Rhaetikon, shared between Switzerland and Austria, with Klosters, at the head of the Prätigau valley, which runs east from Landquart on the Chur–Sargans road to the foot of the high Silvretta Group, the chief and last Swiss resort here (see p. 195).

From Bludenz the Arlberg road rises broad, modern and fast in gentle steps up the meadowland and terraces of the Klostertal to Langen (3,990 feet), where the railway enters the six-mile-long tunnel built in 1880–83 at a cost of £1,300,000. Trucks for car transport are available if the pass is blocked by snow in spite of the new 1,130-foot avalanche-gallery near Innerbraz.

Only about a mile beyond Bludenz, the Montafon–Silvretta toll-road forks off into the mountains on the right. This fine, if narrow, mountain road, opened in 1954, is one of two recently constructed bypasses to ease the heavy Arlberg traffic; the other and less interesting, the Hochtannenberg (5,232 feet) runs through the Allgäu ranges to the north through Lech and Schröcken, and was completed a year earlier. The artificially-created Montafon 'pass' (6,666 feet) affords a splendid mountain drive, with numerous finely engineered hairpins biting deep into the northern aspect of the snowy Silvretta Group (Fluchthorn, Piz Buin, Silvrettahorn and their glaciers – see p. 207, lying so close to the Arlberg road, but hardly seen from it. This longer route, forming two sides of a triangle, rejoins the direct Arlberg road at Wiesberg, just short of Landeck at its eastern foot.

From Langen a steeper section climbs to Stuben (4,600 feet), lately grown to a popular ski-centre, and here the fine Flexenpass road (5,775 feet) climbs away to the north to the more famous winter resorts of Zürs and Lech, and so by the Hochtannenberg into the Allgäu.

Only a short bare slope separates Stuben from the Arlberg Saddle (5,912 feet), the watershed between the North and Black Seas, for here the Rosanna rises to flow eastwards down into the Inn. This is the only point on the whole Arlberg road where the scenery grows for a moment even moderately wild and a fleeting impression of a high mountain crossing is evoked.

On the long descent through St Christoph and the still more famous St Anton (4,275 feet) the home and school of Austrian skiing, the forest-covered slopes, immensely steep and high, allow only restricted views, with an occasional brief glimpse of the tops of the Silvretta peaks as the entrances to steep and narrow lateral valleys flit by. Below St Anton, where the railway emerges from its blind passage under the saddle, the valley opens out somewhat, while the road continues to fall steeply through Strengen (3,350 feet). Here wider views are revealed ahead, over the floor of the Inn Valley, still far below, as the descent, by a series of wide curves, brings you down to Landeck (2,670 feet). This is a charming old town with a castle dominating its ravine from a rocky bluff, lofty bridges and ancient coaching hotels, straddling the Rosanna Valley at its confluence with the Inn, which comes racing down from the Engadine through a narrow gateway to the south. To the north rises the Parseierspitze (9,965 feet), the highest in the Northern Limestone Alps.

If you are bound for Italy and the Dolomites, the old traditional road swings away southeastwards over the Resia Pass (see previous chapter) and down the beautiful Adige Valley to Bolzano, with the great wall of the Austrian Alps to the north and the magnificent Ortler Group (see chapter 15) to the south. The new, more direct road over the Timmlsjoch is described below (p. 216).

From Landeck the main Austrian highway runs straight, level and fast along the Inn's broad and lovely valley to Innsbruck, 48 miles to the east. For its whole length it is bounded on the north by the parallel ranges of the Northern Limestone Alps, along whose higher crests runs the Bavarian frontier. The rocky tops immediately bordering the valley are those of the Mieminger Gebirge, separated from the loftier Wetterstein range to its north by the beautiful Gaistal, at whose foot is Leutasch and, still farther north, Mittenwald (3,000 feet), for centuries the seat of the German violin industry.

This beautiful district is reached from the Inn Valley by a road from Zirl, ten miles short of Innsbruck, through charming Seefeld. A little northwest of Mittenwald, where the Loisachtal falls in from the west, lies the considerable joint summer and winter resort of Garmisch-Partenkirchen (2,295 feet) in a pleasant broadening of the Loisach Valley. The road continues northwards to Oberau, from which a road runs through the hill northwest to Oberammergau, whose world-famous decennial Festival is more easily accessible from Munich, 60 miles to the north, through Murnau.

Nine miles along the Inn Valley from Landeck, at Imst, a very attractive road branches northwards through Nassereit, over the pretty Fern Pass (3,970 feet) with fine views of the Wetterstein Range, to the well-known resorts of Lermoos (3,265 feet) and Ehrwald, close to the foot of the huge Zugspitze (9,720 feet; see below). To the northeast the road continues down the upper Loisach Valley to Garmisch-Partenkirchen. Nassereit can also be approached by the pretty shelf-road running along the north side of the Inn Valley from Telfs seven miles beyond Imst on the valley highway and 17 short of Innsbruck.

The main Wetterstein range of fine rock peaks and steep faces (Hochwanner, 9,010 feet, Hochblassen 8,850 feet and the huge Wettersteinwand, 8,143 feet, all providing interesting rock-climbs) runs from Mittenwald in the east to its western culmination in the massive Zugspitze, the highest mountain in Germany, and the only one possessing its own glaciation, though only two-thirds of the peak are in Bavaria, the rest belonging to the Tyrol and therefore Austrian property. This was once a favourite ascent by seven hours of path from Ehrwald, but who would undergo so much sweat and toil when there are now a railway, two aerial ropeways and three ski-lifts from the Bavarian side, while the Austrian ropeway from Ehrwald leaps its cable-length of 3,413 yards to the summit in 17 minutes? The ski-runs from the Ehrwalderkopf shoulder (7,500 feet) on the ropeway down to the valley are magnificent late-winter runs, but strictly for the expert. By whichever way the ascent is made there is a superb panorama from the summit, over the Inntal, beyond the shattered ridges of the bare Wetterstein and Karwendel ranges, to the main chain of the snowy Ötztal, Stubai and Zillertal Alps southwards and eastwards and ringing the far-distant eastern horizon, the Hohe Tauern, dominated by the Grossglockner and Gross Venediger, the highest peaks in the eastern Alps; not to mention the limitless prospect northwards over the Bavarian highlands to the German plain.

There is a lovely day's walking to the north of the Wetterstein range, far from the busy highways, from Partenkirchen by way of charming Ellmau to Mittenwald; and the short excursion from the former resort to the attractive Eibsee, dotted with islands, at the foot of the enormous Zugspitze precipices is well worthwhile.

The Karwendel Ranges, to the east of Mittenwald, house innumerable rocky summits, the highest among which are the Birkkarspitze (9,040 feet), and Oedkarspitze (9,020 feet). The Karwendeltal, from which the Isar issues at Scharnitz, a few miles south of Mittenwald, cuts through the middle of the region, whose rocky summits and great faces are a climber's delight and offer magnificent path-walking among those mighty cliffs; at its eastern end it emerges at the famous Ahornboden (4,585 feet) at the head of the Johannestal, falling to the north and accessible by path just before Hinter Riss in the long Risstal, which runs west from the Achensee to Vorder Riss in the Isar Valley. This grove of more than a thousand maple trees, some of them more than 800 years old, is one of the most beautiful spots in the Alps, with the limestone walls of the Spritzkarspitze and the Gruber (8,730 feet) soaring 4,000 feet to the sky behind them. Indeed the whole two-mile stretch of this valley floor of the Eng is an oasis of loveliness.

From the Ahornboden by way of the Ladiz Alp and the 6,000-foot Ladiz Jöchl, the Lalidern Alp (5,000 feet) can be reached in two and a half hours of magnificent walking among these towering walls of rock. Here you face one of the most impressive sights in the Limestone Alps – the 3,000-foot high precipices of the vertical Lalidererwand (8,577 feet) and Lalidererspitze, whose north ridge wings up to the summit in a single unbroken sweep. There are five 'Grade VI' ('extreme') routes up face and ridge; it need hardly be said that they are only for the élite of the climbing fraternity.

On the other hand, there are perfectly safe paths, high and low crossing the Karwendel complex from end to end, which could occupy and delight the mountain walker for the three to four days' minimum required up to a fortnight, if he cared to loiter and linger. And all this is only four hours – an hour and a

half by car, two and a half on foot – from Munich. Lucky
Bavarians!

It is time, for the moment, to leave the northern side of the
Inn Valley on our eastward progress towards Innsbruck and turn
south seven miles after Imst at the railway-station called Ötztal, to
explore the very different and even greater delights of the main
Alpine chain, some 25 miles away up the truly beautiful valley of
that name. The snowy Austrian Alps may not have the stature
nor the magnificence of form nor the glaciers (here known as
Ferner or *Kees*) the same cataclysmic downthrust displayed by
their cousins in the great western groups, but this is lovely mountain country by any standards.

The Ötztal is the first of three almost parallel valleys running
south into the great Alpine backbone, heavily glaciated on this
side, falling more abruptly on the other into the deep trench of
the Adige valley. The road climbs typically and purposefully for
27 miles up the narrow valley of the Ache, through the small
resorts of Umhausen, Längenfeld and Sölden (4,465 feet: ropeway
to Hoch Sölden, a recently developed ski-centre on a high shelf to
the west) to Zwieselstein (4,830 feet), where the valley divides into
three, the Ventertal, the Gurglertal and a smaller more easterly
offshoot, the Timmlstal into which the latest of the trans-Alpine
motor passes, the fourth highest, finds its way to the Timmlsjoch
(see below).

Vent (6,250 feet) lies some six miles farther up the longest and
most open arm of the valley, at the foot of the magnificent horseshoe of peaks and glaciers which constitute the Ötztal group, and
directly below the Rofkarferner falling steeply from its highest
peak, the 12,380-foot Wildspitze. The ascent of this great mountain, whose summit commands a superb view, is not a difficult
mountaineering effort and is made in four hours from the beautifully situated Breslauer Hut (9,345 feet), three hours up a steep
path, above Vent. In spring it is possible to ski almost to the
summit.

It is quite impossible to enumerate the glorious walks, mountain huts and hospices, glacier passes, high-level skiing tours and

accessible high peaks in this lovely valley and the splendid group of mountains ringing it, from the Gaislachkogel at its northwestern entrance through the Wildspitze, Fluchtkogel (11,530 feet) to the Weisskugel (12,290 feet) at its southern extremity; then swinging due eastwards to the Similaun's fine pyramid (11,835 feet) and back to the northeast in a slightly lower range topped by the Hintere Schwärze (11,920 feet), Kreuzspitze (11,330 feet), Schalfkogel (11,515 feet) and Ramolkogel (11,050 feet), to divide it from the eastern branch, the Gurglertal.

This is a paradise for the mountain-lover in summer and the ski-addict in winter (though, in all fairness, the twain do sometimes meet). For those to whom long uphill walks are barred by physical handicaps or are anathema owing to spiritual ones, the recent opening of a ropeway to the Gaislachkogel (10,105 feet), just southwest of Sölden, has provided a high summit viewpoint from which the splendours of the whole Ötztal chain can be enjoyed without effort. It has also become, in winter, the starting point for several high-level ski-tours as well as of some headlong down-hill runs to the valley.

The neighbouring, much narrower Gurglertal, at whose head rises the 11,405-foot Hochwilde, runs up from Zwieselstein to Ober Gurgl (6,265 feet), at the foot of the Gurgler Ferner, the longest glacier in the area, and is contained on the west by the Ramolkogel chain, separating it from the Ventertal and forming the northeastern arm of the Ötztal horseshoe.

Obergurgl, one of the highest villages in the Tyrol, has become one of the most popular high-Alpine summer and winter ski resorts, its altitude ensuring an abundance of snow, and its many ropeways and ski-lifts (Hohe Mutt, 8,735 feet, Gaisberg and the rest) providing every degree of difficulty for beginner and expert alike.

In summer, the Karlsruhe Hut (9,460 feet), halfway up the Gurgl Glacier, and the Ramol Haus (10,105 feet) are the starting points for climbs and high passes in the group, the most attractive of the latter being the eight-hour crossing of the Ramoljoch (10,480 feet) to Vent, with wonderful views of all the surrounding mountains and especially of the majestic Wildspitze across the valley on the descent.

As recently as 1969 a new motor road was added to the long-existing 18 trans-Alpine passes which cross saddles on the true backbone at the Timmlsjoch (Passo di Rombo, 8,215 feet). From Zwieselstein it penetrates the Gurglertal as far as Unter Gurgl (5,890 feet), from which point eight finely-engineered miles of completely new road have been thrust up the mountainside to the east to reach the saddle, the mule track over which into Italy has been used for centuries. An entirely new habitation, the last on the Austrian side, consisting of a cluster of hotels, has been built at about 7,200 feet and named Hoch Gurgl. Unlike most of the other great passes, its higher reaches are scenically somewhat uninteresting and the view from the saddle itself is limited, but those on the lower approaches are ample compensation. To the south the road winds down the huge Italian slope, 6,000 feet high, for ten miles, through the villages of Corvara and Moso to S. Leonardo (2,250 feet) the well-known resort in South Tyrol's Val Passeria, from which it is only another 12 miles to Merano.

The opening of this major pass has provided a direct route from central Switzerland over the Arlberg to Landeck and on to Bolzano, the Dolomites and the Venetian plain, short-circuiting by many miles the old Reschen–Scheideck–Adige détour, or the even longer one through Innsbruck and over the Brenner (see below).

Returning to the main Landeck–Innsbruck highway, at Kematen, near Zirl, the Sellraintal, running up through the mountains to the south almost parallel with the Inn Valley, leads through Gries and St Sigmund to Kühtai (6,450 feet), in winter a small ski resort, from which there are short cuts over lofty tracks for walkers from Innsbruck to the Ötztal, to Umhausen or down the Ochsengartental to Ötz. From Zirl to Innsbruck is ten miles along the main valley.

For Innsbruck itself (1,885 feet) with its colonnades, churches and towers, its monuments and balconies, its broad modern shopping streets, its concert halls and theatres, its swift flowing river spanned by bridges old and new, all backed by the splendid mountain range which towers immediately above them all, the established guide-books are the proper mentors. But for lovers of the wider mountain scene, the Hafelkar and Patscherkofel (7,265 feet), splendidly provided with cable-railways, will offer irresistible attractions, with their superb views over city, hill and vale. (For those who do not like the bustle and turmoil of even so lovely an example as Innsbruck, Igls, at the foot of the Patscherkofel only six miles away, is a charming resort set in pleasant meadows and backed by eminently walkable woods.) And if you have not the time or inclination to visit the high places, at least drive or take the old funicular up to the Hungerburg shelf, to look down on the clustered city spread like a map across the plain below and out beyond into the gentle green re-entrant, dominated by the distant rock-pyramid of the Serles, down which the Brenner falls from its historic saddle. Up on that delightful shelf, only a few hundred feet above the busy streets, there are two excellent restaurants from whose terraces the diner, as he consumes a first-class meal, can watch the lights flicker into chains of diamonds in the deepening gloom below, as the summer dusk fades out on the wooded slopes and the faint glow dies from the topmost rocks of the Serles and Habicht far away to the south. It is a very pleasant way of spending an Innsbruck evening, and in high summer it will be much cooler up there than in the hotel dining-room or any of the restaurants bordering the hot, paved streets of the town.

South of the city the great modern motorway over the low and easy but traffic-congested Brenner Pass (4,495 feet) climbs into the hills by great swinging bends and over the beautifully carved Europabrücke viaduct on its way to Vipiteno (formerly Sterzing), beyond the Alpine watershed in Italy. Vipiteno lies just off the main road and it is worth the detour to walk along its beautifully preserved medieval high street.

At Schönberg (3,310 feet), five miles along the ascent, the road to the lovely Stubaital, the second of the parallel valleys diving south into the main range, branches off to the right and having first negotiated a low spur, then ascends gently along the wide, level floor of that hanging valley for ten miles, through Fulpmes,

Neustift, its chief village, to Ranalt, at its lovely head, where the road (narrow and mountainous beyond Neustift) peters out at the foot of the great wall and the mule-tracks to the climbers' club huts which serve its snowy peaks and their glaciers begin.

The main ridge running due west to east throws up a number of summits of 11,000 feet and more, from the Schaufelspitze at its western end to the Wilde Freiger at the other. Almost at its centre rises its highest peak, the 11,520-foot Zuckerhütl, a most rewarding and not difficult climb of about five hours, reached from a number of club huts in the area (Dresdner, 7,570 feet, Nürnberger, 7,555 feet, and several others) with splendid views southwards over the South Tyrol valleys to the Ortler group and the Dolomites. None of the ascents in the range is particularly difficult and there are a number of splendid high-glacier tours from one hut to another. Valley walks abound in this quiet and unspoiled fold in the hills.

A very different and far stiffer proposition are the Kalkkögel (highest peak 9,000 feet), whose savage rock-teeth lift halfway along the western side of the valley and are approached up the Schlickertal from Fulpmes. These are undertakings for expert rock climbers only.

At the eastern entrance to the valley, above Neder, rises the shapely rock-pyramid of the Serles (8,920 feet), such a prominent feature of the Innsbruck skyline, climbed from here or from Medratz on the Brenner road without much difficulty. Farther up the valley's eastern containing range the isolated Habicht, Innsbruck's other showpiece, rises to 10,760 feet, best ascended from the 7,740-foot Innsbrucker Hut above Moser in the next valley to the east, the Gschnitztal, to which long, high passes lead over from Neustift.

Beyond Innsbruck, the Inn takes a slightly more northeasterly course through Hall, Jenbach and Rattenberg till at Wörgl, an important road and rail-junction, it turns sharply northeastwards and forces a passage through the defences of the Northern Range – whose main axis still continues resolutely eastwards – and, broadening out rapidly, runs on down into the German plain at

Rosenheim. This part of its course forms the boundary between North Tyrol and the province of Salzburg.

However, long before this, at Jenbach, 20 miles to the east of Innsbruck, the third long Alpine valley opens up to the south, the Zillertal, at first broad and fertile for 15 miles till beyond Zell am Ziller. Here a lateral valley, the Gerlosertal, strikes off eastwards to Gerlos (4,070 feet), the summer and winter resort which gives it its name, and a track leads on over the Gerlos Pass (4,875 feet) to Wald in the Pinzgau (see p. 258).

The Zillertal now contracts for the five miles to Mayrhofen, its chief village and the terminus of the railway, where the valley splits up into four arms, the southwestern being the immensely long Zemmtal, running for miles at the feet of the main Zillertal Alps to its south, with the shorter parallel range of the Olperer (11,415 feet)–Riffler group between it and the Tuxertal to the west; while to the east the Zillergrund runs up to the foot of the Reichenspitz (10,845 feet) – Wildgerlos comb, projecting separately to the north from the main group and the fine Stilluptal, parallel with it to the south, rising to the Gross Löffler, towards the eastern end of the main group, which continues eastwards, dividing Austria from Italy, on a slightly lower lever, but still thrusting up such summits as the Raudhkofel (10,670 feet) and the Dreiecker.

The main Zillertal range, about ten miles long, rises to its greatest height in the Hochfeiler (11,540 feet) and the Mösele (11,435 feet) at its western end, and the Schwarzenstein (11,055 feet) and Gross Löffler (11,095 feet) to the east. As in the Ötztal and Stubai, there are numerous huts from which the climbs and glacier crossings in the area may be made, most of them of no great difficulty; and there is walking at the lower levels to delight the heart. The mountains here, on the frontier ridge between North and South Tyrol (Italy) naturally command superlative views both north and south. They are also climbed from what, before the transfer of South Tyrol to Italy, used to be the Ahrntal, but is now the Val Aurina, on the Italian side, under the southern wall of the Zillertal peaks. This is a very beautiful and unspoiled valley 15 miles long, rich in flowers, and ideal walking country (see p. 259).

It may perhaps be felt that I have paid very sketchy attention to the country lying to the north of the limestone range, with its pleasant hills, valleys, and lakes, south of Munich. The following brief survey may make good the deficiency to some extent, though it is impossible to do justice to all the sub-Alpine areas in a relatively short book about the Alps.

Suffice it to say that between Munich and Mittenwald lie a number of pleasant lakes – the Starnberger, Wurmser, Walchen, the charming Tégernsee and Schliersee, the Kochelsee and, far to the east beyond the Inn gap, the very large Chiemsee. South of the Austrian frontier I have already mentioned the long Risstal corridor, running from the Isar Valley along the northern flank of the Karwendel complex to Pertisau at the southern end of the Achensee, just north of Jenbach, a lovely green pasture facing the Sonnengebirge and with beautiful views up the six-mile-long lake, as well as southwards across the Inn Valley to the Zillertal peaks.

The Northern Limestone Range continues due eastwards beyond the Inn's break-through at Kufstein, through the rocky Loferer Steinberge, the Steinerne Meer and the Tennengebirge, forming the Bavarian–Austrian frontier, to the Dachstein Group, south of the Salzkammergut; then losing height gradually to Liezen in the fine valley of the Ober-Enns. Just to the east between Admont and Hieflau are the fine gorges and rapids 12 miles long, made famous by canoe experts, of a section of the Enns known as the Gesäuse (Styria).

This tremendous defile, with its raging waters, is flanked on either side by steep rocky mountains, to the north the Grosse Buchstein (7,295 feet), to the south by a chain containing the Planspitze, Hochtor (7,780 feet), Oedstein (7,660 feet) and Reichenstein. These peaks, seen from the lovely Johnsbachtal valley at their feet, form one of the most impressive and varied of the lower Alpine ranges. They also constitute the climbing-ground in which most of the great Austrian alpinists learned their first lessons on difficult rock. For here there are routes of every degree of difficulty, from the Hochtor–Oedstein ridge-traverse entailing nothing more than Grade II ('moderate') in its several hours of climbing delights, to such classical Grade IV (very difficult) routes as the famous northwest ridge of the Oedstein. The Johnsbachtal paths can be recommended to all walkers in search of glorious scenery.

Farther east, the range declines gradually in height along the north side of the Mürrental, past Leoben and Bruck an der Mur to the north of Graz, until they peter out into the delightful wooded hills of the Wienerwald 20 miles to the west of Vienna, where the city-dwellers can still find comparative peace and quiet along a network of footpaths which can be combined to provide delightful walking tours covering several days, with more than 40 huts.

Even here the Alps are not quite finished with. On several craggy outcrops serious rock-climbers pursue their training for more taxing assignments and novices come to learn their craft and win their spurs. The best known of these practice grounds is the Peilstein, on which there are routes ranging from 'moderates' suitable for novices to those involving the expert briefly in 'severe' difficulties – on one of which an extremely airy traverse has been appropriately decorated with a notice stolen from a Vienna tram car – *'Nicht hinausehnen'* – 'Don't lean out'. Here again, many a great Austrian climber has made his first acquaintance with rocky joys before moving on to the Gesäuse.

Returning to the Wörgl–Kufstein bend of the Inn and a little to the southeast of it, the Alps of Kitzbühel extend eastwards through that famous resort to St Johann in Tyrol, consisting of the Hintere and Vordere Kaiser (Kaisergebirge) and the minor range separating the areas from the upper valley of the Salzach to the south. To the northwest of St Johann lies Lofer, at the foot of the rocky comb of the Loferer Steinberge, on the Bavarian–Austrian frontier. The main feature is, however, the magnificent rocky range of the Wilde Kaiser, seen to great advantage from the Wörgl–St Johann road at its feet, from the Schwarzsee near

Kitzbühel and all high vantage points in its neighbourhood, such
as the Gross Rettenstein (7,745 feet) to its south, which offers a tre-
mendous view over the Hohe Tauern to the south, the Zillertal
Alps to the west and all the northern ranges beyond the Inn
Valley. Another famous and much lower viewpoint is the Hohe
Salve (5,985 feet) to the north of Hopfgarten on the Wörgl–
Kitzbühel road.

The Wilde Kaiser itself runs for nearly ten miles from Kufstein
to St Johann and is an extraordinary jumble of savage rock towers
and vertical walls supporting them. Its cliffs and gulleys are those
among which, after the first war, the Munich school of young
climbers pioneered a new climbing technique – with artificial aids
since universally adopted and developed – and mastered faces and
ridges, such as the Fleischbank's tremendous east face, previously
considered impossible. It has since become the 'great Munich
climbing ground', where during summer weekends every climber
in the city from the novice to the 'extremist' can be found on his
appropriate route – and he can be at its starting point in two and
a half hours from the city centre.

The range is equally attractive for walkers, the walk through
the Kaisertal at its heart, between the Hintere and Vordere Kaiser,
being one of the most enjoyable in the Limestone Alps. Artificially
protected club-paths also cross the main ridge at a number of
places, and there are several huts for rest and refreshment. The
best approach is from Ellmau (2,700 feet) on the Wörgl–St
Johann road by the great central re-entrant of the Ellmauer Tor.
The summits are all about 7,000 feet high, the Ellmauer Halt-
spitze (7,690 feet) being the local monarch in this Kaiserdom.

To the northeast of the Kitzbühel Alps, sharing with Austria the
frontier combs of the Loferer Steinberge and the Steinerne Meer,
a southern tongue of Bavaria licks southwards deep into the ridge
they crown; at its northern base are the resorts of Reichenhall and
Traunstein (Chiemsee), while its highest peak is the sharp, rocky
Watzmann. The main centre in this attractive mountain region is
Berchtesgaden (1,875 feet), where beside the natural delights of
rugged peaks and one of the most beautiful lakes on earth, the

Königssee, some man-made fantasies of one of the least prepossessing human beings ever seen on its face are still available for inspection by those in pursuit of the macabre – or should I say eerie?

The little town is beautifully situated, looking out on an impressive ring of rock peaks, from the Hohe Göll (8,265 feet) round to the jagged mass of the Grosser and Kleiner Watzmann (8,710 feet), their modest altitude belied by the low level from which you look up at them. 'The Environs', to quote the insatiable compiler of the best guide-books ever published, 'afford an almost inexhaustible variety of beautiful walks and excursions.'

The one nobody should miss is that to the narrow five-mile-long Königssee, from whose dark green waters the grey mountains on either side rise almost sheer for 6,000 feet. The head of the lake, round whose precipitous edges there are paths, is only three miles from Berchtesgaden. The best way, however, to enjoy this true marvel of nature is to make the journey by boat to St Bartholomä, a little promontory graced by a chapel with twin towers, a small, trim green lawn at the foot of the Watzmann's grim, grey precipices. This is altogether a scene of rare and quiet loveliness. There is, moreover, another smaller lake of great beauty not a mile to the south of the Königssee's southern tip, separated from it by a low, barren ridge – the Obersee, with huge limestone cliffs soaring thousands of feet above it, and a fine backward view of the Watzmann's massive flank.

This triple-headed peak (8,710 feet) can be ascended from its northern side by good paths starting from Ilsank, three miles from Berchtesgaden or from the Ramsau – a particularly lovely valley a mile or two farther on, well worth a visit on its own account for the wonderful contrast between its luxuriant foliation and the gloomy grey cliffs surrounding it. The long grind of seven or eight hours can be broken at the Watzmann Haus (6,330 feet). The views from the summit ridges over the lakes sheer below, southwards to the Hohe Tauern, north to the wide Bavarian plain and the whole Salzkammergut lake-district to the east are certainly worth the effort. The mountain's eastern precipices house a number of 'extreme' climbing routes, the scene of hair-raising achievements in winter as well as summer conditions and, inevitably, of a number of grizzly tragedies.

To the south of the lakes rises the extraordinary jumble of stone, running up to 8,700 feet in the Schönfeldspitze, aptly named the Steinerne Meer and forming the frontier ridge between Bavaria and the Austrian Tyrol. It is approached by tracks from St Bartholomä or the Sallet Alp which divides the Königssee from the Obersee. Experienced mountain ramblers can traverse this huge rock plateau, eight miles by three, by a number of passes, the best being by way of the Ramseider Saddle (6,895 feet) on which stands one of several huts, the Riemann Haus, and down a somewhat vertiginous path to the charming little resort of Alm (2,600 feet), four miles east of Saalfelden, one of the popular skiing centres in the Pinzgau on the main road and rail route from St Johann to Zell am See (see chapter 16). This traverse should only be undertaken in settled weather, for in misty conditions there is a serious danger of losing the way.

To the east of the Berchtesgaden area the Bavarian–Austrian frontier runs sharply back from south to north, with Salzburg and the Salzkammergut close at hand to the east beyond it. Salzburg, the home of Mozart and music, an enchanting city clustering up and down wooded spurs and looking out across the boulders of the stony Salzach to the green ridges of its own lovely province, needs no further description.

The celebrated lake district of the Salzkammergut contains a dozen charming lakes in pockets between the relatively low ridges of the Höllengebirge, the Todtes Gebirge and, to the south, close beyond the most beautiful of them all (the Hallstatter See), the much loftier and truly mountainous Dachstein–Kammergebirge ridge, which separates the Salzkammergut from the upper course of the Enns Valley between Bischofstein and Admont (see p. 220). The many pretty lakes include the Attersee and Wolfgang See, famous for an operettic hostelry, between Salzburg and the resort of Ischl; the Traunsee further to the northeast, and other smaller ones, the whole district being extremely picturesque, with a lovely sub-Alpine flavour all its own. The long plateau-like tract of the

Höllengebirge, eight miles long, only 6,000 feet high and accessible by the Feuerkogel railway, is ideal, almost level, walking country on well made footpaths with lovely views over the lakes. (Memories of Julie Andrews and the children in *The Sound of Music*.)

Hallstatt's deep-set fjord-like lake offers equally attractive walking on its forest covered slopes, as well as good, stiff climbs in the Dachstein Group. Behind Hallstatt itself a narrow ravine, the Salzbergtal, has over a number of years yielded the secrets of the civilisation known as the Hallstatt Age (900–390 B.C.) which reached its peak when the Bronze Age passed over into the Iron. A few of the finds are in the local museum, but the bulk of them have gone to Vienna.

The Dachstein (9,815 feet), higher than the Zugspitze and the second highest in the Northern Limestone Alps after Landeck's Parseierspitze (9,965 feet), can now be ascended by ropeway from its southern foot. The view extends as far as Terglou (Triglav, 9,400 feet) in Jugoslavia (see p. 268). None the less, the southern faces of the Torstein, Mitterspitz, the Dachstein itself and the Dirndl, all over 9,000 feet high, remain favourite sites for Grade IV (very difficult) climbing. This is a splendid group of rock peaks, and a fine, safe footpath runs the whole length of its three-mile southern wall.

The lower ranges to the east have already received attention and it is time to return far to the west to the lovely sectors to the south of the main Alpine chain, bypassed in our eastward rush.

15. South of the Backbone: 1. From Aosta to the Ortler

Before moving south, it may be useful to take a look, for the motorist's benefit, at the 19 major passes and two purely road tunnels across the main spine of the Alps from the temperate lands to their west and north to the sunshine and softness of the southland plains. This may perhaps also help to place in their proper perspective the two isolated mountain masses south of the main range and the sub-Alpine lake areas still farther south.

1. From south-west to east, the first, the Colle di Tenda (4,331 feet: perhaps this one is more accurately from one sun-drenched southland to another) links Nice with Turin and has already been described (p. 86).
2. The next to the north, the Col de Larche (6,545 feet) is an easy passage from Guillestre and Barcelonnette in the Cottians (chapter 7), joining the Tenda route at Cuneo. It provides the most direct link between the Rhône Valley, south of Valence, and the Plain of Piedmont and Turin.
3. Thirty miles farther north, the Mont Genèvre (6,100 feet), easiest and most historic of these western passages since Roman times, links Briançon with Turin and, by use of the associated Lautaret Pass (chapter 6) provides the shortest journey (in mileage) from Lyon and central France through Grenoble to northern Italy.
4. Less direct, but in the end little, if any, longer in terms of time, because it is a main European highway with long sections of fast valley road to the foot of its single pass, the Mont Cenis

(6,834 feet) links the same two areas, eventually sharing the last 30 miles to Turin with the Mont Genèvre route. This is one of the scenically more beautiful passes and worth motoring for that reason alone (see chapter 7).

5. Branching northeastwards from the Mont Cenis route at St Pierre d'Albigny, just short of Albertville, the Petit St Bernard (7,178 feet) crosses the watershed between the Isère in France and the Dora Baltsea in Italy, falling into the latter's valley at Pré St Didier, a mile or two below Courmayeur (chapters 8 and 15). Even more beautiful, especially on its eastern side.

6. At Aosta, in the Dora's great valley, the Great St Bernard (8,110 feet) falls in from the north having climbed over the backbone from Martigny in the Rhône Valley (see chapter 10). The new tunnel under the summit is not truly a trans-Alpine tunnel but a bypass of the last 1,000 feet of the old road, which have still to be driven if the world-famous monastery at the top is to be visited. Except on its southern side, this is scenically a rather grim road for long stretches of the way. Here also, through Entrèves and Courmayeur, the seven-mile-long Chamonix tunnel emerges to join the motorway down to Aosta and Turin (see p. 122).

7. Thirty miles to the east, the Simplon (6,594 feet) is the next motorable pass, linking the eastern end of the Rhône Valley and its connection with the Oberland to Domodossola, Lago Maggiore and Milan. This is a glorious road in every way, traversing superb scenery and one of the truly 'great' passes (see chapter 11).

8. The next to the east, another of the 'greats', is the St Gotthard (6,926 feet), the major north–south link between central Switzerland, Lucerne and, down the long Ticino road, to Lugano and Milan. Scenically wonderful, if less liberally supplied with mighty snow peaks. The traffic is usually extremely heavy and is swelled by the outflow over the next two passes on its southern end (chapter 12).

9. The Lukmanier (6,289 feet) is the shortest link between the western end of the Upper Rhine Valley, at Disentis, and Milan,

by way of Biasca in the Ticino where it joins the St Gotthard (chapter 12).

10. The San Bernardino (6,768 feet) provides a useful link between the eastern end of the Upper Rhine Valley at Chur, and the same region, joining the Gotthard route still farther down at Bellinzona (chapter 12).

11. The Splügen (6,930 feet) affords the shortest link between Chur and Milan by way of Chiavenna and the Lake Como area, the main highway bypassing the lake and Como itself to the east through Varenna and Lecco (chapters 13 and 15).

None of the three above passes, attractive as they all are, lie close to great peaks, though they all command view of the somewhat retiring Rheinwald Group which is especially well seen from the Splügen.

12. The Maloja (6,000 feet) provides the most direct route from Austria (Innsbruck–Landeck–Engadine) to the Italian lakes and Milan. Scenically lovely, especially the Upper Engadine section of the true pass from St Moritz to Maloja and the descent through the Bregaglia Valley to Chiavenna, where it joins the Splügen at its southern foot (chapter 15).

13. The Bernina (7,644 feet) linking the Upper Engadine with the Valtellina at Tirano disperses its considerable traffic; westwards to join the previous route at Colico, just south of Chiavenna; southwards over the little Aprica to Edolo, Iseo and Brescia; or eastwards over the Aprica and Tonale to Bolzano and the Dolomites, whence a number of roads offer outlets southwards to Brescia, Lake Garda, Belluno in the Venetian Alps, Venice or Trieste (see chapters 13 and 15).

14. The unexciting Ofen (7,070 feet) is a useful link between the Engadine and the Adige, Bolzano and the Dolomites, otherwise it is of minor importance.

15. The Resia (4,947 feet) is of far greater importance, since it still provides the least mountainous main route from eastern Switzerland over the Arlberg to the same points in South Tyrol and beyond, into the Italian plain (chapters 14 and 15).

16. The shorter but much loftier route over the Timmlsjoch

(8,213 feet), the latest addition to the major trans-Alpine passes (1969), helps to syphon off some of the heavy traffic from the traditional main road over the Resia (chapter 14).

17. The Brenner (4,495 feet), the lowest, easiest and most used crossing from north to south Europe throughout history, has in recent times become increasingly traffic-jammed, in spite of the modernisation of the old road into a motor highway. The opening of the Timmlsjoch to its west and the new Felber–Tauern road tunnel between Mittersill and Matrei should have helped to ease the situation to some extent (chapter 14).

This second trans-Alpine road tunnel (opened in 1967) at about the 5,000-foot level provides a fast 'lowland' link between Kitzbühl, points along the Inn Valley to its west and north and Lienz, a northern gateway to the Dolomites.

18. Only a few miles to its east, the Grossglockner (8,212 feet), the most easterly of the truly 'great' passes and the fifth highest, has for years past taken not only the immense daily sightseeing coach traffic but that passing through from Munich via Kufstein and St Johann, as well as that from Salzburg over the little 'Steinpass' through Lofer, Saalfelden and Zell am See to its northern foot. The opening of the neighbouring tunnel should greatly relieve the congestion. The pass is scenically magnificent, and even more so the *cul de sac* spur road it throws out to the Franz Joseph's Höhe above the Glockner glaciers (chapter 18).

19. The remaining 'backbone' pass, 20 miles to the east, the Radstadter Tauern–Katschberg (5,334 feet): Salzburg–Lueg 'Pass'–Bischofshofen, Radstadt, Mauterndorf) remains a steep, difficult and unattractive road over the Niedere Tauern range to Carinthia (see chapter 17); the provision of the two routes just described has rendered it of less importance than ever. To the east of the Tauern there are eight minor passages through the diminishing range, none of them over 4,500 feet high and none of them sufficiently important to be included in the list.

.　.　.　.　.

Such are the great road arteries leading down into the wide arc of territory at the foot of the immense Alpine wall, the sub-alpine belt of foothills, lakes, and occasionally isolated high groups of peaks, lying between it and the great plain of Northern Italy; a belt varying in depth from less than 30 to 60 miles.

The valleys running up into the Cottians and the Graians to the west of Turin have already been examined (chapter 7). As you drive down the Dora Valley highway from Aosta to Châtillon, Ivrea and Turin, there are several beautiful valleys running up into the great Pennine barrier to the north, with resorts in them from which the mountain lover can find walks, short and long, of the most delectable kind, as well as mountaineering among the great peaks at their head. (Skiing, of course, in winter and from some of them in summer too.)

The first, the long and lovely Valpelline, branches northeast not far out of Aosta on the road northwards to the Great St Bernard and bites deep into the main chain of the Pennines for 20 miles almost to the foot of the Dent d'Hérens (13,715 feet) and the Matterhorn. This is the valley of the Buthier and its main villages are Oyace, Bionaz and, at its far end, Prarayé (6,538 feet), in a most beautiful setting of grand mountains, with the Rifugio Aosta (9,350 feet) four hours farther on above it. There are high passes from the valley to Breuil (Cervinia) at the south foot of the Matterhorn in the next valley; to the Val de Bagnes (see p. 150); to Arolla and Ferpècle by the Col des Bouquetins (11,214 feet); and the long, magnificent glacier tour over the 11,687-foot Col de Valpelline to the Schönbuhl Hut (p. 153) and Zermatt.

The second, and most famous, leaves the valley road to the flourishing resort of Châtillon-St Vincent and runs due north for 15 miles up the historic Val Tournanche through the village of that name – from which Carrel fought his losing battle against Whymper for the conquest of the Matterhorn in 1865 – to what was once the picturesque huddle of châlets known as Breuil (6,575 feet) at the south foot of the great peak. The historic hamlet has been transformed, in the name of progress and profits, to a hideous eyesore of tall concrete high-rise hotels and renamed Cervinia in honour of Il Cervino, as the Italians call the mountain.

Ropeways run to Furggen (11,360 feet) high up at the base of the Matterhorn's towering precipices, and to Plan Rosa (11,314 feet), the huge snow-plateau at the foot of the Breithorn, crowded in summer and winter with skiers. The glacier crossing of the Theodule Pass (10,899 feet), that traditional trade route between Zermatt and Breuil, is thus shortened to next to nothing by ropeways looping up either side. The walks in and around the valley are glorious, with the blunt and rocky southern aspect of the great peak dominating everything. And if half an hour's stroll is your limit, do not fail to visit the little green tarn among the pines just off the road outside the town, an ideal spot for reflection and reflections; it alone would, I think, justify the journey up the valley. The chief snags about the road from Châtillon to Cervinia are its narrowness and the fact that in the high season it is jammed bonnet to tail with 40-seater monsters bringing tourists up from the plains on day-trips.

At Verres, ten miles down the valley from Châtillon, a third attractive valley, the Val d'Ayas, runs up to Champoluc (5,151 feet) and St Jacques, pleasant summer resorts at the foot of the Breithorn (13,685 feet), well equipped with a ropeway and ski-lifts for winter sports. The high glacier crossings to Zermatt have been described in chapter 10.

Still farther down the main valley, at Pont St Martin, an even more lovely fourth lateral valley nearly 25 miles long, the Val di Gressoney, passes through the small resorts of Issime and Champsil to Gressoney St Jean and Gressoney La Trinité, beautifully situated at the foot of the Lys glacier falling from the Lyskamm (14,889 feet). The resorts are equally frequented in summer and winter and there is a ropeway under construction (1973) from La Trinité up to the skiing slopes at 10,000 feet on the Punta dei Salati, as well as ski-lifts to the neighbouring Punta Jolanda and to the Weissmatten runs above St Jean. There are fine high walking passes to Alagna in the Val Sesia to the east.

Just short of Pont St Martin, at Bard, a short road runs westwards to the small Graian resort of Champorcher (4,682 feet) from which a fine bridle-path leads over the Finestra de Champorcher (9,311 feet) to Cogne (see chapter 7).

(Owing to these northern valleys having once belonged to the Franconian Empire, the French language still lingers on in them.)

At Ivrea, 20 miles short of Turin by *autostrada*, the main road to the east through the foothills to Biella, Borgomanero and Sesto Calende at the foot of Lago Maggiore winds away along the lower slopes on a kind of shelf, with wide views over the plains, to Biella, a large town in which the work of Vittorio Sella, the great Alpine photographer, is commemorated in a museum (see p. 77).

At Borgomanero a road up the long and lovely Val Sesia branches off northwards for 23 miles through Mollia to Alagna Sesia (3,907 feet), a summer and winter resort charmingly situated at the base of Monte Rosa's southeast bastion, the Punta Gnifetti (14,965 feet). Here, as everywhere, there are high ropeways and ski-lifts and in summer a fine and easy walking pass over the Col d'Olen back to Gressoney.

Five miles beyond Borgomanero we are at the foot of Lago Maggiore and join the main Simplon road from Switzerland to Milan at Arona, a few miles from Sesto Calende, where the 45-mile *autostrada* to Milan begins.

In chapter 12 our north–south journey from the Appenzell to the Ticino brought us to the Italian frontier at Brissago, half-way down the west shore of Lago Maggiore. From there the road southwards, skirting the lower half of the lake, twisting in and out of its little bays and round its small rocky promontories, is a long chain of pleasing prospects, but being far too narrow for the prodigious traffic it has to take, vile to drive. (This stricture applies generally to all the main coastal roads round Maggiore and Como, which is a pity, for the scenery is beautiful.) Passing through the oleander- and verbena-scented Intra-Verbania region – it would be tedious to remark every time that these lakeside resorts are lovely, though terribly over-populated – at Baveno the road takes a sharp-angled eastward turn along the southern arm of the lake.

Here, Domodossola and the foot of the Simplon are only 20

miles away to the northwest along a fast valley highway. Just short of Domodossola the exciting mountain road up the Val Anzasca climbs away up the beautiful 25 miles of that valley to Macugnaga (4,350 feet), the popular summer-and-winter-sports resort in a high hanging valley at the base of Monte Rosa's enormous southeastern precipices – one of the great sights in the Alps, magnificently seen by taking the chair lift to Belvedère at their very feet. Mention has already been made of the great walk over the Monte Moro pass by way of the Alp Bill to the Saas valley in Switzerland (p. 172). There are shorter walks, scrambles and climbs of no great difficulty on both sides of the Macugnaga valley in summer, and the scenery is everywhere glorious. The surrounding peaks and classic glacier crossings to Zermatt and Saas have been dealt with in chapter 10.

From Baveno the lakeside road continues through tourist-swamped Stresa – whose view to the north up the lake, with the Borromean islands, Isola Bella and Pescatori in the foreground, has proved its fortune and its ruin – and then through the almost unbroken built-up area of Lesa, Meina and Arona to Sesto Calende at the foot of the lake. The Stresa view, by the way, is infinitely more enjoyable from the quietude of the lovely road winding just behind it, which will, in a few miles, bring you to Monte Mottarone (4,890 feet), one of the classic viewpoints south of the Alps, whose enormous prospect over lake and mountain swings round from Monte Rosa, in the ascendant, to the remote Bernina and Ortler in a gorgeous arc and back over the plain of Lombardy.

If you turn west at Arona as far as Borgomanero on the road to Biella already mentioned and then turn north again you will come to the charming little lake of Orta, with its wooded promontory projecting into its quiet waters; the road leads on back to Baveno, from which the visit can equally well be made.

If you are not bound for Milan and the plains, but eastwards to the foothills and, beyond Como, into the mountains again, the main road strikes off at Sesto Calende and leads on the level to the industrial city of Varese, on a small lake of its own. Industrialised as it is and excessively hot, it still commands a lovely, if distant, view of Monte Rosa by morning light and, on a hill a mile or two outside the city, a unique flower garden of rare beauty. From Varese to Como is less than 20 miles.

Como itself – the approach from the Gotthard by way of the Ticino and Lugano has been described above in chapter 12 – is low-lying, hemmed in by its hills, exceedingly stuffy, rather ugly and prone to sudden appalling thunderstorms. Its narrow two-pronged lake, however, so different in character from Maggiore, is very beautiful, and along the 30 miles of its west shore lie a dozen famous and lovely resorts – Cernobbio, Lenno, Cadenabbia and Menaggio among them. The best-known on the east shore is beautiful Bellagio, beloved of honeymooners, reached by less frequented roads on that side of the lake or by ferry from Cadenabbia.

At the northern end of the lake, at Colico, two important Alpine roads diverge. The one to the north reaches Chiavenna in another 15 miles and there the Splügen and Maloja passes fall in from Splügen and Thusis due north and the Engadine to the northeast (see chapter 13). The other runs due east from Colico for 40 miles up the deep trench of the Valtellina, the valley of the Adda, through Sondrio (for Chiesa in the Val Malenco see p. 202) to Tirano at the southern foot of the Bernina Pass. That magnificent road crosses the Swiss frontier only a mile away to the north at Campocologno, ascends gently past the blue lakelet of Le Prese to Poschiavo (3,315 feet) and then climbs, twisting and writhing its way up the enormous southern flank of the Alps, through La Rösa (6,162 feet) to the summit at 7,644 feet (see p. 206).

Beyond Tirano the Adda Valley contracts gradually as it swings northwards and rises steadily in steepening steps for another 25 miles to the large resort of Bormio (4,020 feet), at the foot of the Stelvio Pass which leaps across the huge ridges of the isolated Ortler Group ahead, separated from the main Ötztal–Zillertal–Tauern 'backbone' farther north by the deep score of the Adige Valley.

Before exploring this splendid mountain complex and the incomparable road which slashes its way along its western fringe, it is necessary to mention a number of passes, major and minor, relevant to communications in the area, between it and the main Alpine area and with the Dolomites to the northeast.

At Tresenda, just short of Tirano, the gentle Aprica (3,875 feet) runs east to Edolo, the road beyond which connects at Ponte di Legno with the Tonale Pass (6,181 feet), a lovely road skirting the western feet of the Adamello–Presanella massif (11,694 feet), another isolated group south of the Ortler, and the last high peaks north of the Italian plain. This in turn gives access, by way of a long tedious valley road and the low Mendola Pass (4,475 feet), to Bolzano, the Brenner 30 miles to its north and the Dolomite region close at hand to its east. While from Bormio the high and difficult Gavia (8,604 feet) swings back south through the Baths of Santa Caterina (5,700 feet) whose neighbourhood has a lovely view of the southern summits of the Ortler range – particularly the 11,818-foot Tresero – to join the Tonale at Ponte di Legno. Back at Edolo again the long valley road runs south through the Val Camonica, past the pretty jade-green Lago d'Iseo (620 feet) to Brescia on the Milan–Verona–Venice *autostrada*.

The Ortler Group is one of the grandest and most beautiful in the Alps. Its main range stretches for some 20 miles from above Bormio through the Cristallospitze, Schneeglocke, Eiskögele, Gran Zebru, Königsspitze and Suldenspitze, with the enormous bulk of the Ortler itself (12,800 feet) and its cascading glaciers thrust out as a separate bastion to the north, to Monte Cevedale (Zufallspitze). (Here, as in the Dolomites, after long usage when the whole territory was Austrian and German-speaking, I find myself unable to adopt *all* the Italianised version of mountain names I have known since childhood by their originals, which are mainly retained to this day by the Austro-German fraternity of climbers and mountain lovers.) At this point the range divides, the eastern arm continuing through a number of slightly lower summits to the Zufrittspitze (11,170 feet) above Gand in the Martelltal (see below); while the other arm is thrust southwards and eventually westwards in a beautiful curve through the Punta della Mare to the Tresero above Sta Caterina in the Val Furva. Nearly all the peaks named are 12,000 feet or more high.

Half a dozen valleys run up to the foot of the heavily glaciated peaks, and the walks up and around them yield a feast of superb mountain scenery in every direction. From Bormio the Val Furva, carrying the lower sector of the Gavia motor road, whose summit commands a fine view of the range, leads beyond Sta Caterina to the southern foot of the 12,380-foot Cevedale, with the whole horseshoe from it to the Tresero and the huge Forno Glacier falling from them. Only a mile or two from Bormio, the six-mile-long Val Zebru strikes off to the north, curving along the foot of the whole wall from the Cristallo to the Königsspitze – this is a glorious walk.

From Fucine on the Tonale road, to the south of the group, a road runs north to the mineral springs of Péjo (4,430 feet) above which the beautiful Val del Mare bites north into the heart of the group at the eastern foot of the Cevedale, with the Cevedale Hut (8,550 feet) perched high on a green ledge opposite: another day's magnificent hill walking.

The other great valley penetrating the group is the very long Martelltal, leaving the Adige Valley to its east at Mortez near Latsch and running up for 12 miles through Gand to the Zufall Alp, on which stands the Zufall Hut (7,455 feet) at its head, close opposite the enormous Langen and Zufall glaciers, falling from between the Cevedale and the Suldenspitze. This long trek, which can be conveniently split into two days, and the paths high up on the slopes and up the short lateral re-entrants, are a delight to the heart.

For those who want to make closer acquaintance with the Ortler Group, but do not like to stray far from their car, there is the Stelvio, which surely deserves its sobriquet 'The King of the Passes'. If you visit it first from the southern side at Bormio you will have the bonus of the 'surprise' view at the summit; if from the north, you will have the dominant peaks and glaciers continually ahead of you instead of leaving them, with a regretful glance over your shoulder every second yard, as you descend to the Adige Valley. Starting from Bormio, the road forces its way up the rocky ravine of the Braulio by a series of tunnels, then mounts the frontal face of the Alpine wall by the 12 magnificent hairpins of the *Spondolungha* into an open, rock-girt basin at about 8,000 feet, where the (Swiss) Umbrail road – a 'non-pass' this, since it is unilateral – comes up to join it from Sta Maria at the foot of the Ofen (see p. 207). For the last ten minutes from the junction at the fourth Cantoniera to the saddle, you are still shut in by ridges lifting high overhead as indeed you have been all the 12 miles from Bormio. Then as you swing out onto the tiny plateau at the Stelvio summit, at 9,042 feet second only by 40 to the Iseran, the overwhelming view to the north is revealed with breath-taking suddenness. (Its foreground has not been exactly improved by the network of pylons (leading up the nearer snow slopes to the new ski-buildings of Monte Livrio 1,500 feet higher up, but this is a small detail in the vast canvas.)

The impact of the Ortler's great snowy dome, still lifting the height of Snowdon overhead, crowning 6,000 feet of precipitous rock, with the riven tongue of the Unter Ortler glacier cascading below you into the depths is such that at first it seems to fill the whole earth and sky, and it is difficult to take in anything else. Then gradually the eye swings away towards the valley levels, out to where, beyond the bewildering pattern of the road's incredible hairpin descent of the rock face to the west and the deep V-shaped rift to the north, the distant Ötztal and Zillertal Alps lift their snow-crowned battlements in a long wall from the Wildspitze to the Similaun.

The whole thing is, as usual, vastly improved if time is taken to walk up one of the neighbouring bumps that flank the narrow balcony of the pass and so broaden the prospect, which is slightly restricted by the containing slopes. Certainly the ten minutes' path towards the one-time trilingual peak, the Dreisprachenspitze

(9,325 feet) should be taken, till you look steeply down on the roofs of the Hospice buildings and more widely out over icefall and rock-curtain and the piled-up maze of the windings staggering up the left-hand wall of the (ex-) Austrian side's narrow rift to meet you.

The 4,000-foot descent by those superb, swirling, looping hairpins to Trafoi (5,055 feet) is a supreme half-hour of motor-mountaineering. All the way down you are at close quarters, across the narrow ravine of the Trafoital – a walk well worth taking from the tiny resort – to the fantastic rock-buttresses and creaming glaciers of the group's western wall – the magnificent Madatsch Glacier and its smaller neighbour of Trafoi, the Ortler itself dominating the four-mile crest along which its mighty 12,000-foot neighbours, the Gran Zebru, Eiskögele, Thurwieserspitze, Trafoier Eiswand and the spotless snow-dome of the Schneeglocke lift their impressive summits. There are frequent lay-bys along the descent as well as vantage points above it; and at Trafoi there is a chair-lift to the 7,290-foot Furkelspitze from which the panorama is seen at its most splendid.

At Trafoi we are among pinewoods again and the road falls through them by further hairpins to the village of Gomagoi (4,175 feet). Here a narrow spur road climbs away southeastwards up the remaining valley to penetrate the heart of the group, the Suldental, leading in seven lovely, flower-starred miles to Sulden (Solda, 6,000 feet), the charming little resort at the head of this cul de sac, where most of the climbs and glacier routes in the Ortler Group are begun, either from the Payer (9,940 feet) or from a number of other famous club huts. This is a delightful, unspoiled spot, where a fortnight's stay would not exhaust all the local walks through the woods and up the splendid paths to the huts and other wonderful viewpoints. The head of the valley, which is flanked on the south by the huge bulk of the Ortler, is dominated by the superb Königsspitze (12,655 feet), rising above the Suldenferner Glacier, whose summit cornice is one of the marvels of Alpine ice.

Below Gomagoi the Stelvio road runs prettily down to the

Adige Valley levels at Prato, with the snow-capped Austrian Alps rising ever nearer and higher ahead, till at Spondigna (2,903 feet) it crosses the river by a historic bridge, immediately after which it strikes into the valley highway coming down from Landeck over the Resia to the west and continuing eastwards along the lovely, sunny trench for 30 miles to Merano and Bolzano.

16. South of the Backbone: 2. The Dolomites

Bolzano, that fine city (880 feet) sprawling hugely across its hot wide plain, surrounded on all sides by wooded mountain ridges is, in terms of converging routes, to the Eastern Alps what Crewe is to the Midlands. For not only does it sit astride the main north–south road and rail link, descending over the Brenner, 30 miles to the north, from Innsbruck and continuing due south to Lake Garda, Verona and the plain of the Po, 80 miles away, but at least five road links of major importance radiate from it.

The first is the highway by which we have come, from Central Switzerland by way of the Arlberg and the Resia (or over the Timmlsjoch), the Adige Valley and Merano. The second is the Brenner itself. The third, following that traffic-saturated highway up the Isarco (Eisack) Valley for 25 miles to Fortezza, branches off due east there, follows the eastern Val Pusteria (Pustertal) through Brunico (Bruneck) and Dobbiaco (Toblach), skirting the northern fringe of the Dolomites, on across the Austrian frontier at Sillian to Lienz, from which the Felber–Tauern tunnel road and the Grossglockner Pass (pp. 261–5) strike off northwards to Innsbruck and Salzburg respectively. Beyond Lienz lies the Drave Valley road to Klagenfurt, Carinthia, Eastern Austria (Spittal–Villach–Leoben–Bruck–Semmering–Vienna) and Jugoslavia (Bruck–Graz–Maribor).

The fourth, over the Mendola, Tonale and Aprica passes is the westwards link with the Adda Valley and Lake Como (see p. 235), throwing out at Dimaro the road to Brescia over the Carlomagno

Pass, through Madonna di Campiglio and Tione, and at Edolo the Val Camonica route southwestward to Bergamo and Milan.

The fifth, opening up the whole Dolomite area to the east, is the Costalunga–Pordoi–Falzarego ('Dolomite Road') link with Cortina, where it gives access by way of Pieve di Cadore and the Mauria Pass to Tolmezzo, Udine and Trieste, as well as to Carinthia through Tarvisio and on to the Jugoslavia frontier close by; while at Pieve di Cadore the main highway strikes due south to Vittorio Veneto, Treviso and Venice.

To the lover of mountain scenery and mountaineers, however, Bolzano's chief attraction remains that it is truly the western gateway to the Dolomites, that isolated, extraordinary and unique mountain area, some 40 by 50 miles in extent, lying immediately to its east.

Since only two light railways penetrate the 'enclave' and there are none anywhere in the central area, I am assuming it will be explored by car, the feet being called into use wherever the enchanted driver may decide to stop by the wayside.

From Bolzano, then, there are three road approaches. Fifteen miles north along the Isarco–Brenner highway at Ponte Gardena (1,545 feet) an iron girder-bridge to the right crosses the river and climbs purposefully into the Val Gardena (Grödnertal), a lovely, secluded upland valley. The road, accompanied by one of the district's two narrow-gauge railways threads the meadows below the woods, climbing from green level to green level for eight miles to Ortisei (St Ulrich: 4,055 feet) the home of an ancient wood-carving industry. Ortisei and Sta Cristina (4,685 feet) three miles farther on are both delightful summer and winter resorts at the foot of the huge Seiser Alp. Here, all of a sudden, there is a first thrilling hint of Dolomite marvels to come, as the rounded fang of the Langkofel's (Sasso Lungo, 10,455 feet) utmost tip shoots up above the woods, unbelievably big, sheer and high.

At Sta Cristina, where the enormous wall of the Sella's cliffs (10,340 feet) looms up ahead, the valley contracts and the Sella Pass road begins its steep climb up the great turfy slopes at their feet to the 7,264-foot saddle between the Sella and Langkofel groups. As the road, the latest of the mule-tracks to be converted to a motor highway, climbs steadily to the saddle, the three fantastic spikes composing the Langkofel group shoot higher and higher into the sky on the right. Not far below the summit the few short windings of the Gardena Pass (6,970 feet) swing off to the left to a low green col at the northern end of the Sella Group, over which it drops steeply down to Corvara (5,110 feet), another charming holiday centre at the head of a lovely valley road coming up from Brunico due north in the Val Pusteria (see also p. 251).

At the Sella saddle, where there is a modern hotel and car park, the vast view eastwards is suddenly disclosed. From between the solid ochre-coloured mass of the Sella's great unbroken blocks and the riven, fluted spires of the blue-grey Langkofel trio – Langkofel, Fünffingerspitze, Grohmannspitze – you look out, as from a high balcony, across the depths of the Avisio valley with Canazei 2,500 feet below in its green bowl, to the rocky ridges heaped beyond, away to the distant San Martino peaks. Through the dark pine-woods on the opposing slope to the left, the upper windings of the Pordoi Pass slash their way to the Pordoi Saddle, only a mile or two away as the crow flies, but ten miles and many thousands of feet away by road, first down the Sella, then up the Pordoi's southern flank. And behind the Pordoi, in middle distance, its wings outspread like those of some huge grey sea-bird, her breast glittering bluish with the great glacier pouring down from her blunt snowy head, the Marmolata's lovely mass lies dreaming against the sky. For the 'Queen of the Dolomites' (10,970 feet) alone in this vast area of barren rock peaks boasts the shining raiment of a full-sized glacier-robe.

The road drops down, hairpin after hairpin, into and through the woods at the base of those astonishing Sella cliffs. Not long before the junction, 2,000 feet below, with the Pordoi road, almost at the bottom, there is a point at which the whole stupendous screen with hardly a wrinkle in it stands unfolded above the pines – surely one of the most marvellous bastions of smooth, vertical rock in the world. To point a contrast, across the way the dark

Langkofel spikes stand ruined to the sky like shattered lanceheads. It is a truly lovely pass, the Sella.

Here at Canazei we are on the 'Strada dei Dolomiti', described in details below (pp. 248–253).

The direct approach from Bolzano itself is by the Costalunga (Karer) Pass (5,752 feet), recently and not by any means too soon widened and modernised on the Bolzano side, and uniquely free of hairpins. The road climbs for 20 miles through the interesting ravines of the Eggental and later over wide grassy slopes dotted with pines. A few hundred yards short of Carezza al Lago is the world-famous Lago di Carezza (Karersee), which might easily be missed in its steep hollow to the right of the road were it not for the hideous ornamental fencing and the cluster of snack-bars and ice-cream booths advertising its presence. This widely-published emerald of the mountains, admittedly glorious in colour and superbly set among the pines at the foot of the stupendous flutings of the grey Latemar cliffs behind it (9,165 feet), is, in my view, a disappointingly small chipping, hardly more than a pond, ringed by muddy shallows and contained on its far side by an unpicturesque bank of shingle. Perversely I always take one look at it and spend the rest of the time marvelling at that wonderful screen of rock winging skyward beyond it.

Carezza, the resort (5,400 feet), has another rock-marvel to offer at its back, in the opposite direction above its grassy alp – the pale-beige walls of the Rosengarten Group (Catenaccio: 9,780 feet), which has a talent for turning rose-petal pink or blazing orange and coal-fire red in the light of the setting sun. (The Rosengarten is not alone in this respect: most of the Dolomite groups know how to blaze with fantastic colours at times.) There are charming walks at its feet, magnificent expeditions high into it recesses and by paths across the range to the Val di Fassa; and, of course, inexhaustible rock-climbing of every degree of difficulty, in both Rosengarten and Latemar groups. There are also chair-lifts and, for the horizontally-minded, a nine-hole golf course.

There is a minor but scenically fine road to the left just beyond

Carezza skirting the base of the Rosengarten all its great length, to the Col Nigre (5,500 feet) on the way to St Cyprian in the Val Tires. A couple of miles along you can find as wide and lovely a view as can be found in the Alps without leaving your car. The eye roves out over the heads of the valley pines, far across the distant Adige rift, far beyond the green hills which range from the Mendola, above Bolzano, southwards to the Brenta and the Adamello, and then out and away across the grey-green distances to where, suspended in the vast horizon sky some 50 miles away, the great snow-capped summits of the Alps from the Ortler to the Ötztal float in ethereal detachment, minute links in a long-drawn chain of silver. Close behind you the creamy cliffs of the Rosengarten sweep prodigiously upwards, and it need hardly be said that the same lovely prospect is greatly enhanced by taking any of the paths leading high up among them.

St Cyprian (3,560 feet) is high up in the Val Tires, above whose head rise the fantastic Vajolet Towers, a handful of spiny fingers at the northern end of the Rosengarten. The three hours' path to the Vajolet Hut (7,430 feet), at their very base, leads to a truly fantastic world of spires and pinnacles, and the journey through it can be extended down the Val Vajolet into the Val di Fassa near Vigo (see next page, also p. 253), a wonderful walking tour. Most of the climbs among the towers are of extreme difficulty, and the scenery is the most dramatic in the western Dolomites.

Lower down the valley is Tires itself, from which the valley road runs down to fall into the main Isarco Valley only a mile or two from the point where the Costalunga leaves it. That amazing Dolomite peak the Schlern (8,405 feet) can be 'climbed', in spite of its precipitous appearance, by a path from this valley : but the ascent is best made by the long though easy path from Seis and Bad Ratzes (3,935 feet) at the head of the next valley to the north, the Schwarzgries, the road to which diverges southwards from the Gardena Valley–Sella Pass route just after crossing the Isarco bridge at Ponte Gardena (see p. 241). It can also be tackled from Ortisei and Sta Christina up the enormous slopes of the lovely Seiser Alp, the largest pasture in the South Tyrol, dotted with châlets and hay-huts – a skiing paradise in winter – and the Praliner-Schwaige. In spite of its daunting verticality, which provides several extremely difficult face climbs, the Schlern is so accessible by its paths that there is a cluster of buildings, the Schlern Haüser, with accommodation for 100, close to its highest summit, which commands a sensational view. Not only are all the important peaks and ridges of the nearer Dolomites visible to the east and the Brenta, Presanella and Adamello away to the southeast; but, westwards beyond the Adige rift, the splendid chain of the Ortler and, ringing the horizon from northwest to east, the Ötztal, Stubai and Zillertal Alps and the continuation of the main chain to the Venediger in the Hohe Tauern.

There is one more valley branching eastwards from the main Isarco highway at a point midway between Chiusa (Klausen) and Bressanone, which should not be missed by the searcher for the most fantastic Dolomite scenery. This is the Villnöstal, nine miles long, with Villnös (3,600 feet) and Sta Magdalena (4,700 feet) its highest villages. To the southeast of the latter the tremendous wall of the Geislerspitzen, the Saas Ragais and Furchetta, both 9,930 feet high, goes streaming to the sky in a seemingly vertical leap of 3,000 feet. The north face of the Furchetta, which only catches the sun in the early morning offers the climber nothing less than 'extreme' Grade VI routes; oddly enough the summit can be reached by a novice in an hour by a Grade I 'easy', starting from the Geisler Hut, high up on its reverse side, the long approach being made by a path from Sta Cristina in the Val Gardena.

Returning to Carezza and the Costalunga, we soon reach the narrow neck of the pass (5,722 feet). The road then contours its tortuous way along a narrow ledge at the base of the Rosengarten spurs and presently descends gently across the flower-starred meadows to Vigo di Fassa, only 1,200 feet and five miles below the col. The chief joy of the descent is a series of lovely views up the vale of the Avisio to the distant Sella group and the Marmolata's snows. At Vigo the pass falls into the main 'Strada dei Dolomiti', described later (pp. 248–253).

Bolzano's third approach dives into the hills at Ora, five miles south of the city on the highway south to Trento, Lake Garda and Verona, climbs over a low saddle, the 'San Lugano', through the beautiful Val Fiemme past Cavalese, and meets the Avisio Valley and the southern end of the 'Dolomite Road' at Predazzo, a busy little market town. Here, to the east, begins one of the finest Dolomite passes, the Rolle, leading to San Martino di Castrozza then southwards to Primiero and Primolano, whence the road to Vicenza and Padua, some 40 miles away in the plains, wriggles south through some exciting gorges by way of Bassano, the birthplace of two famous painter brothers, who adopted its name. To the east of Primolano another road runs due eastwards to Feltre and Belluno, just beyond which it meets the Pieve di Cadore–Vittorio Veneto–Venice highway (see above, p. 241). There is also a direct west–east link between Trento, on the Bolzano–Verona Adige Valley highway, through the lovely Val Sugana and Borgo to Primolano, skirting the southern fringes of the main Dolomite area.

From Predazzo (3,337 feet) the Rolle Pass heads gently enough for some miles up a green valley, then climbs nearly 2,000 feet up the broad breast of a meadow-covered slope into a narrow ravine below the pinewoods. Hereabouts the jagged skyline, still some miles away, of the San Martino peaks suddenly heaves itself up above the forest to unearthly heights, to be lost again as the road winds through the deep and narrow gorge above a small, dark unruffled lakelet. Above the ravine, wide modern curves swing up through the glorious pines till, beyond their topmost rim, the road crosses the last bare slope to the turfy saddle of the pass (6,463 feet) and its fantastic background of the Cimone della Pala (10,450 feet), the 'Matterhorn of the Dolomites'.

At first the eye is held entirely by the sky-raking surge of the Cimone's narrow shaft, 4,000 feet of slender uprightness and slabby verticality. Presently one notices the immediate presence of the Vezzana and other adjoining cliffs. Five minutes' stroll from the unbeautiful knot of summit hotels and other tin-roofed buildings up the grassy knolls behind them will discover not only a charmingly situated chapel but a variety of new views of the great massif ahead, including its extension to the startling crags and pinnacles of the Rosetta and the endless bastion of peaks beyond, overlooking San Martino and the long valley down to Primiero. There is a chairlift to the Baita Segantini a little hostelry at 7,400 feet named after the great Swiss painter, if you wish to inspect the cliffs from closer to their base. If there were nothing but the summit views to draw me to the bare, humpy saddle of the Rolle, I should still turn east at Predazzo every time. Fortunately, it leads to more, and much more, though nothing quite so magnificent beyond, where the road tumbles in a terraced series of spasmodic hairpins into the wonderful mat of pine forest sloping to the valley below, and then down and down, looping among gigantic firs for four miles and 2,000 feet, with vista after vista of beige and grey rock-pinnacles above their tufty tops, till suddenly at one of the innumerable hairpin bends the topmost hotels of San Martino emerge from the woods.

San Martino (4,740 feet), with its ancient church tower brave against the cliffs, is a lovely spot in which to stay. Its meadows are a veritable sun-trap; the pine-woods above them on every side, whose trees grow to exceptional heights, offer a cool shade and a glut of woodland strawberries at the side of their paths. There are strolls and walks, short or long, and of course mountaineering of all standards of severity.

Dominating the northeastern side of the little clearing and bordering the whole length of the valley, rises the mighty, precipitous wall of extraordinary towers, spires, crags and pinnacles stretching for ten miles from the southwest face of the Cimone, here broad and castellate, through the Rosetta, Saas Maor and the organ-pipes of the Pala di San Martino to the Cima di Ball.

The finest all-day expedition is to the 9,000-foot peak of the Rosetta, 20 minutes by chairlift to above the tree level and then seven more by a fantastic cable-loop to the Rosetta saddle between it and the Cimone, leaving only 500 feet of steep rock-path to be dealt with on foot, over the almost snow-white summit rocks. Those who still enjoy a day's exercise will find the truly remarkable path cut in the apparently vertical face of the mountain, with a few really exposed corners protected by railings and wire ropes, well worthwhile for its three hours of real delights from the top of the chair-lift. Not far from the top station of the ropeway across the almost level saddle stands the Rifugio Rosetta (8,530 feet) for rest and refreshment. The view from the Rosetta's gently tilted summit slabs are superb.

For those who prefer woodland shade and an entire absence of vertiginous places there is the broad and less steep track, through some of the most magnificent pine forest in the Alps, leading in three hours to the very attractive Malga (Alp) Tognola (6,510 feet) on the gentler side of the valley, where the hostelry commands wonderful views across the valley of the whole elongated chain of the San Martino peaks opposite.

Below San Martino the Rolle road continues pleasantly down the long straight valley for nine miles to Fiera di Primiero, where it reaches the floor of the wider Primiero Valley and the roads leading southwards and eastwards to the plains (see p. 241).

For the motorist on his way to Italy, who has only limited time to devote to the Dolomites, it would be best to enter the region from the north at Dobbiaco (Toblach) in the Val Pusteria and drive straight down the linked passes of the 'Strada dei Dolomiti': the Tre Croci to Cortina and thence over the Falzarego and Pordoi to Canazei, on down the Avisio Valley to Predazzo, over the Rolle and so down to the plains and the *autostrada*.

At Dobbiaco the road enters a narrow gateway in the tall hills and ascends the deep Rienz Valley to Carbonin (4,730 feet). Only a mile or two up the valley, to the right of the road, there is the first little Dolomite gem – the small, sombre lake of Dobbiaco, hidden by a shallow screen of firs and only 100 yards from a parked car. You could easily miss it if you did not know it was there. To my mind, this smooth sheet of dark-green water, trapped at the foot of high ridges, with the first distant lift of a great Dolomite peak, the Tofana, beyond, is far lovelier than its bigger, more celebrated sister of Misurina, a few miles ahead.

At Carbonin the Tre Croci road leaves the direct valley road to Cortina and climbs along an uninteresting defile, with an unsatisfactory distant glimpse of the Drei Zinnen high up on the left, to the open bowl which cradles the pretty, almost oval lake and resort of Misurina (5,760 feet), backed to the south by the long grey serrated comb of the Marmarole (9,620 feet), while to the east the twin summits of Monte Cadini (9,320 feet) stand up mightily. (There is lovely walking country in and around their massif.)

If time allows, you should take the narrow mountain road penetrating the hills on the left up to Rimbianco, no great distance from the base of three of the most remarkable of all the Dolomite peaks – the famous 9,500-foot Drei Zinnen or Tre Cime di Lavoredo. These three massive absolutely vertical upheavals of smooth-faced stone, standing in a row almost touching each other, can boast some of the most appallingly difficult climbing routes in the world, and are almost frighteningly impressive.

From Misurina the Tre Croci road runs almost level for five miles till it meets the road falling away to Auronzo, Pieve di Cadore and the Mauria Pass (see p. 241), then winds gently up through vast acres of pines to the unspectacular summit which, however, commands a fine if greatly foreshortened view up Monte Cristallo's towering cliffs (10,495 feet). The view ahead over the heads of the pines is pleasant and peaceful.

And yet here stands – in the form of a memorial – an incredible reminder that these vertical cliffs and apparently inaccessible pinnacles, thousands of feet overhead, were the scene of some of the bitterest fighting between Austrian and Italian Alpine troops during the First War. And up there, among the beige crags and gullies, machine-gun emplacements, trench systems, dugouts and a labyrinth of connecting tunnels, all blown out of the living rock, festooned with rusty coils of barbed wire, still bear witness to an unbelievable form of warfare, the possibility of which even the toughest commando-trained plainsman of today might doubt.

The road then winds amiably down through more pinewoods, out of them onto the sunny slopes of a wide valley and in 20 minutes you are right among the shops and hotels of Cortina d'Ampezzo (3,983 feet), the undisputed queen of the Dolomite resorts.

A secluded mountain village, rapidly grown into a large, sophisticated town, Cortina has somehow contrived to maintain its native charm. Everything the pampered tourist demands is here – luxury hotels, cafés, bars, dance-places, tennis courts, swimming pools, a golf course, chair-lift and ropeways to a variety of view-points, to say nothing of the vast and, I think, beautiful Olympic open-air stadium of 1955–6, on whose rink ice-skating is enjoyed by hundreds on the hottest summer day. Yet Cortina, sitting firmly with her foot on the neck of the Dolomite road, remains a lovely place.

The first ten miles of the 6,913-foot Falzarego really demand a great deal of parking and looking back, as successive banks of hairpins surmount the wide meadows, swing up through the pine-woods and eventually enter the long corridor leading to the saddle itself. For at each turn of the road the Ampezzo bowl falls farther away and the sharp outlines of the Sorapis, Antelao and Cristallo, dove-grey, vast and all over 10,000 feet, lift higher and higher above it.

The straight, almost level, corridor above the pine forests is beautifully withdrawn from the world. On the right the tre-mendous precipices of the Cima Bois (8,393 feet) and the Tofana present the aspect of a vertical wall rising thousands of feet into the sky. On the left, beyond the wooded ravine down which the torrent dashes valleywards, the beautiful slender spires of the wine-coloured Croda del Lago (8,885 feet) cluster high above the shallow vale and the incredible blocks of the much lower Cinque Torri stand jumbled like some fantastic outsize Stonehenge above the bare wilderness of scree at their feet.

The best view of the Tofana (10,585 feet) is from the summit of the pass, where you are far enough away from the great cascading curtain of beige cliffs, and the huge domed belfry of rock which crowns them, and which in certain lights shines as white as any snow-peak. On the opposite side well set back from the saddle rises the Nuvolao range (8,460 feet).

The southern descent is by a magnificent 'staircase' down the very steep slope to Raggazzi, consisting not only of built-out hairpins and some tunnels, but of several hairpin tunnels. It continues less steeply, but too hemmed in to allow of any wide views, through pinewoods to Andraz (4,665 feet), the true foot of the pass, and up again over a low spur to picturesque Pieve di Livinalongo (4,815 feet), from which you should look back to the Civetta's immense rock screen (10,565 feet). This is the nearest point to that masterpiece of Dolomite architecture, ten miles away to the north.

For the celebrated close-up view of those gigantic organ pipes, splendid beyond description, in the great wall rising from the blue depths of the tiny lake of Alleghe (3,170 feet) at its very base, it is necessary to take a long detour by a road winding monumentally down from Andraz first to Caprile (see also p. 253), and then on to Alleghe, a charmingly situated resort in a little bay – 12 slow and seemingly endless miles. Moreover, the famous view is half an hour on foot from the car parked at the village, up a slope round the head of the lake. It is a wonderful view, worth all these tribulations, but it would be wise to budget two and a half hours for the digression.

From Pieve to Arabba the road clings high up on the flank of the beautifully wooded Livinalongo valley, contouring for four miles above the gorges and the deep green lake formed by the river at one point, with the snows of the Marmolata appearing occasionally ahead.

At Arabba (5,255 feet) the 6,125-foot Campolungo Pass comes in on the right from delightful Corvara, finely situated in the lovely Val Badia (see above, p. 242). There Colfosco, at the foot of the immense Dolomite cliffs, is one of the most picturesque villages in this whole region and Corvara is a perfect holiday resort in summer or winter.

The Pordoi Pass, the third in the Dolomite road, immediately climbs out of the Livinalongo Valley through meadows and then up a long green slope by a bewildering pattern of long, looped windings to a bare alp, where the angle eases somewhat, and so to the 7,346-foot summit, a distance of six miles from Arabba. The

Pordoi saddle consists of a brief upland dell about a mile long, containing a considerable village of hotels and other buildings, between the Cima di Boë (10,340 feet), the easternmost of the Sella peaks and the low comb of the Cima di Rossi (7,790 feet). The rather restricted view to the east can be greatly improved by ascending the grassy slope towards the screes below Cima Boë for only ten minutes, when the Marmolata with her beautiful snow-cap and pale blue glacier shield – the only sizeable sheet of ice in the Dolomites – lifts into view to the east, soaring more grandly the farther you go up towards the marked viewpoint about three-quarters of an hour above the pass. On the other side of the road, behind the hotels, a relatively level path strikes off around the rocky spurs (the 'Bindelweg') and leads in half an hour to a point where the whole mass of the Marmolata stands up even more magnificently across the valley below. The path, which eventually reaches the Fedaja Pass (6,150 feet), with its famous view, in two and a half hours, can also be used for the ascent of the Belvedère (8,695 feet) and the easy Cima di Rossi, each about an hour from the path. The view back towards the Falzarego and Cortina from the saddle, with the heads of all the distant Ampezzo and Cadore peaks on the skyline, is wide and unrestricted.

Beyond the summit saddle the road passes through the jaws of a narrow 'gateway' where the view over the Avisio Valley (Val di Fassa) opens up, with Canazei at your feet. Beyond the sheer Sella cliffs to the right, above the green Sella saddle (p. 242) the huge wedges of the Langkofel shoot incredibly into the sky. Snaking down a bare slope by short, steep windings, the road then reaches out in wide, less steep dog-legs through the pines, with the ochre cliffs of the enormous Sella massif streaming up above them, for seven miles, to drop into the main street of Canazei (4,086 feet).

Beautifully situated in a green plainlet, the little resort is backed by a fine view of the Marmolata and offers an attractive diversion, the side road to the east leading up the Contrintal to Penia and the foot of the ropeway which now goes almost to the summit of the great mountain for the delight of summer and winter skiers. High up in this lateral valley stands the Contrinhaus (6,585 feet) from which the great Grade VI climbs on the almost vertical, huge south face of the Marmolata are undertaken.

At Canazei the long link of high passes ends, and the road – broad, mostly straight and always maintained in top condition for the heavy traffic it understandably attracts – continues for 17 miles down the truly beautiful valley of the Avisio, whose stream bubbles merrily alongside through the meadows, to Predazzo. All the way, through a string of charming little resorts with melodious names – Campitello, Vigo di Fassa, Moena – a delicious corridor of flowery meadows, pine-covered slopes, white-walled villages and their slender church towers, there are glimpses on either hand of famous groups and summits. To the right, first the Latemar, then the lengthy east wall of the Rosengarten with the Vajolet Towers (the reverse side of that described on p. 243); to the left, the minor but lovely Punta Vallaccia (8,665 feet). At Vigo, which lies just off the road to its right, the Costalunga starts up the slope on its way to Carezza and Bolzano (ibid). At Predazzo, where the Dolomite Road ends, the Rolle Pass goes off to the southeast, and the road to Ora, Trento and Lake Garda to the southwest. If the Rolle has not been visited separately, it should definitely be included as the finale to this symphony of Dolomite passes.

The only major Dolomite peak I have so far neglected is one of the finest, the great triple-headed Pelmo (10,395 feet) not far from Cortina. It can (and should) be approached either from the main Ampezzo Valley highway running from Cortina to Pieve di Cadore, at San Vito (3,315 feet), above which the mountain towers colossally, and up the Val Fedarola, at whose head stands the Rifugio Venetia (6,624 feet); or, more picturesquely, from its other side, by the road climbing eastwards from Caprile (p. 251) up the Val Fiorentina to Selva, prettily situated against the three great rocky heads of the peak, and Pescul closer to its base, from which a pleasant track leads over to the Ampezzo Valley by way of the 6,480-foot Forcella Forada. A third approach is by the road from Forno due south of the peak, ten miles up the attractive Val di Zoldo, biting northwest into the hills at Longarone, 15 miles south of Pieve di Cadore on the main valley highway to Belluno and Vittorio Veneto. It will be recalled that Longarone was completely destroyed in 1966 when a disastrous landslide, precipitated by the bursting of the Vaiont dam in the gorge high to its east overwhelmed it, with heavy loss of life.

Forty miles south of Bolzano and to the west of the main Dolomite area's southern fringe (Belluno–Feltre–Trento) rise the two last southernmost groups of high mountains between the main Alpine chain and the Lombardy plain – the rocky Brenta Dolomites and the snowy Adamello.

The area is neatly bisected by the easy 5,580-foot Campiglio Pass, which leaves the Bolzano–Mendola–Tonale link at Fondo, the eastern foot of the Tonale (p. 235), and leads over the Carlomagno saddle to nearby Madonna di Campiglio (4,970 feet), one of the loveliest of the larger Dolomite resorts. A little to the east rise the astonishing castles and spires (Crozzon di Brenta, Cima Tosa and the fantastic needles of the Guglia and Torre di Brenta), of the short but splendid Brenta group of the Dolomites. The whole range is visible from the road at 'Panorama Corner' a mile or two below Madonna, itself nestling too deeply under the wooded spurs to allow a wide view. Even moderate walkers can, however, see the great peaks with minimum effort, for chair-lifts go up on either side of the valley to crests 1,500 feet higher up, above the treeline.

At the top of the 20-minute 'ride' to Monte Spinale (6,900 feet) there is, without further journeying, a wide and splendid view westwards to the broad Adamello snowfields (11,640 feet) and the long serrated rock ridge to the Presanella's dark ice-fluted pyramid (11,690 feet); while closer at hand behind a billowing green alp rise the fantastic blocks, wedges, whorls and spikes of beige rock, flecked with small hanging glaciers, which are the Brenta (9,000–10,500 feet). A gentle track leads across the alp in an hour and a half to the Graffler Hut (8,200 feet), where the magnificence of the Ortler chain, only 20 miles away, and the much more distant Ötztal Alps are added to the view. This is the starting place for the crossing of the range by the 8,715-foot Bocca di Tuckett. The terrific 4,000-foot vertical face of the Crozzon, lit by the westering sun, will be with you all the way down in the afternoon, a stupendous sight.

For those who want a close-up view of the incredible Brenta needles, there is a wonderful path up the terraced rock steps of the Val Brenta, in four hours, to the Bocca di Brenta (8,375 feet) above the Tosa Hut, through some of the most savagely impressive rock scenery in the world.

The lifts on the western side yield closer views of the Adamello–Presanella snows, by contrast, and there is wonderful walking up the valleys at their feet, the Val Nambino with its lakelets from Madonna itself and the glorious Val di Genova, 12 miles long, from Pinzolo, the resort five miles down the road to Tione and Lake Garda. Its road and paths lead high into the coronet of snows to the Mandron Hut (7,900 feet) grandly placed half-way between the two peaks at its opposite ends. (Their most impressive aspect from the Tonale road and the lovely walking country around Fucine and Ponte di Legno on their western side have already been mentioned (p. 236).

On the eastern side of the Brenta, towering close behind, lies Molveno (2,835 feet) on its pretty lake. The approach here is by roads from near Mezzolombardo or from Arco on the main Adige highway from Bolzano to the south, below Trento. The connecting road from Arco runs through to Tione at the foot of the Campiglio Pass, tunnelling and clinging remarkably along the vertical walls of impressive gorges past Stenico (2,190 feet), just before which the Molveno road strikes off to the north.

With the Brenta and the Adamello we come to the southern limits of an Alpine survey. The area to the south is occupied by the 40-mile-long Lago di Garda and its foothills, petering out rapidly into the Lombardy plain at its southern end, where Brescia and Verona are only 20 miles away on either hand. In my view it is incomparably the loveliest of the Italian lakes, with its wide, open base, redolent of the warm south and its narrowing tongue piercing northwards into the foothills and a hint of the Dolomites behind them.

There is surely no more wonderful lakeside road than the one tunnelling 40 times above clear turquoise waters from Gardone to Riva along its western cliffs. On the opposite short a whaleback of green hills rises steadily to Monte Baldo (7,000 feet) above Malcesine (ropeway) with a magnificent view over lake, plain and distant Dolomites. Its shores are trimmed with enchanting Salò, Gardone Riviera, Sirmione, Torri, Torbole – all desperately overcrowded, it is true – but all lovely to look upon. Yes, here there is everything the holidaymaker could ask for; since we are no longer in the Alps, let the guidebooks of Northern Italy tell him what, where and how.

17. The Eastern Alps

With one digression far to the east, from the Northern Limestone Alps beyond Salzburg and through the subsidiary ranges providing a continuation to the extreme eastern end of the Alps on Vienna's doorstep, our journey along the main range of the Alpine system has so far not taken us beyond the eastern end of the Zillertal group, where we paused for an exploration of the vast mountainous area between it and the northern plain of Italy. It is high time, therefore, to return to the Brenner and follow the backbone and the areas adjoining it to its ultimate conclusion on and beyond the Jugoslav frontiers.

For the main range, continuing unbroken from the Zillertal Alps through the Hohe Tauern, in which rise Austria's (and the eastern Alps') two highest peaks – the Gross Glockner and the Gross Venediger – in fact fragments at the eastern end of the Hohe Tauern into two more or less distinct arms; the northern running through Styria's Niedere Tauern – a much lower range, as its name suggests – and the still lower foothill ranges already dealt with in chapter 14; the southern, with further fragmentations on either side, swinging southeastwards through the Carinthian Alps to peter out near Leoben. While some distance to the south, below Lienz, the eastward extension of the Dolomite group, the Carnic Alps and the Julians beyond them, with a southwestward offshoot in the Venetians – take on the characteristics of the main west-to-east watershed, separating the parallel basins of the Drave and Save to their north, heading for the Black Sea from the headwaters of the Piave and Isonzo flowing southwards to the Adriatic.

This 'backbone' ends in a final mighty upthrust in the Julians, with Triglav (9,400 feet) and its high and splendid stony neighbours, 40 miles short of Ljubljana. A little to the north, the Karawanken range sticks a long finger out eastwards below Klagenfurt, but these are only pleasant hills. With that tremendous flourish, where Austria, Italy and Jugoslavia meet, we have come to the coda of the long Alpine symphony.

Fully to understand the very complicated geography of this eastern sector of the declining Alps, it is best to take the reader back to the Inn Valley, east of Innsbruck and the Kitzbühel area (see p. 221), where two parallel roads run due south, to fall into the broad, straight trench of the Upper Pinzgau (Salzach Valley): the first from Kitzbühel over the minor 'Pass in Thurn' to Mittersill (also approached direct from Innsbruck through Zell am Ziller and Wald); the other being the road mentioned below (p. 265) from St Johann and Zell am See to Bruck im Pinzgau, at the central foot of the Hohe Tauern and the point where the Grossglockner Pass, having climbed over them from the south, debouches into the sunny Pinzgau.

Zell am See (2,470 feet), with a fine view to the south of the Kitzsteinhorn (10,512 feet), is a sizeable but delightful township on the west bank of its pretty lake, around whose shores nestle minor and quieter resorts for those who abhor the gallimaufry – Thumersbach is particularly secluded and charming. Behind Zell there is a ropeway up to the Schmittenhöhe (6,455 feet) above the wooded slope; this is one of the famous lower viewpoints, embracing the whole Hohe Tauern range to the south and the stony ranges to the north on the Bavarian frontier – Watzmann, Steinerne Meer, Loferer Steinberge – almost equidistant, with the lake forming a lovely middle-ground.

The Hohe Tauern, the true continuation of the Alpine watershed, runs due east from the last of the Zillertal peaks for some distance before curving southeastwards to near Gmünd, a distance of 60 miles. Besides the Venediger and Glockner it boasts 30 peaks of over 10,000 feet. The first big peak, only five miles east of the Dreiecker, the last of the Zillertal range (p. 219), is the Dreiherrenspitze (11,500 feet) with the slightly lower Grosse Geiger between it and the huge Gross Venediger (12,008 feet), again five miles to the east. The Venediger is the most heavily glaciated mountain in the eastern Alps, its glaciers covering more than a fifth of the whole massif. It is also one of the easiest of all high mountains to climb, several of its approaches demanding nothing but a very long snow-trudge.

The group is bounded on the north by the upper valley of the Salzach, on its way to Mittersill and Bruck, from which a number of valleys – such as the Sulzbachtal near Wald and the Habachtal – liberally supplied with paths and huts, run up into its recesses. To the east its limit is the Felber Tauern, through which runs the new motorway (Mittersill–Matrei–Lienz), piercing the Alpine chain in a tunnel three and threequarter miles long under the Venediger, and the Matrei–Tauern valleys; to the south it is bounded by the Virgental, Dabertal and Defereggental and to the west by the Ahrntal (Val Aurina, see p. 219), which runs all the way up below the Ziller peaks on a northeasterly diagonal almost to the foot of the Venediger's glaciers; and by the Birnlücke and the valley of the Krimmler Ache.

A short way up the Isel- (Tauern-) tal from Lienz at charming Winddisch-Matrei, the Virgental branches off to the west; 11 miles up it lies Prägraten (4,305 feet), another pleasant centre from which a track up the Klein Iseltal leads to the Johannis Hut, the starting point for an easy route up the Venediger and equally easy glacier crossings to the Pinzgau. The motor road up the Tauerntal above Matrei leads to the Tauern Haus and the guesthouse at Inner Gschlöss (5,530 feet), with splendid views of the glaciers and peaks – the best views of the Venediger are from this eastern aspect. An easy route up the mountain by way of the Neu Prager Hütte (9,205 feet), starts here; one of the finest views of the group is about an hour and a half up the path to the hut. All the valleys here, to the south of the massif, radiating from Matrei, provide lovely walking and there are numerous huts and refuges high up in its re-entrants.

Fifteen miles to the east, beyond the intervening Sonnblick (10,101 feet), stands the highest peak in the Tauern and in Austria, the Gross Glockner (12,461 feet), rising above a fine glacier complex, the Pasterzen being the third longest in the Alps. The sharp spearhead of the great peak dominates the group which curves away to the northeast through a number of snowy peaks to the Grosse Wiessbachhorn (11,713 feet) at its northern end. The normal route up the Glockner from the Hoffmann's Hütte on the Pasterzen's edge (see below) up to the Franz Joseph Hut on the Adlersruhe (11,370 feet) is steep and long, but not difficult; I wonder how many have made the ascents as the only 'big Alpine adventure' of their lifetime, to enjoy the marvellous views from the summit and its adjacent ridges. The climbs on its western face, approached from Kals and the Dorferertal to its south or the Stubachtal from near Mittersill in the Pinzgau, are much tougher propositions, while the Kaprun Valley from that village farther along the Pinzgau to the east gives access to the northern peaks in the group – Hohe Riffl, Hocheiser, Johannisberg (11,375 feet) and the rest.

The classic approach for non-climbers and motor mountaineers is, of course, the marvellous 'Gross Glockner Hochalpenstrasse', which rivals the Stelvio and Bernina for magnificent views of glaciers and snowpeaks from the road. Lienz is the starting point if you have come from the foot of the Brenner at Fortezza along the Val Pusteria, or from Dobbiaco, the northern gateway to the Dolomites, across the Italo–Austrian frontier at Sillian (see p. 240). If you are coming from the north – the Inn Valley, Salzburg or Kitzbühel – the wonderful journey begins at Bruck in the Pinzgau.

Lienz, that beautifully clean and tidy town, is an important road junction, for besides being at the southern end of the (comparatively) new Matrei tunnel road and the parallel Glocknerstrasse, it commands, owing to a geographical freak, two main valley routes eastwards, which reunite at Spittal (for the lake of Millstatt) and run on to Villach, the other lakes of the Carinthian Lake District and the direct high road northeast to Klagenfurt through Bruck an der Mur, the road junction for Graz, a few miles to its south, and Maribor in Jugoslavia; and, eventually to Vienna.

The odd geographical feature is that between Lienz and Villach the more or less parallel valleys of the Drave and its tributary, falling into it at Villach, the Gail, are only separated by the long narrow ridge of the 'Gailtal Alps', whose summits, except at its western extremity close to Lienz, rarely exceed 7,000 feet, and whose eastern end, the Dobratsch, that delightful upland area close to Villach, is described below (p. 267).

At the western end, however, the Gailtal range suddenly sticks up the spiny fingers of the 'Dolomites of Lienz', so impressive from the deep valley, and providing the men of Lienz with their own private climbing and rambling paradise. This isolated group is about 20 miles long and six miles deep from north to south, and its peaks are truly Dolomite in character .It takes six hours to reach the Karlsbader Hut (7,390 feet) close to the little jewel of the Laserzsee, set among the rocky teeth of the Laserz peaks, almost all of them difficult climbs – the Sandspitze (9,350 feet) being the highest, and half a dozen rocky towers nearly as high. 'Mere trippers' do not go in any great number to high places it takes six hours to reach on foot, and there is as yet no ropeway – I wonder for how long? – so the lover of solitary walks among silent summits can still find here an unspoiled tract of glorious mountain country. And he can look out across that deep valley to where Lienz's other climbing ground, the Schober Group, so prominent a feature from the southern side of the Glocknerstrasse, lifts its higher but un-Dolomitic ridges to the summits of the Petzeck (10,770 feet) and the Hochschober (10,660 feet). The Glockner route leaves the Villach road a little to the east of Lienz and climbs over a spur called the Iselberg into the Mölltal, a beautiful valley which soon splits into two arms, the wider of them leading away eastwards to Spittal. The road to the pass climbs gently up the narrower one between pine forests, through pretty Mörtschach and Döllach, then steepens appreciably up to Heiligenblut on its green spur, with the tip of the Gross Glockner lifting its sharp snowy spear head into the remote sky.

Heiligenblut (4,265 feet), in spite of all the efforts of commercialism and touristic fame to spoil it, remains a unique and charming village, narrowly perched at the gateway to the great mountains, its lovely tall church dominating the huddled châlet roofs, its unusually slender spire lifting proudly yet humbly as a kind of human recognition and reflection of the great snow spire so serenely poised many thousands of feet directly above it.

The car parks may be wedged with cars and coaches, children and *portiers* may besiege you touting with offers of accommodation, the place may be packed to overflowing; but I defy anyone to come back unimpressed from a visit to the cool high-vaulted shrine housing the relic of the Holy Blood St Briccius brought back six centuries ago, and to the little terraced acre of the dead above the valley's edge where the rude forefathers of a mountain hamlet lie buried. And if a smile be needed to temper a deeper emotion, there in the crypt is the little grinning negro boy, whose china head and shoulders keep watch over the offertory box, bowing his thanks with greater or less enthusiasm according to the weight of the coin inserted.

Here the Glockner road proper begins, after a compulsory halt at the toll-house, winding very steeply in terraced hairpins, with the Möll Valley falling away deeper and deeper at every turn and the view over it to the distant Lienz Dolomites widening every minute. After a short slightly downhill contour of the Tauernbach's re-entrant it mounts again to Guttal (6,310 feet), where at the first control the spur-road to the Franz Joseph's Höhe and its wonderful glacier view leaves the main road to the pass. This marvellous 'side-show' is a dead-end, involving four miles and 1,600 feet in each direction, but it is the real glory of the Glocknerstrasse.

It climbs by bare slopes with fine views of the rocky Schober peaks across the blue rift of the valley till at the Glocknerhaus (6,985 feet) the Glockner peaks and the tongue of the Pasterzen glacier, hidden till now by great stony spurs, come into sight. Should you want to see the ineffable spectacle of the dawn on the Glockner's spire and graceful shoulders, there is good plain overnight accommodation here (this is a Refuge of the Austrian Alpine Club, not a hotel) at a very reasonable cost.

A thousand feet higher up (7,935 feet), at the end of the spur road, stands the Franz Joseph's Haus, a modern luxury hotel with all comforts, high above the glacier world and commanding the superb view denied the old Club Hut below. A night spent there will cost you at least twice as much. (We solved the economic problem by sleeping at the Glocknerhaus, being called at three a.m., and after a splendid breakfast driving up with the headlights on, in plenty of time for the unimaginable beauties of the dawn.)

The Höhe is an extraordinary place, a vast terrace of smooth car parks, below which are enough modern lavatories to accommodate a football crowd (a necessary provision here during the high coaching season), all hewn out of the dark rock of the mountainside. All the traffic and bustle does not seem to disturb the marmots, whole families of which, accepting the motor age philosophically, can be seen scampering in out of of their holes, close to the hubbub.

The view is breathtaking in its magnificence. The flat, straight, crevassed course of the huge Pasterzen Glacier is dominated by the long, snowy, rock-buttressed wall of the Glockner range, from the Schwerteck through the 12,460-foot Glockner itself and the broad Glocknerwand to the spotlessly white Eiskogel, all rising sheer from its farther shore. To see it when the rosy fingers of dawn are charming it back to life out of the night is an unforgettable experience, once reserved for hardy mountain-walkers, now available to the imaginative motorist. Beyond the car parks a good path cut into the rock and at points tunnelling through it provides an almost level walk of about an hour, contouring close above the glacier, to the Hofmann's Hut, the starting point for the Glockner and other climbs (arrangements for a guide can be made at Heiligenblut, the Glocknerhaus, the hotel or even on the spot at the hut).

Back at Guttal, the main road to the true pass at the Hochtor Saddle, 2,000 feet above, immediately tackles the great green spur ahead and traces bewildering designs and loops up it for the five intervening miles. The summit is at the Hochtor tunnel (8,212 feet), 300 yards long, at whose northern end – inscribed with the words '*In te Domine speravi*', to commemorate 12 years of faith, fervour and human toil and sweat which forced this great road through a stony wilderness in the teeth of the mountain's menace and the fury of the winter winds – a completely different scene meets the eye. Before and below you, the thin, taut thread of the road stretches downwards through a wide, bleak basin of greenish-grey rock, with the unmelted snow-shields sweeping down to the roadside even in summer, for four grim miles, to the lower rim of the high cauldron. There it is forced to take a wide loop, writhing round the intervening spur, to double back on its far side to the hotel and resaurant buildings on the Fuschertörl ridge (7,890 feet), with their enormous car park and terrace overlooking the narrow abyss to the north, above which the snowy domes and pyramids of the Baerenkopf–Grosse Wiessbachhorn range (11,700 feet) leap up against the blue.

The builders of this marvel among roads, however, were not satisfied with the restrictions imposed on the prospect by its containing slopes and ridges. Close by, directly to the north rises a sharp, conical peak, the Edelweiss-spitze (8,550 feet) only 600 feet higher. So, yet another spur road was thrown out, demolishing the abrupt mountainside in six marvellous windings, steeply banked one above the other (wisely barred to coaches), to the small flat platform which has replaced what was once the rough summit of the sharp little peak. From there the whole road slashing back to the Hochtor tunnel becomes visible, the Wiessbachhorn soars more grandly than ever, and a unique treasure is added to the Fuschertörl view: the immense panorama northwards, beyond that mountain's lower spurs and the Hohe Tenn (11,060 feet), over the plummeting depths of the Salzach ravine and valley below them, opening out on the Pinzgau plain, the blue eye of the Lake of Zell serenely set in it, and away to the cloud-topped, stony barrier ranges of Lofer and the Steinerne Meere, floating in the haze of the Bavarian border, 25 miles away.

This brief side-show, involving ten minutes each way, is a touch of sheer genius. If the weather is fine, the clouds and the traffic not too thick, it would be a crime to miss it.

From Fuschertörl to the Ferleiten toll-gate at the northern end of the road is a drop of 4,200 feet, breathtakingly accomplished in eight wonderful miles. Just before the bottom of this continuous descent, carved down a colossal mountain slope, down, down and always steeply down into the deep, green-carpeted floor of the Salzach valley, there is a lovely and well-named waterfall, the Schleierwasserfall (Cascade of the Veils). Three miles beyond Ferleiten, at Fusch, there is a final ticket-control and the Grossglocknerstrasse – all 42 miles of it, if both the spur roads are traversed – comes to an end.

At Bruck, in the smiling Pinzgau trench, it meets the main valley highway through Lend, St Johann im Pongau, Bischofshofen (for Salzburg over the minor Lueg pass to the north) and eastwards through Radstadt to Liezen, the gateway to the Gesäuse (Admont-Hieflau, see p. 220) and Leoben on the road to Vienna.

At Taxenbach, five miles east of Bruck, a lovely and unspoiled valley runs south into the heart of the Hohe Goldberg sector of the Tauern, the Rauristal. Beyond Rauris (3,110 feet) it leads to Kolm-Saigurn (5,240 feet), where the track divides to the Knappenhaus (7,680 feet) magnificently situated on the moraine of the Goldberg Glacier, while the path to the right leads all the way to the summit of the Sonnblick (10,190 feet), which has an inn, the Zittelhaus, a meteorological station and a superlative view to recommend it. Heiligenblut to the southwest can be reached by a short glacier descent and the Kleine Fleisstal in about five hours from the Sonnblick.

The main southern offshoot some miles farther east at Lend leads to Bad Gastein (3,480 feet), the celebrated and fashionable resort on the river Ache, famed for its gentle and beautiful walks and low, easily ascended viewpoints like the Hüttenkogel (7,315 feet), with paths running up to them, commanding the snows and glaciers of the eastern Hohe Tauern – Hohe Sonnblick, Schareck and Ankogel – all nearly 11,000 feet high. The railway tunnels under them (trucks for motor transport) to Ober Vellach; there is no road exit to the south of this beautiful valley.

These peaks at the eastern end of the Hohe Tauern – Ankogel, Hafnereck and Hochalmspitze – are approach from the south by the Maltatal coming up above Gmünd on the road from Radstadt over the Radstadter Tauern pass and the notorious Katschberg to Spittal down the Katschtal, which divides the Hohe Tauern from the lower Niedere Tauern, running east to Leoben along the north side of the Upper Enns Valley, but in a sense only a northeasterly continuation thrown out by the main range. The lower ranges to the east along the Enns Valley, losing height rapidly to the lowlands beyond, have already been covered as properly forming the easterly extension of the Northern Limestone Alps, in chapter 14. At the same time they are, in effect, the continuation and eventual extinction of the Alpine backbone, declining for the remaining 60 miles of the Alpine and sub-Alpine area in the direction of Graz and Vienna.

It might however be argued that the short curved range of the Carinthian (as distinct from the Carnic) Alps, running almost due east from Spittal to near Leoben, is the true termination of the main range. The truth is that there is a confusion of minor ranges to the north of the Drave Valley from Lienz onwards, and no major spine emerges – as will be seen by consulting a map – any more as the true north–south watershed.

What is quite clear, however, is that the Carnic Alps, running parallel with the Drave but some miles to the south, and separated from it by the narrow Gailtal ridge and the Gailtal (Lessach Valley), uniting at Villach, 20 miles to the east of Lienz, are the direct continuation of the northern spurs of the Dolomites, with the long, low Karawanken range straggling on beyond into Styria for another 40 miles, to peter out in foothills at the extreme limit of the Alpine area near Maribor, south of Graz. While to the south of the Carnics the 40-mile-long much loftier chain of the Venetian and Julian Alps, in Italy and Jugoslavia respectively, carry the central and southern Dolomite ranges to their logical conclusion in one last high upthrust in the western corner of Jugoslavia.

If we follow the Drave valley road from Lienz eastwards through Oberdrauburg, where the low Plöcken Pass (4,470 feet) strikes off southwards to Mauthen, Tolmezzo and Udine, to meet the Venice–Trieste *autostrada*, we come to Spittal (1,770 feet) at the southern foot of the Katschberg (Salzburg–Hüttau–Radstadt–Mauterndorf), just east of which lies the charming Millstatter See with the favourite resort of Millstatt on its north shore, the first of the Carinthian Lakes.

Fifteen miles farther east, Villach (1,640 feet) is the gateway to two more of the Carinthian Lake District's pretty lakes – the Ossiacher See (Ossiach and Sattendorf) and the ten-mile-long Wörthersee, with Pörtschach being world-famous, Sattendorf perhaps less so, but very attractive.

In the other direction, immediately to the west of Villach, there rises an upland ridge ten miles long and three wide, part of the Gailtal range, the Dobratsch, whose highest point reaches 7,110 feet. There is a road up into its eastern end, several huts at the disposal of ramblers and skiers, and the people of Villach have long since turned it into their local playground, which they call the Alps of Villach. From its ridge there are splendid views southwards, across the Gailtal steeply embedded in the foreground, over the low wooded spurs which form the outliers of the Karawanken range, to the rocky north faces of the Julian Alps, towering up only about 12 miles away in Jugoslavia – Grosse Mojstrovska, Travnik, Jalovec and the huge Mangart.

Into this magnificent range a number of short valleys run south from the Save Valley, separated from that of the Drave only by the low Karawanken ridge, and not more than 15 miles from Villach to its south. Here is mountain country no one can afford to miss if he has come so far east in his exploration of the Alps. Here too is the meeting point of Austria, Italy and Jugoslavia, the frontiers dodging about in the most alarming fashion due to adjustments following two world wars.

The northern aspect of Mangart (8,785 feet) is seen to full advantage from the small Fusine lakes (3,060 feet: Italian now, ex-Weissenberg) an hour's walk to the south of the village, which stands close to the source of the Save and only three miles from Tarvisio on the Villach–Ljubljana motor road, soon after the junction with the road which crosses the gap between the eastern and western Julians by the little Predil pass (3,810 feet) and then down the Isonzo Valley to Chiusaforte. Above the lakes there is lovely walking up on the broad Mangart Alp at the foot of the immense grey wall towering 5,000 feet overhead. There is in fact a 'club-path' all the way to the summit for those who enjoy six hours of strenuous uphill work, but some familiarity with steep rock and a complete immunity to vertigo are essential assets on this 'walk'.

From Ratece (Jugoslavia), a mile or two to the east of Fusine, to the head of the Planica Valley is only four miles and its scenery is as impressive as anything in the eastern Alps. The valley is closed by the wonderfully stratified north-west face of the Mojstrovska (7,765 feet) flanked by its huge neighbours Travnik and Jalovek (8,711 feet). In the woods at the foot of this immense wall and dwarfed by it, stands the Tamar Hut (3,635 feet), from which starts every walk and climb (Grades IV to VI only) in the upper reaches of this wonderful valley.

Prisank (8,380 feet), standing a little behind this group to the southeast (the easy rambler's path over the Mojstrovska Pass crosses a saddle above the hut and descends into the head of the Isonzo valley (Italy) to the south, with magnificent views of Triglav to the east), is the only peak in the eastern Julians to present an array of separate towers and gulleys, starting quite close to the larch forests at their feet, as against solid masses of rock. The scenery here is magnificent, the climbs on the faces of the Prisank Towers very exacting, but for the mountain walker there are five protected 'club paths' to the top.

Triglav (Terglou : 9,400 feet) is the highest peak in the Julian Alps, a truly tremendous mountain upheaval, famous and awe-inspiring. It is approached on its northern side by the startlingly beautiful and wild Vrata Valley, which dives southwards from Moistrana (Jugoslavia) in the main valley of the Save 20 miles east of Tarvisio (Italy). Little more than a mile from the foot of the mountain's 5,000-foot north face, one of the highest in the Alps, at 3,300 feet stands the Aljaz Haus (150 beds and floor-mattresses for 60 more) in surroundings offering the rambler days of rewards and delights.

Rock climbers have mastered more than 20 named routes, from 'moderate' Grade II to 'extreme' Grade VI up the faces, arêtes and buttresses of that enormous wall of rock, but non-climbers can safely reach the summit from the south and west on clearly marked and protected 'club-paths'. It seems superfluous to say that the view from that summit, dominating the eastern Alps and itself visible as far afield as the Dachstein (see p. 225) commands a matchless panorama of the piled-up Alps and Dolomites to its west. A rough path also leads from the hut by way of the Luknia Pass (5,835 feet) between Terglou and the Steiner (8,220 feet) to join the track already mentioned, coming over the Mojstrovska Pass from the Tamar hut, in the upper Isonzo glen to the south of the group.

The southern approach to all the peaks in the eastern Julian group is from Flitsch (now Bovec), five miles down the Isonzo road below the Predil Pass, which is equidistant from the eastern and western groups. Mangart and its near neighbours are also accessible from Raibl (Cave del Predil), to the west and to the north of the Pass, which also gives access to the peaks behind it in the Western Julian group.

The western group of the Julian Alps rises a little to the south-west of Tarvisio and contains the imposing but easily climbed Montasch (9,039 feet) and to the south of it Monte Canin (8,468 feet) and Prestreljnik (8,202 feet), the former being approachable from Tarvisio to its north, Raibl to its east or Dogna to its west on the Pontebba–Chiusaforte road running down the Valle di Ferro; the other two from Flitsch, close under them to the east. The separate Wischberg group, whose northern precipices are rarely lit by the sun and then only in summer, is grimly impressive. Its chief peaks are the Gamsmutter, Innominata (Kleinspitze), Gamsmutter Turm and the 8,755-foot Wischberg itself. (I have retained the original German names for many of the above peaks and places, though there are Italian versions such as, for one, Monte Montasio.) A wonderful close-up can be had from the Luigi Pellarini Hut (4,920 feet), at the heart of this vast semicircle of grey rock-faces, three hours above the valley, the path starting to the north of Valbruna and leading up the lovely glen of that name.

This is all magnificent mountain country and all too little known to British and other tourists, which gives it the great advantage of being still unspoiled and less crowded than other, better advertised, areas of the Alps.

It may be thought that I have given too little attention to the Carnic Alps, running west to east all the way from the Cadore Dolomites to the Julians for fully 30 miles, with the Gail Valley to their north, except for my coverage of the Lienz Dolomites. It is a fine mountainous area throwing up a number of high peaks – Monte Coglians (9,128 feet), the Kellerwand, only a few feet lower, Monte Paralba (8,829 feet) and others. It shares some lovely valleys with the eastern fringe of the Dolomites such as the Upper Piave, in which, at the foot of the precipitous Siera chain and not far from the Paralba, is the little hamlet of Bladen (Sappada) whose inhabitants have remained resolutely German in culture and language since migrating, owing to unbearable oppression, from the Pustertal nearly a thousand years ago. Here you will find the Bladens (the original family to lead the exodus), the Hofers, Krettners, Obertalers and Waschingers, against the background of the fine Siera peaks (8,040 feet). On the whole, however, the area does not compare with all the magnificence to be found to its west and east. And, if I have been neglectful, I am in good company. For Coolidge's dry comment in *The Alps in Nature and History* is: 'It is a great fall in every way, from the Dolomites to the last of our twenty groups (South-eastern Alps)', while R. L. G. Irving refused to include them in *his* Alps at all. Yet, if one had never visited any other mountain area, they would seem wonderful indeed.

Southeastwards of the Julians the ranges fall away towards Ljubljana and Trieste. The low Karawanken fade gently due east to Maribor. Westwards, to the south of the Carnics, the Alps of Venetia put up as moderate resistance to the encroachment of the plains as their army did in a historic campaign many years ago to an invading enemy. They swing round in a modest arc, with Udine to their south, towards Vittorio Veneto, without throwing up any peaks of note. This does not, of course, mean that there is not a great deal of scenery to delight the eye, as among mountains, large and small, everywhere; by Alpine standards, however, it is not the most exciting.

I think what I am trying to say is that I have run out of Alps. I might also be running out of words, under the limitation imposed. I hope my editor will not have counted them too meticulously; but I have a feeling that, had I been a betting man like Phineas – which I am not – I might have scraped home by just about the same whisker as he did, and collected.

Index